THE HIDDEN PLACES OF
THE LAKE DISTRICT AND CUMBRIA

By Barbara Vesey

© Travel Publishing Ltd.

Regional Hidden Places

Cornwall
Devon
Dorset, Hants & Isle of Wight
East Anglia
Lake District & Cumbria
Northumberland & Durham
Peak District and Derbyshire
Sussex
Yorkshire

National Hidden Places

England
Ireland
Scotland
Wales

Hidden Inns

East Anglia
Heart of England
North of England
South
South East
Wales
West Country
Yorkshire

Country Pubs and Inns

Cornwall
Devon
Sussex
Wales

Country Living Rural Guides

East Anglia
Heart of England
Ireland
North East of England
North West of England
Scotland
South
South East
Wales
West Country

Other Guides

Off the Motorway

Published by: Travel Publishing Ltd, 7a Apollo House, Calleva Park, Aldermaston, Berks, RG7 8TN

ISBN 1-904-434-32-0

© Travel Publishing Ltd

First published 1990, second edition 1993, third edition 1996, fourth edition 1998, fifth edition 2001, sixth edition 2003, seventh edition 2005

Printing by: Scotprint, Haddington

Maps by: © Maps in Minutes ™ (2005)
© Crown Copyright, Ordnance Survey 2005

Editor: Peter Long

Cover Design: jpbstudio, Whitchurch, Hampshire

Cover Photograph: Ashness Bridge overlooking Derwent Water, Lake District © www.britainonview.com

Text Photographs: © www.britainonview.com

Foreword

This is the 7th edition of the *Hidden Places of The Lake District & Cumbria* which has been fully updated. In this respect we would like to thank the many Tourist Information Centres in Cumbria and The Lake District for helping us update the editorial content. Regular readers will note that the pages of the guide have been extensively redesigned to allow more information to be presented on the many places to visit in *Cumbria* and "the jewel in its crown", *The Lake District* . In addition, although you will still find details of places of interest and advertisers of places to stay, eat and drink included under each village, town or city, these are now cross referenced to more detailed information contained in a separate, easy-to-use section of the book. This section is also available as a free supplement from the local Tourist Information Offices.

The delightful county of *Cumbria* in which the Lakes reside is England's second largest county, but surprisingly has a relatively small population of only 490,000 people which is only slightly more numerous than the city of Leeds. The *Lake District* is most famous for its impressive mountain scenery but also encompasses green rolling hills, fast flowing rivers, deep lush forests and of course the enchanting and languid lakes. Below the fells, peaceful country lanes meander through beautiful little hamlets and tiny rural villages, many steeped in history. This wonderful scenery is of course celebrated by the "Lake Poets" - Wordswoth, Coleridge and Southey. Apart from the Lake District, Cumbria offers the visitor gentle moorland, craggy coastal headlands, scattered woodlands and a fascinating history and cultural heritage.

The *Hidden Places* series is a collection of easy to use local and national travel guides taking you on a relaxed but informative tour of Britain and Ireland. Our books contain a wealth of interesting information on the history, the countryside, the towns and villages and the more established places of interest. But they also promote the more secluded and little known visitor attractions and places to stay, eat and drink many of which are easy to miss unless you know exactly where you are going.

We include hotels, inns, restaurants, public houses, teashops, various types of accommodation, historic houses, museums, gardens, and many other attractions all of which are comprehensively indexed. Most places are accompanied by an attractive photograph and are easily located by using the map at the beginning of each chapter. We do not award merit marks or rankings but concentrate on describing the more interesting, unusual or unique features of each place with the aim of making the reader's stay in the local area an enjoyable and stimulating experience.

Whether you are visiting Cumbria or the Lake District for business or pleasure or are a local inhabitant, we do hope that you enjoy reading and using this book. We are always interested in what readers think of places covered (or not covered) in our guides so please do not hesitate to use the reader reaction forms provided to give us your considered comments. We also welcome any general comments which will help us improve the guides themselves. Finally if you are planning to visit any other corner of the British Isles we would like to refer you to the order form for other *Hidden Places* titles to be found at the rear of the book and to the Travel Publishing website at **www.travelpublishing.co.uk**.

Travel Publishing

Contents

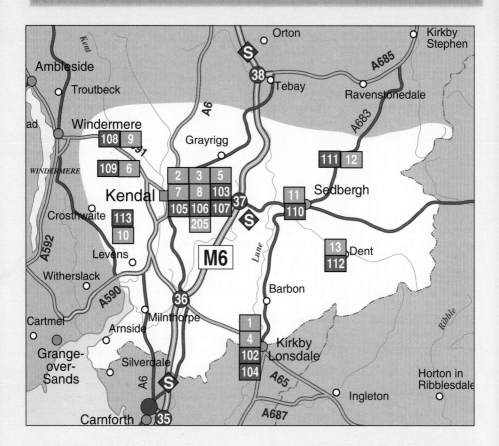

Gateway to the Lakes

An irresistible combination of enchanting lakes, picturesque villages and some of the most dramatic scenery in England draws millions of visitors from all over the world to the Lake District. The region boasts England's highest mountain – Scafell Pike (3,205 feet) – its largest and deepest lakes – Windermere and Wast Water – along with hundreds of other mountains, another 14 lakes (known for the most part as 'meres' or 'waters'), challenging crags and lovely wooded valleys.

Though it is a draw for millions, most of these keep themselves to the main tourist attractions, so the region retains many peaceful glades and windswept, isolated fells, as celebrated by the Lake Poets Wordsworth, Coleridge and Southey. Between them, this lyrical trio transformed the pervading 18th-century perception of this most northwesterly corner of England from that of an intimidating wilderness to an oasis of majestic scenery.

Cumbria is England's second-largest county in size, though its population numbers just under half a million. Almost one-third of the county's 2,636 square miles lies within the boundaries of the Lake District National Park, created in 1951 to protect the area from 'inappropriate development' and to provide 'access to the land for public enjoyment'. Its 22,292 square kilometres include a wonderfully varied landscape, and the opportunities for enjoying the great outdoors are almost boundless.

Cumbria is much more than the Lake District National Park, however. It was here that the British Celts managed to preserve their independence from the Saxons; the Norse influence can still be detected in the place names here. Not a single mile of motorway has penetrated its borders, with only the very occasional stretch of dual-carriageway. Access to the area is very easy, however, as the M6 runs right along its eastern edge. For many visitors travelling from the south into Cumbria, their first experience of the county is the area around Kendal and Kirkby Lonsdale. These ancient settlements provide an excellent introduction to the history, people, culture and economy of Cumbria. Ideally placed for the Lake District National Park and the south Cumbrian coast, it is easy to forget that this area is also close to the northern Pennines and the Yorkshire Dales National Park.

Topiary Gardens, Levens Hall

3

1/102 THE KINGS ARMS

Kirkby Lonsdale

Ancient traditional inn with great food, real ales and cottage accommodation.

🍴 🛏 see pages 136,178

4/104 THE PHEASANT INN

Casterton, Kirkby Lonsdale

Traditional inn in peaceful village. Oak beams, open fires and 10 individually furnished guest bedrooms.

🍴 🛏 see pages 136,178

KIRKBY LONSDALE

One fine day in 1875, John Ruskin came to Kirkby Lonsdale and stood on the stone terrace overlooking the valley of the River Lune. It was, he declared, 'one of the loveliest scenes in England, therefore in the world'. He was equally enthusiastic about the busy little market town – 'I do not know in all my country a place more naturally divine than Kirkby Lonsdale.'

Ruskin had been inspired to visit the town after seeing JMW Turner's painting of that view. Turner himself had come in 1816 on the recommendation of William Wordsworth. These three artists and friends made a point of going to see the **Devil's Bridge** over the Lune – a handsome, lofty structure of three fluted arches. The Devil's Bridge was reputedly built by Satan himself in three days. According to legend, an old woman, unable to cross the deep river with her cattle,

had asked the Devil to build her a bridge. He agreed, but demanded in return the soul of the first creature to cross. Cumbrian cunning outwitted him, however: The old woman threw a bun across the bridge for her dog to run and fetch; thus she cheated the Devil of a human soul.

The bridge is at least 700 years old. Its exact age is a mystery but we do know that some repairs were carried out in 1275, making it certainly the oldest surviving bridge in Westmorland. By the 1920s this narrow bridge, originally designed for pack-horses, proved quite inadequate for motorised transport. A new bridge was built and this, together with one of the country's first by-pass roads, has saved this lovely old town from further destructive road-widening schemes.

Kirkby's Main Street is a picturesque jumble of houses spanning several centuries, with intriguing passages and alleyways skittering off in all directions, all of them worth exploring. It's still a pleasure to stroll along the narrow streets bearing names such as Jingling Lane, past the 16th-century weavers' cottages in Fairbank, across the **Swine Market** with its 600-year-old cross where traders have displayed their wares every Thursday for more than 700 years, past ancient hostelries to the even more venerable **St Mary's Church** with its noble Norman doorway and massive pillars. In the

Devil's Bridge, Kirkby Lonsdale

churchyard, a late Georgian gazebo looks across to the enchanting view of the Lune Valley as painted by Turner.

The town has won the Britain in Bloom competition three times, and also attracts thousands of visitors for its **Victorian Fair**, held on the first full weekend in September, and again in December for the Yuletide procession through streets ablaze with coloured lights and decorated Christmas trees.

AROUND KIRKBY LONSDALE

HALE

7 miles W of Kirkby Lonsdale off the A6

This tiny village close to the Lancashire border is surrounded by woodland. It is also home to the **Lakeland Wildlife Oasis** where a wide range of animals and birds can be seen. A hands-on exhibition tells the story of evolution. Visitors can drape a snake around their neck, exchange inquisitive glances with a ruffled lemur or a meerkat up on its haunches, and admire creatures rarely seen in captivity such as flying foxes and poison arrow frogs. The Tropical Hall is the home of numerous free-flying birds, bats and butterflies; other exhibits range from leaf-cutter ants to pygmy marmosets. The Oasis was established in 1991 by Dave and Jo Marsden, who were keepers at Chester Zoo before setting up this popular family attraction, which is open throughout the year.

About 3 miles south of the town, **Leighton Hall** is actually in

Kirkby Lonsdale

Lancashire but well worth a short diversion. The Hall has been described as the most beautifully situated house in the British Isles, with the dramatic panorama of the Lakeland Fells providing a striking backdrop. The elaborate neo-Gothic façade cloaks an 18th-century mansion which in turn stands on the site of the original medieval house built in 1246 by Adam d'Avranches, whose descendants still live here.

Leighton Hall is famed for its collection of Gillow furniture.

Inland from Arnside, and found down a quiet lane, Arnside Tower is one of the many pele towers that were built in the area in the 14th century. This particular tower dates from the 1370s and may have been part of the chain of towers designed to form a ring of protection around Morecambe Bay. Pele towers are unique to the north of England and were built by the people of Cumberland and Westmorland to withstand invasion. Usually three-story buildings 3 to 10 feet thick, about 90 were built in the region.

During restoration work in the 1830s, a hoard of around 100 coins, minted in Norman times, was discovered inside the base of a pillar in the Church of St Michael and All Saints, Beetham.

ARNSIDE

10 miles W of Kirkby Lonsdale off the B5282

This quiet town on the Kent Estuary, with its short but elegant promenade, was once a busy port with its own shipbuilding and sea salt-refining industry. As the Estuary silted up during the 19th century – a process accelerated by the construction of the striking 50-arch railway viaduct – so the port declined. Today it is a favourite retirement destination and a peaceful holiday resort.

Around Arnside there is a wonderful choice of country walks, particularly over and around **Arnside Knott**. This limestone headland, now a nature reserve rich in old woods and wild flowers, is part of the Arnside and Silverdale Area of Outstanding Natural Beauty. *Knott* comes from the Saxon word meaning 'rounded hill', which in this case rises 521 feet above sea level and gives extensive views of the Lakeland fells, the Pennines and the southern Cumbrian coast. There is a beautiful path around the headland and along the shoreline past Blackstone Point.

BEETHAM

8 miles W of Kirkby Lonsdale on the A6

Approached through a pergola of rambling roses, the **Church of St Michael and All Angels** dates from Saxon times. Although the church was badly damaged during the Civil War, when its windows were smashed and effigies broken, a glass fragment of Henry IV in an ermine robe has survived the centuries. The village of Beetham is also home to an unusual 19th-century **Post Office** with a distinctive black-and-white studded door.

Just outside the village lies **Heron Corn Mill**, a restored and working watermill with fully operational grinding machinery. A fine example of a traditional corn mill which operated for trade in the Westmorland farming area, the mill ceased trading as recently as the 1950s. The situation of Heron Mill is ideal, as a natural shelf of rock in the River Bela forms a waterfall, providing the necessary head of water to drive the waterwheel. This made the site an obvious one when, in 1220, the Lords of the Manor of Haverback granted lands to the Canons of Coningshead for the construction of a mill. Referred to several times in archives from the Middle Ages, the land was transferred to Sir William Thorneburghe when Coningshead was destroyed in 1538. Visitors to the mill can see an exhibition about its history and view the milling process. Also here is the **Museum of Paper Making**, which was established in 1988 to commemorate 500 years of papermaking in England.

MILNTHORPE

8 miles W of Kirkby Lonsdale on A6

Just north of the Lancashire border, Milnthorpe has been a market town since the 14th century. It originally flourished as a port on the banks of the River Bela, but the harbour has long since silted up.

The mill of the town's name refers to the waterfalls that once stood alongside the river. A small folly tower on **St Andrew's Hill** was built in the 1830s by the architect George Webster as a means of occupying his idle hours while restoring the town's church.

SANDSIDE

9 miles W of Kirkby Lonsdale on the B5282

From this small village situated on the banks of the Kent Estuary, pack-horses and drovers during the Middle Ages, together with their sheep and cattle, would set off across the treacherous sands into Cumbria rather than take the longer, inland route. Consequently many lives were lost. The route remains as dangerous today as it was then.

KENDAL

A survey a few years back by Strathclyde University revealed that the highest quality of life of any town in England was to be found in Kendal, the unofficial capital of South Lakeland. That assessment came as no surprise to the residents of this lively, bustling town, which was once one of the most important woollen textile centres in northern England. The Kendal woollen industry was founded in 1331 by John Kemp, a Flemish weaver, and it flourished and sustained the town for almost 600 years until the development of competition from the huge West Riding of Yorkshire mills during the Industrial Revolution. The fame of the local wool was so great that Shakespeare refers to archers clad in Kendal Green cloth in his play *Henry IV*. These archers were the famous **Kendal Bowmen** whose lethal longbows were made from local yew trees culled from the nearby limestone crags. It was these men who clinched the English victories at Agincourt and Crécy, and fought so decisively against the Scots at the Battle of Flodden Field in 1513.

Kendal has royal connections, too. The Parr family lived at **Kendal Castle** until 1483 – their most famous descendant being Catherine Parr, the last of Henry VIII's six wives. Today, the castle's gaunt ruins stand high on a hill overlooking the town, with most of the castle wall and one of the towers still standing, and two underground vaults still complete. Castle Hill is a popular place for walking and picnics. In summer the hillside is smothered with wild flowers. From the hilltop there are spectacular views; a panorama panel here assists in identifying the distant fells.

The largest settlement in the old county of Westmorland, Kendal has always been a bustling town, from the days when it was on the main route to Scotland. Nowadays the M6 and a by-pass divert much of the traffic away from the town centre, but its narrow main streets, Highgate, Stramongate, and Stricklandgate, are always busy during the season. The fine coaching inns of the 17th and 18th centuries, to which Bonnie Prince

Kendal's motto, 'Wool is my Bread', reveals the extent to which the town's economy depended on the wool from the flocks of Herdwick sheep that roamed the surrounding fells.

3/106   THE BLACK SWAN

Kendal

Jennings Brewery ales, home-made dishes and four good-sized guest bedrooms in the centre of Kendal.

🍴 🛏 *see pages 136,179*

205   ABBOT HALL ART GALLERY AND MUSEUM

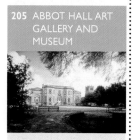

Kendal

Gallery including works by John Ruskin and George Romney.

🏛 *see page 219*

Charlie is said to have retreated after his abortive 1745 rebellion, still line these streets.

Anyone wandering around the town cannot help but notice the numerous alleyways, locally known as yards, that are such a distinctive feature of Kendal. An integral part of the old town, they are a reminder that the people of Kendal used to live under the constant threat of raids by the Scots. The yards were a line of defence against these attacks, an area that could be secured by sealing the one small entrance, with families and livestock safe inside.

Shoppers are spoilt for choice in Kendal. In addition to all the familiar High Street names, the **Westmorland Shopping Centre**, **Blackhall Yard** and **Elephant Yard**, all in the heart of the town, and the **K Village Factory**

Shopping complex on the outskirts, make it easy to shop until you drop. One local product well worth sampling is **Kendal Mint Cake**, a tasty, sugary confection which is cherished by climbers and walkers for its instant infusion of energy. Another once-popular local medication, **Kendal Black Drop**, is sadly no longer available. 'A more than commonly strong mixture of opium and alcohol', Kendal Black Drop was a favourite of poets Samuel Taylor Coleridge and Thomas de Quincey.

Kendal's excellent sporting facilities include the **Kendal Leisure Centre**, which offers a one-week tourist pass, Kendal Wall, which is one of the highest indoor climbing facilities in the country, Kendal ski slope, two local golf courses and a driving range. Drama, music and the visual arts are represented in a regularly changing programme of exhibitions, live music, theatre productions and craft workshops at the **Brewery Arts Centre**. The Centre also houses Kendal's cinema, which presents a mixture of mainstream, classic and art house films.

A number of interesting museums and galleries are also located in Kendal. The **Museum of Lakeland Life and Industry** takes as its theme the traditional rural trades of the region, and together with the **Abbot Hall Art Gallery** forms part of a complex within Abbot Hall Park. The museum, in re-created farmhouse rooms, contains a wide variety of exhibits, including Arthur Ransome

Kendal Castle

memorabilia, craft workshops, a Victorian street scene, artefacts from the Arts and Crafts movement, nautical displays and Captain Flint's Locker, a pirate-themed activity area for children and families. The Gallery, in an elegant Georgian villa, houses a collection of society portraits by the locally born George Romney, and watercolour scenes by Ruskin and Turner, as well as works by 20th-century and contemporary artists such as Walter Sickert, Ben Nicholson, Lucien Freud and Bridget Riley. The **Museum of Natural History and Archaeology**, founded in 1796, is one of the oldest museums in the country. Based on the collection first exhibited by William Todhunter in the late 18th century, the Museum takes visitors on a journey from prehistoric times, a trip which includes an interactive exhibit recounting the story of Kendal Castle.

The famous fellwalker and writer, Alfred Wainwright, whose handwritten guides to the Lakeland hills will be found in the backpack of any serious walker, was honorary clerk here between 1945 and 1974. Many of his original drawings are on display.

Adjacent to the elegant Georgian Abbot Hall and Museum is the 13th-century **Parish Church of Kendal**, 'the Church of the Angels', one of the widest in England, with five aisles and a peal of 10 bells. Among the many interesting things to see are the carved reredos of the Parr Chapel,

Farmland near Kendal

the stained glass windows, and the sculpture *The Family of Man* by Josephina de Vasconcellos. The church also contains a sword that is said to have belonged to Robert Philipson, a Cavalier during the Civil War. While away fighting in Carlisle, Cromwell's supporters laid siege to Philipson's house at Windermere. On his return, the Cavalier attacked the Kendal church when he thought the Roundheads would be at prayer. Riding his horse right into the church, he found it empty save for one innocent man, whom he despatched with his trusty sword.

Perhaps the most unusual attraction in Kendal is the **Quaker Tapestry Exhibition** at the Friends Meeting House in the centre of the town. This unique exhibition of 77 panels of community embroidery explores Quaker history from the 17th century to the present day. These

7   PRELUDE OF KENDAL

Kendal

Licensed coffee house and restaurant open Mon-Sat 8.30 a.m.–5 p.m. for breakfast, morning coffee, hot and cold lunches and afternoon tea.

 see page 137

9

Kendal

Gracious, attractive and tasteful establishment in the heart of Kendal. Refurbished bar and restaurant; 11 cosy and comfortable guest bedrooms.

see pages 138,179

Staveley, Kendal

Superb café with tasteful décor and even tastier breakfasts, sandwiches, hot and cold snacks and an excellent range of mouth-watering cakes.

see page 138

Staveley, Kendal

Four beautiful refurbished cottages sleeping up to five each set in 18 acres of working farmland within the Lake District National Park.

see page 180

colourful, beautifully crafted tapestries are the work of some 4,000 people aged between 4 and 90, from 15 countries. A Quaker costume display, embroidery demonstrations, workshops, courses and a large-screen video programme combine to provide a fascinating insight into the Quaker movement and its development.

AROUND KENDAL

LEVENS

5 miles S of Kendal off the A590

At the southern tip of Scout Scar, overlooking the Lyth Valley and the lower reaches of the River Kent, stands **Levens Hall** with its unique topiary gardens. The superb Elizabethan mansion (described as 'one of the wonders of Lakeland') developed from a 14th-century pele tower. The gardens were first laid out in 1694, and were the work of Colonel James Grahme, a keen gardener who purchased the hall in 1688 and employed a Frenchman, Guillaume Beaumont, to create the amazing topiary work (Beaumont also redesigned the gardens at Hampton Court for James II). The fame of the Levens Hall gardens spread quickly, and ever since they have been a popular attraction. Today there are more 90 individual specimens, some almost 20 feet high, with the ancient yew trees cut

into often surreal shapes. The topiary is by no means the only attraction in the grounds, however, which also include a Fountain Garden created in 1994 to mark the tercentenary of the gardens. The interior of the house is equally rewarding – a wealth of period furniture, fine panelling and plasterwork, a dining room with walls covered in goatskin, and paintings by Rubens, Lely and Cuyp. The Hall is said to be haunted by three ghosts: a black dog, a lady in pink, and a gypsy woman who, legend has it, put a curse on the family saying that they would have no heir until the River Kent ceased to flow and a white fawn was born in the park. In fact, after many years without a direct heir, in 1896 the River Kent froze

Levens Hall

over, a white fawn was seen, and a son and heir was born. A major location for the BBC-TV serial *Wives and Daughters*, the Hall's other attractions include a collection of working steam engines, a tea room, gift shop and plant centre.

Only a couple of miles north of Levens Hall, just off the A591, is another stately old residence, **Sizergh Castle**, the impressive home of the Strickland family since 1239 (although the property is now administered by the National Trust). Originally a pele tower built to withstand border raiders, the house has been added to and altered over the intervening centuries to provide the family, as times became less violent, with a more comfortable home. Now boasting intricately carved chimney mantels, fine oak panelling and a collection of portraits of the Stuart royal family, the castle offers an additional 'attraction' in the form of the ghost of a medieval lady. She is said to haunt the castle, screaming to be released from the room in which she was locked by her fiercely jealous husband. It was here that she starved to death while he was away in battle. More reliable (and less gruesome!) attractions at Sizergh are the well laid-out gardens and 1,500 acres of grounds which provide superb views over the Lakeland fells.

BRIGSTEER

3 miles SW of Kendal off A591

This tiny hamlet lies under the limestone escarpment of Scout Scar. From this pretty settlement

the road leads into the National Trust property of **Brigsteer Woods** where, as the climate is milder here due to its sheltered position, there are wild daffodils in spring.

BURNESIDE

2 miles N of Kendal off the A591

The remains of an ancient stone circle can be seen close by Burneside, on **Potter Fell**. By the 15th century Burneside was a settled agricultural area, and a rich variety of mills sprang up along the River Sprint – corn, cotton, wool, bobbin and the original rag paper mill at **Cowan Head**. There has been a settlement at Burneside since Stone-Age times.

The River Sprint, which meets the River Kent just south of the village, has its own remarkably beautiful Longsleddale Valley which curves past Garnett Bridge deep into the high fell country. A bridle path climbs from the head of the valley into Kentmere, another spectacularly beautiful walk.

GRAYRIGG

5 miles NE of Kendal on the A685

This is a fine village with a cluster of almshouses, cottages and a simple church found in a lovely rural setting. It was the birthplace of Francis Howgill (1610-69), who was responsible for introducing founding Quaker father George Fox to the **Westmorland Seekers**, a group of radical Christians from the area.

6 THE SUN INN

Crook, Kendal

Traditional hand-drawn ales and home-cooked food in a proper village pub in a quiet setting yet close to all local attractions.

see page 137

109 MITCHELLAND HOUSE

Crook, Kendal

Scenic views and first-class accommodation in a characterful listed building in seven acres of beautiful countryside.

see page 180

10/113 THE WHEATSHEAF AT BRIGSTEER

Brigsteer

First-class food, drink and accommodation at this superior inn with a truly impressive menu and four tasteful and comfortable bedrooms.

see pages 139, 181

11

•

Religious tolerance has long been a feature of Sedbergh: at St Andrew's Church, for example, Protestants and Roman Catholics take turns to use the building for their own services, an arrangement believed to be rare in England.

•

SEDBERGH

In 1974 Sedbergh was brusquely removed from the West Riding of Yorkshire and became part of Cumbria. However, it still lies within the Yorkshire Dales National Park – the surrounding scenery certainly belongs to the Dales, as the mighty **Howgill Fells**, great pear-shaped drumlins shaped by glaciers that soar to more than 2,200 feet (670 metres), attest. **Winder Hill**, which provides a dramatic backdrop to the little market town, is half that height, but with its sleek grassy flanks and domed top, seems much loftier. Four valleys and four mountain streams meet here. For centuries Sedbergh (pronounced Sedber) has been an important centre for cross-Pennine travellers. During the golden age of stage-coach travel, the town became a staging post on the route between Lancaster and Newcastle-upon-Tyne. The complete journey took from 4 o'clock in the morning to 7 o'clock at night: 15 hours to cover a distance of about 120 miles, an average speed of 8 miles per hour. At the **King's Arms Hotel**, the four horses would be swiftly changed before the equipage rattled off again across the moors to Teesdale, Durham and Newcastle.

In those days, the stage-coach would have been used frequently by the boys attending Sedbergh's famous **Public School**. Its founder was Roger Lupton, a Howgill boy who rose to become Provost of

Eton: he established the school because he felt that one was desperately needed 'in the north country amongst the people rude in knowledge'. In later years Wordsworth's son studied here, and Coleridge's son, Hartley, became a master. The school's extensive grounds, through which visitors are welcome to wander, seem to place the old-world town within a park.

This impression is reinforced if you follow the path beside the River Rawthey to **Brigflatts**. Close to where George Fox stayed overnight with his friend Richard Robinson is the oldest **Quaker Meeting House** in the north of England. Built in 1675, and still with its original oak interior, this beautiful, simple building has changed little over the years.

This area is filled with Quaker history and **Firbank Knott**, on nearby Firbank Fell, can be said to be the birthplace of Quakerism: it was here, in 1652, that the visionary George Fox gave his great sermon to inspire a huge gathering from the whole of the north of England. This meeting was to lead to the development of the **Quaker Movement**. The simple boulder on the fell, from which Fox delivered his momentous words, is marked by a plaque and is now known as **Fox's Pulpit**.

Many of the town's older buildings have survived, in particular the stone-built cottages on both sides of the cobbled yard known as **The Folly**, just off Main Street, have not only survived unscathed but remain dwellings rather than having been converted to other uses. Much of the heart of Sedbergh has been deemed a Conservation Area.

To the east of town, on a small wooded hilltop, lies **Castlehaw**, the remains of an ancient motte-and-bailey castle. Built by the Normans in the 11th century, the castle guarded the valleys of the River Rawthey and the River Lune against the marauding Scots. Also just outside town, on the A683 Garsdale road, is **Farfield Mill** Heritage and Arts Centre, where spinners, weavers, potters, woodcarvers and other craftspeople use traditional skills to produce high-quality goods, all of it for sale in the shop. Also on site are an arts and crafts gallery, a heritage display depicting the history of the mill, and a riverside restaurant. The mill is accessible to all visitors, with disabled facilities and a lift to all three levels.

One important recent development is the establishment of Sedburgh as a Book Town. A number of bookshops and other businesses based on writing, reading and publishing have been brought together, the main aim being to concentrate on selling hard-to-find second hand books. The hope is that over the next months and years, Sedburgh will grow into a book lover's paradise where thousands of enthusiasts will come to find an out-of-print volume to add to their collection.

AROUND SEDBERGH

DENT

4 miles SE of Sedbergh off the A684

This charming village, the only one in Dentdale – one of Cumbria's finest dales – has a delightful cobbled main street with tall cottages lining the road. Visitors to this tranquil place will find it hard to believe that, in the 18th century, Dent was of greater importance

13/112   STONE CLOSE TEA ROOM & GUEST HOUSE

Dent, Sedbergh

Traditional tea room and accommodation in a picturesque village with magnificent views.

see pages 140,180

Dent Village

Viaduct, Dent

Dent stone, with no iron pyrites likely to cause sparks, was popular for the millstones used in gunpowder works. The little valley of Dentdale winds from the village up past old farms and hamlets to **Lea Yeat** where a steep lane hairpins up to Dent Station, almost 5 miles from the village. This is a marvellous place to begin a ramble into Dentdale or over the Whernside. In the shadow of Whernside itself, **Whernside Manor** is a famous house with associations with the slave trade. Dent is the highest railway station in Britain, over 1,100 feet above sea level, and it lies on the famous Settle-Carlisle railway line.

•

Dent's most famous son is undoubtedly the 'Father of Geology', Adam Sedgwick. Born the son of the local vicar in 1785, Sedgwick went on to become the Woodwardian Professor of Geology at Cambridge University and also a friend of Queen Victoria and Prince Albert. The fountain of pinkish Shap granite in the village centre is Dent's memorial to this great geologist.

•

than nearby Sedbergh. The impressive **St Andrew's Church** is Norman in origin, though it underwent almost complete renovation in the early 15th century. Inside can be seen a Jacobean three-decker pulpit that is still in use and also the local marble which paves the chancel.

Farming has dominated the local economy for many years, though knitting, too, has played its part. During the 17th and 18th centuries the women and children on whom this work fell became known as the '**Terrible Knitters of Dent**', which may sound uncomplimentary but in fact, at that time, meant quite the opposite (like 'wicked' today!). Large amounts of dressed wool were turned by the knitters into stockings and gloves which were then exported out of the dale to local towns.

GARSDALE

5 miles E of Sedbergh on the A683

Lying just north of Dentdale, Garsdale is both a dale and a village, both overlooked by the dramatic **Baugh Fell**. The River Clough follows down the dale from Garsdale Head, the watershed into Wensleydale where a row of Midland Railway cottages lies alongside the former junction station on the Settle-Carlisle line. This is now a surprisingly busy little place during the summer months when, from time to time, preserved steam locomotives pause to take water from a moorland spring.

Around Windermere & Ambleside

This southeastern corner of the extensive Lake District National Park is Cumbria's best known and most popular area, with the main resort towns of Windermere, Bowness-on-Windermere and Ambleside – and, of course, Lake Windermere itself. The area is certainly busy with tourists during the summer months, but this does not in any way attract from its charm. Also, with the unpredictability of Lakeland weather, the region is well equipped with a host of indoor amusements to appeal to all ages.

The area opened up to tourism as a result of the Victorians' growing interest in the natural world and their engineering ability in providing a railway service. Thus these villages, once little more than places where the fell farmers congregated to buy and sell their livestock and exchange gossip, grew into inland resorts with fine Victorian and Edwardian villas, houses and municipal buildings.

There are also many beautiful places close to the bustling and crowded towns that provide solitude. To the southeast lies Cartmel Fell, while further north is isolated Kentmere.

Walkers near Ambleside

Lake Windermere

15

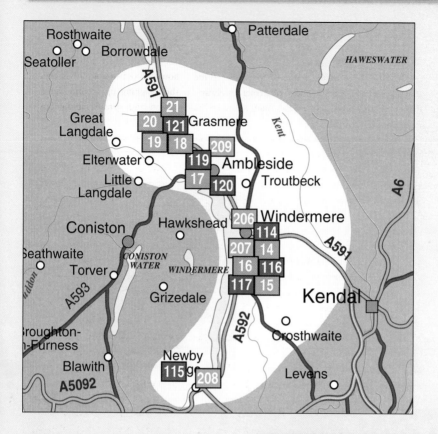

206 WINDERMERE STEAMBOATS & MUSEUM

Windermere

A unique collection of Victorian and Edwardian steam launches, some of which are still in working order.

🏛 *see page 220*

WINDERMERE

Birthwaite village no longer features on any map, thanks to the Kendal and Windermere Railway Company which built a branch line to it in 1847. With an eye on tourist traffic, and considering the name Birthwaite had little appeal, they named the station 'Windermere' even though the lake is over a mile distant. In the early days carriages and, in later years, buses linked the station with the landing stages in the village of Bowness on the shores of the lake. As the village burgeoned into a prosperous Victorian resort, it became popularly, and then officially, known by the name of its station, while Windermere Water was given the redundant prefix of Lake.

The town's Victorian heritage still predominates in the many large houses here, originally built as country retreats for Manchester businessmen – the railway made it possible for them to reach this idyllic countryside in just over two hours. Hotels, boarding houses, comfortable villas and shops sprang up around the station and spread rapidly down the hill towards the lake until Birthwaite and Bowness were linked together.

Windermere's railway is still operating, albeit now as a single track branch line. Diesel railcars run along the **Lakes Line**, providing a busy shuttle service to and from the main line at Oxenholme. The route, through Kendal, Burneside and Staveley, is a delight and provides a very pleasant alternative to the often-crowded A591. The Lakes Line is now the only surviving Railtrack line to run into the heart of the Lake District..

Within a few yards of Windermere Station, just across the busy main road, is a footpath that leads through the woods to one of the finest viewpoints in Lakeland, **Orrest Head**. This spectacular vantage point provides a 360-degree panoramic view that takes in the ten-mile length of Windermere, the Cumbrian hills and even the fells of the Yorkshire Pennines. In a region where glorious views open up at every turn, the vista from Orrest Head remains exceptional. In Victorian times,

Lake Windermere

17

114 MAY COTTAGE

Bowness-on-Windermere

Charming Victorian cottage with excellent accommodation. Hearty breakfasts, Leisure facilities, Parking.

see page 182

14 THE TWO EGGCUPS RESTAURANT

Bowness-on-Windermere

Home-made dishes from breakfast to tea-time in a charming and welcoming setting.

see page 140

•

The remains of one of Thomas West's famous 'stations', described in his Guide to the Lakes (1778) on the western shore of Windermere below Claife Heights, can be visited today. In its heyday each of the windows of the drawing room at Claife Station had a different aspect and could be viewed through different-coloured glass to enhance lighting effects in the landscape: Yellow represented summer, orange was for autumn, light green for spring and light blue for winter. There was also a dark blue for moonlight and a lilac tint to give the impression of a thunderstorm.

•

Steamer on Lake Windermere

visitors wandered through such ravishing scenery carrying, not cameras, but small, tinted mirrors mounted in elaborate frames. Arriving at a picturesque spot, they placed themselves with their back to the view, held the mirrors above them and so observed the view framed, as in a painting. The image they saw recalled the romantic landscapes of Claude Lorraine: the mirrors, accordingly, were known as **Claude Glasses**.

AROUND WINDERMERE

BOWNESS-ON-WINDERMERE

2 miles S of Windermere on the A592

It is from this attractive but seasonally very busy town right on the edge of Windermere that most of the lake cruises operate. Lasting between 45 and 90 minutes, the cruises operate daily and provide connections to the **Lakeside & Haverthwaite Steam Railway**, the

Fell Foot Country Park and the **Visitor Centre** at Brockhole – this centre (also easily reached by road) is idyllically situated in 30 acres of gardens and grounds and has two floors of interactive exhibitions. There are evening wine/champagne cruises during the summer months, and rowing boats and self-drive motor boats are also available for hire all year round.

Not only is **Windermere** the largest lake in Cumbria but it is, at 11 miles long, the largest in England. Formed in the Ice Age by the action of moving glaciers, the lake is fed by the Rivers Brathay and Rothay at the northern end, while the outlet is into the River Leven, at Newby Bridge. Windermere is actually a public highway or, more correctly, waterway, and this stretch of water, with its thickly wooded banks and scattered islands, has been used since Roman times as a means of transport. Later, the monks of Furness Abbey fished here for pike

18

and char. The name 'Windermere', however, comes from Viking times and is derived from *Vinand's Mere*, *Vinand* being the name of a Nordic chief.

Roman Legionnaires used Lake Windermere for transporting stone to their fort at *Galava*, near present-day Ambleside at the head of the lake

Across from Bowness, the lake is almost divided in two by **Belle Island,** which is believed to have been inhabited by the Romans. During the Civil War it was owned by Colonel Phillipson (the Royalist supporter who disgraced himself by riding into Kendal Parish Church), whose family had to withstand an 80-day siege, successfully, while the Colonel was away on another campaign. In 1774 the island was bought by a Mr English, who constructed the round house which, at the time, caused such consternation that he sold the property and the island to Isabella Curwen, who planted the surrounding trees.

Fishermen, too, find great enjoyment practising their skills on this well-stocked lake. Once considered a great delicacy in the 17th and 18th centuries, the char, a deep-water trout, is still found here – though catching it is a special art.

Away from the marinas and car parks is the old village where **St Martin's Church** is of particular interest. It has a magnificent east window filled with 14th and 15th century glass, and an unusual 300-year-old carved wooden figure of St Martin depicted sharing his cloak with a beggar.

On the lake shore just to the north of the village is the **Windermere Steamboat Centre**. Housed here is a unique collection of Lake Windermere's nautical heritage. The exhibits, mainly Victorian and Edwardian craft, include *Dolly*, the oldest mechanically-powered boat in the world, and Beatrix Potter's rowing boat. The 'Swallows and Amazons' exhibition features guided tours of *Esperance*, Arthur Ransome's inspiration for Captain Flint's houseboat. The Museum grounds also include a model boat pond, shop, tea room and picnic area.

Just down the road from the Steamboat Museum is the Old Laundry Visitor Centre, the home of **The World of Beatrix Potter**, one of the most popular visitor

116 PACKWAY HOUSE

Bowness-on-Windermere

Five charming and attractive apartments set in wooded grounds, tranquil yet within an easy walk of Bowness centre.

🛏 see page 182

15 THE NISSI RESTAURANT

Bowness-on-Windermere

Genuine Greek and Mediterranean cuisine expertly prepared and presented.

🍴 see page 140

Rowing Boats at Bowness-on-Windermere

16/117 THE MARINERS INN

Bowness-on-Windermere

Friendly and welcoming inn with accommodation conveniently located on the main road linking Bowness and Windermere.

 see *pages 141, 182*

207 BLACKWELL

Bowness-on-Windermere

In a superb location overlooking Lake Windermere, Blackwell is a treasure trove of the Arts & Crafts movement.

see *page 220*

attractions in the country. Here visitors can enjoy fascinating re-creations of the Lakeland author's books, complete with the sounds, sights and even the smells of the countryside. The year 2002 saw the centenary of the publication of the first *Tale of Peter Rabbit*, and to mark the occasion the Peter Rabbit Centenary springs to life every 15 minutes and features some previously unpublished illustrations from the stories. Open all year, the complex also includes the Tailor of Gloucester Tea Room (children's menu and colouring sheets available) and the Beatrix Potter shop.

About a mile and a half south of Bowness, **Blackwell** is a treasure trove of the Arts and Crafts Movement. Completed in 1900, it is the largest and most important surviving masterpiece of the architect MH Baillie Scott (1865-1945). Inspired by Lakeland flora and fauna, he designed every last detail of this outstanding house, creating a symphony of Art Nouveau stained glass, oak panelling, intricate plasterwork and fanciful metalwork. From the gardens there are wonderful views of Windermere and the Coniston fells.

WINSTER

4 miles S of Windermere on the A5074

This charming hamlet has an old post office, originally built in the early 17th century as a cottage, that is much photographed. South from the village runs the Winster Valley, which provided Wordsworth with

one of his favourite walks. It was at **Low Ludderburn**, a couple of miles to the south, that Arthur Ransome settled in 1925 and here that he wrote his classic children's novel *Swallows and Amazons*. The house is still there, but is not open to the public.

While living here, Ransome discovered the peaceful churchyard at **Rusland** and decided that was where he wanted to be buried. When he passed away in 1967, he was duly buried here, to be joined later by his second wife Eugenia.

WITHERSLACK

9 miles S of Windermere off the A590

On the edge of the village is the **Latterbarrow Reserve** of the Cumbrian Wildlife Trust, a relatively small reserve that is home to some 200 species of flowering plants and ferns. Butterflies and birds, including the spotted flycatcher, are a common sight among the plants that grow in the thin soil between the rocky outcrops. Further from the village is **Witherslack Hall**, once the summer residence of the Earls of Derby; now a school.

NEWBY BRIDGE

8 miles S of Windermere on the A592

The bridge here crosses the River Leven which runs from the southern tip of Windermere to Morecambe Bay. According to geologists, the mass of end moraines seen here show clearly that the village lay at the southernmost point of Windermere, since they were deposited by the glacier while it paused, having carved out the lake. Today, however, the village is some distance from the water's edge, which can be reached on foot, by car or by taking the steam train on the **Lakeside & Haverthwaite Railway**.

One mile north of the village, **Fell Foot Country Park** (National Trust) is a delightful 18-acre site of landscaped gardens and woodland laid out in late-Victorian times. Admission is free (although there's a car parking charge), and the grounds include picnic areas, a children's adventure playground, a splendid rhododendron garden, a gift shop and a tea room with outside tables where you can watch the lake traffic and also the steam trains chugging into Lakeside on the western bank. Rowing boats can be hired at the piers from which there are regular ferries across to Lakeside, and pleasure cruises operate during the summer school holidays.

BACKBARROW

9 miles S of Windermere on the A592

This small village in the valley of the River Leven, which drains Windermere, was a hive of industry at one time. In 1711, the most ambitious iron furnace in Cumbria was built here; its remains can still be seen, along with the relics of the heyday of water power in the village.

LAKESIDE

10 miles S of Windermere off the A590

Located at the southwestern tip of

Windermere, Lakeside sits beneath gentle wooded hills. It's the northern terminus of the Lakeside & Haverthwaite Railway, a 4-mile route through the beautiful Leven Valley which was once part of a line stretching to Ulverston and Barrow-in-Furness. Throughout the season, hard-working steam locomotives chug along the track, their departure times set to coincide with boat arrivals from Bowness – a joint boat and train return ticket is available. The locomotives in use include 42073 and 42085, ex-LMR Fairburn 0-6-4 tank engines, and 5643, an ex-GWR 0-6-0 tank. Also present on display or under steam (when not occasionally required elsewhere) is FR20, built for the Furness Railway and Britain's oldest working standard-gauge steam locomotive. Nearby lies the **Aquarium of the Lakes** with the largest collection of freshwater fish in the UK and also a number of playful otters and diving ducks. A unique attraction for visitors is to walk along a re-creation of Windermere's lake bed along an underwater tunnel. The Aquarium of the Lakes is Britain's only freshwater aquarium. There's also a shop and a café.

A mile or so north of Lakeside, **Stott Park Bobbin Mill** (English Heritage) is a must for anyone interested in the area's industrial heritage. One of the best preserved in the country, it's a genuine working 19th-century mill and stands in a lovely woodland setting at the southern end of the Lake. Visitors can join the inclusive 45-

115 TRUNDLE BROW COTTAGE

Brow Edge, Newby Bridge

In stunning location overlooking the Leven Valley, superior accommodation with comfortable and attractive décor and furnishings.

see page 182

208 THE AQUARIUM OF THE LAKES

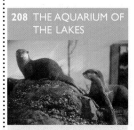

Lakeside, Newby Bridge

The life of the fish and wildlife that live in and beside the waters here, is told through a series of over 30 displays.

see page 220

•

Just north of Troutbeck Bridge lies the Royal Horticultural Society's 4-acre garden at Holehird. In 1945, Edward Leigh Groves bequeathed the mansion and the estate 'for the better development of the health, education and social welfare services of the County of Westmoreland'. Some time later, the Lakeland Horticultural Society took over responsibility for the garden, which is still run by volunteers of that society, whose primary aim is to promote 'knowledge on the cultivation of plants, shrubs and trees, especially those suited to Lakeland conditions'. Highlights of the garden include the borders in the walled garden, the many specimen trees, the summer-autumn heathers and the National Collections of astilbes and hydrangeas.

•

The Lake District

minute tour, watch wooden bobbins being made as they were 200 years ago, and browse over the informative exhibition.

INGS

3 miles E of Windermere off the A591

A pleasant little village set alongside the River Gowan, Ings owes its fine Georgian church and charming almshouses to a certain Robert Bateman, who was born here in the late 1600s. Wordsworth commemorated Bateman in a rather pedestrian poem which recounts how the villagers made a collection so that the young boy could travel to London. He prospered greatly, became a major ship owner and devoted a sizeable portion of his wealth to the benefit of his native village. Sadly, he never saw the completed church: less than a year after building began, he was murdered by pirates.

TROUTBECK BRIDGE

1 mile NE of Windermere on the A591

This small village in the valley of Trout Beck takes its name from the bridge here over the Beck, just before the water runs into Windermere. During the 17th century, **Calgarth Hall** was owned by Myles Phillipson, a local Justice of the Peace who wished to gain possession of nearby farmland. He duly invited the landowner and his wife to a banquet at the Hall and then, having hidden a silver cup in their luggage, accused them of stealing.

At the resulting trial, Phillipson, who was the presiding judge, sentenced the couple to death as well as appropriating their land. As she was led away, the wife placed a curse on the judge, saying that not only would his victims never leave him but that his family would also perish in poverty. The couple were executed, but their skulls reappeared at Calgarth Hall and, no matter what Phillipson did (including burning them and throwing them into Lake Windermere) the skulls kept returning to the Hall. Moreover, the Phillipson family grew poorer and poorer. Finally, in 1705, the family died out altogether.

TROUTBECK

3 miles NE of Windermere off the A592

Designated a conservation area, Troutbeck has no recognisable centre as the houses and cottages are grouped around a number of wells and springs which, until recently, were the only form of water supply. Dating from the 16th, 17th and 18th centuries, the houses retain many of their original features, including mullioned windows, heavy cylindrical chimneys and, in some cases, exposed spinning galleries, and are of great interest to lovers of vernacular architecture. **Troutbeck Church**, too, is worthy of a visit as there is a fine east window, dating from 1873, that is the combined work of Edward Burne-Jones, Ford Maddox Brown and William Morris.

However, perhaps the best-known building at Troutbeck is **Townend** (National Trust), another enchanting example of Lake District vernacular architecture. Built in 1626, the stone-and-slate house contains some fine carved woodwork, books, furniture and domestic implements collected by the Browne family, wealthy farmers

who lived here for more than 300 years until 1944. Open from April to October the house runs a regular 'living history' programme, so if you visit on a Thursday you can meet Mr George Browne – circa 1900.

Another notable resident of Troutbeck was 'the Troutbeck Giant' – Thomas Hogarth, uncle of the painter William Hogarth.

KENTMERE

8 miles NE of Windermere off the A591

This hamlet, as its name implies, lies in part of the valley that was once a lake, later drained to provide precious bottom pasture land. A large mill pond remains to provide a head of water on the River Kent for use at a paper mill.

The beautiful valley of the River Kent is best explored on foot. A public footpath runs up its western side, past **Kentmere Hall**, a fortified pele tower that is now a private farmhouse. Following the river southwards, the **Dales Way** runs down into Kendal and on into the Yorkshire Dales.

BROCKHOLE

3 miles NW of Windermere off the A591

The **Lake District Visitor Centre** at Brockhole provides enough activities for a full family day out. Lake cruises depart from the jetty here for 45-minute circular trips – groups of 20 or more can organise their own private boat. The gardens and grounds were the work of Thomas H Mawson, a Lancastrian who trained in London and set up in business in Windermere in 1885.

Inside St Cuthbert's Church in Kentmere is a bronze memorial to Bernard Gilpin, who was born at Kentmere Hall in 1517 and went on to become Archdeacon of Durham Cathedral. Known as The Apostle of the North, Gilpin was also a leader of the Reformation and, in 1558, he travelled to London to face charges of heresy against the Roman Catholic Church. During the journey Gilpin fell and broke his leg but, fortunately, while he was recovering, Catholic Queen Mary died and was succeeded by Protestant Queen Elizabeth. The new queen restored Gilpin to favour and saved him from being burnt at the stake.

- Events at the Lake District Visitor Centre at Brockhole include the Medieval Living Weekend, Taste of Cumbria Food Fair, Christmas Craft Fair and much more.

- Many of Ambleside's buildings are constructed in the distinctive grey-green stone of the area which blends in well with the green of the fields and fells all around.

The Bridge House, Ambleside

He soon became fashionable, and landscaped the gardens of many wealthy industrialists. Within the beautifully landscaped grounds at Brockhole visitors can join an organised walk accompanied by one of the gardening team, while their children can enjoy the well-equipped adventure playground. There are also lakeside picnic areas and a rare breeds centre. Brockhole itself is a fine Victorian mansion, originally built for a Manchester silk merchant. Here visitors can watch an audio-visual presentation about the area, browse in the gift shop (which stocks an excellent range of books, guides and maps), or take a break in the comfortable café which has an outdoor terrace

overlooking the lake. Home baking to traditional Cumbrian recipes is the speciality, and many dishes feature local produce. There is good wheelchair access to all parts of the Visitor Centre and most of the grounds.

AMBLESIDE

5 miles NW of Windermere on the A591

Standing less than a mile from the head of Lake Windermere, Ambleside is one of the busiest of the Lakeland towns, a popular centre for walkers and tourers, with glorious walks and drives radiating from the town in all directions. Ambleside offers a huge choice of pubs, restaurants, cafés, hotels and guest houses, as well as art galleries, two two-screen cinemas and a mix of traditional family-run shops supplemented by a modern range of retailers in the **Market Cross Centre**. Because of its many shops specialising in outdoor clothing, the town was recently described as 'the anorak capital of the world'. It would certainly be hard to find a wider selection anywhere of climbing, camping and walking gear.

The centre of the town is now a conservation area; its most picturesque building perhaps being **The Bridge House**, a tiny cottage perched on a packhorse bridge across Stock Ghyll. Today it's a National Trust shop and information centre, but during the 1850s it was the home of Mr and Mrs Rigg and their six children. The main room of this one-up, one-down residence measures just 13 feet by 6 feet, so living chez Rigg was decidedly cosy. Close by, at **Adrian Sankey's Glass Works**, visitors can watch craftsmen transform molten material into glass in the age-old way and also purchase the elegant results – wine glasses, perfume bottles, lampshades, huge bowls and much more. The studio stands next to an 18th-century water mill which Adrian Sankey, together with other local craftsmen, restored in 1995. Now, water flow permitting, you can watch the wheel in full working order and enjoy a coffee in

the café-restaurant housed in a restored 15th-century building.

A short walk from the mill brings the visitor to the **Armitt Museum** and Library, dedicated to the area's history since Roman times and to its most famous literary luminaries, John Ruskin and Beatrix Potter. Among the highlights are Beatrix Potter's early watercolours – exquisite studies of fungi and mosses – and a fascinating collection of photographs by Herbert Bell, an Ambleside chemist who became an accomplished photographer.

The popular panoramic view of Ambleside, looking north from the path up **Loughrigg Fell**, reveals the town cradled within the apron of the massive Fairfield Horseshoe, which rises to nearly 3,000 feet. Within the townscape itself, the most impressive feature is the rocket-like spire, 180 feet high, of **St Mary's Church**. The church was completed in 1854 to a design

17   BIZZY LIZZY'S

Ambleside

Charming coffee house and takeaway open mornings to late afternoon for light lunches, cakes and more.

see page 141

209   THE ARMITT MUSEUM

Ambleside

Gallery, museum and library dedicated to the history of the Lakeland area and its most famous inhabitants.

see page 221

Hills near Ambleside

120 COTTAGES ON THE GREEN

Ambleside

Three comfortable and attractive self-catering cottages near the town centre yet secluded and peaceful.

see page 183

by Sir George Gilbert Scott, the architect of London's St Pancras Station and the Albert Memorial. Inside the church is a chapel devoted to the memory of William Wordsworth, and an interesting 1940s mural depicting the ancient ceremony of rush-bearing. The mural was painted by Gordon Ransome of the Royal College of Art during the Second World War,

when the college was evacuated to the town. The rush-bearing ceremony dates back to the days when the floor of the church was covered by rushes, and is still enacted on the first Saturday in July. Some 400 children process through the town bearing colourful decorated rushes and singing the specially-commissioned Ambleside Rushbearer's Hymn.

A few weeks later every July, the famous **Ambleside Sports** take place, an event distinguished by the variety of local traditional sports it features. In addition to carriage-driving, ferret- or pigeon-racing, and tugs of war, the Sports include Cumberland and Westmorland wrestling (a little like Sumo wrestling but without the rolls of fat), fell-racing and hound-trailing.

Another experience not to be missed while at Ambleside is a boat cruise on Lake Windermere to Bowness. There are daily departures from the pier at **Waterhead**, about a mile south of the town. At Bowness there are connections to other lakeland attractions and, during the summer months, evening wine cruises. Rowing boats and self-drive motor boats can also be hired. Just to the west of the pier is **Borrans Park**, a pleasant lakeside park with plenty of picnic spots, and to the west of the park, the site of Galava Roman Fort. There is little to be seen of the fort, but the setting is enchanting. Also well worth a visit is nearby **Stagshaw Gardens** (National Trust), a spring woodland garden which contains a fine

Waterhead

collection of shrubs, including some impressive rhododendrons, azaleas and camellias. Parking is very limited and vehicular access is hazardous, so it's best to park at Waterhead car park and walk.

Perhaps the most unusual visitor attraction in Ambleside is the **Homes of Football**, described by the *Sunday Times* as a national treasure. It began as a travelling exhibition of football photographs and memorabilia, but now has a permanent home in Lake Road. Photographer Stuart Clarke recorded games and grounds at every kind of venue from the Premier League down to amateur village teams. There are now 60,000 photographs on file and a massive selection on show, framed and for sale. Some of the memorabilia retail for £200 or more, but entrance is free.

From Ambleside town centre, a steep road climbs sharply up to the dramatic **Kirkstone Pass** and over to Ullswater. The pass is so called because of the rock at the top which looks like a church steeple. Rising to some 1,489 feet above sea level, the road is the highest in the Lake District and, though today's vehicles make light work of the climb, for centuries the Pass presented a formidable obstacle. The severest incline, known as **The Struggle**, necessitated passengers to step out of their coach and to make

Kirkstone Pass

their way on foot, leaving the horses to make the steep haul with just the empty coach.

RYDAL

7 miles NW of Windermere on the A591

In 1813, following the deaths of their young children Catherine and Thomas, William and Mary Wordsworth were too grief-stricken to stay on at the Old Rectory in Grasmere. They moved a couple of miles down the road to **Rydal Mount**, a handsome house overlooking tiny **Rydal Water**. By now, the poet was well established and comparatively prosperous. A salaried position as Westmorland's Distributor of Stamps (a tax official) supplemented his earnings from poetry. Although Wordsworth only ever rented the house, it is now owned by his descendants and has been open to the public since 1970. The interior has seen little change, retaining a lived-in atmosphere. It contains first editions of the poet's work and

27

Wordsworth's House, Rydal Mount

**19   THE WILD
      DAFFODIL**

Grasmere

Superb café and restaurant
open for breakfast to last
orders at 9 p.m. for delicious
home-made food.

🍴   *see page 141*

many personal possessions, among
them the only surviving portrait of
his beloved sister, Dorothy.

William Wordsworth was a
keen gardener, and the 4-acre
garden at Rydal Mount remains
very much as he designed it.

GRASMERE

9 miles NW of Windermere on the A591

In 1799, Wordsworth described
Grasmere as 'the loveliest spot that
man hath ever found'. Certainly
Grasmere enjoys one of the finest
settings in all Lakeland, its small
lake nestling in a natural scenic
amphitheatre beside the compact,
rough-stone village.

For lovers of Wordsworth's
poetry, Grasmere is the pre-
eminent place of pilgrimage. They
come to visit **Dove Cottage** where

Wordsworth lived in dire poverty
from 1799 to 1808, obliged to line
the walls with newspaper for
warmth. The great poet shared this
very basic accommodation with his
wife Mary, his sister Dorothy, his
sister-in-law Alice and, as almost
permanent guests, Coleridge and
De Quincey. (Sir Walter Scott also
stayed, though he often sneaked off
to the Swan Hotel for a dram, since
the Wordsworths were virtually
teetotal.) Located on the outskirts
of the village, Dove Cottage has
been preserved intact: next door is
an award-winning museum
dedicated to Wordsworth's life and
works. Dove Cottage, Rydal Mount
(another of the poet's homes near
Grasmere), and his birthplace,
Wordsworth House at
Cockermouth, are all owned by the

Wordsworth Trust which offers a discount ticket covering entrance to all three properties.

In 1808 Wordsworth moved to **The Rectory** (private) opposite St Oswald's Church. In his long poem *The Excursion*, he describes the house and its lovely garden beside the River Rothay. The church, too, is remembered in the same poem:

Not raised in nice proportions was the pile
But large and massy, for duration built,
With pillars crowded and the roof upheld
By naked rafters intricately crossed,
Like leafless underboughs in some thick wood.

In 1850 the Poet Laureate was buried beneath yew trees he himself had planted in **St Oswald's** churchyard. He was joined here by his sister Dorothy in 1885, and his wife Mary in 1889. In Grasmere town cemetery is the grave of

William Archibald Spooner, sometime Warden of New College, Oxford. He gave his name to Spoonerisms, in which the initial letters of two words are transposed, with amusing results. Here are a few of his gems, some genuine, others perhaps apocryphal, such as *'You have hissed all my mystery lessons'* and *'Yes indeed: the Lord is a shoving leopard.'* Spooner spent many holidays in Grasmere with his wife at her house, How Foot.

Like Ambleside, Grasmere is famous for its **Sports**, first recorded in 1852, which still take place in late August. The most celebrated event in the Lake District, they attract some 10,000 visitors and feature many pursuits unique to Cumbria, such as Cumberland and Westmorland wrestling as well as the more straightforward, if arduous, fell-running.

20/121   DALE LODGE HOTEL

Grasmere

Gracious and elegant hotel, bar and restaurant in acres of beautiful gardens surrounded by stunning scenery.

⊨ ‖   *see pages 142, 184*

Dove Cottage

29

Wordsworth Relics at Dove Cottage

Collectors of curiosities who happen to be travelling north on the A591 from Grasmere should look out for the vintage black-and-yellow AA telephone box on the right-hand side of the road. Still functioning, **Box 487** has been accorded Grade II listed building status by the Department of the Environment.

The Cartmel & Furness Peninsulas

The southernmost coast of Cumbria is sometimes overlooked by visitors, but this is a great pity as it has much to offer, including a rich history as well as some truly splendid scenery. Lying between the lakes and mountains of the Lake District and the sandy estuaries of Morecambe Bay, this is an area of gentle moorland, craggy headlands, scattered woodlands and vast expanses of sand.

It was once a stronghold of the Cistercian monks, whose influence can still be seen in the buildings and fabric of the landscape. This was Cumbria's ecclesiastical centre, and several monasteries remain. Two in particular are well worth visiting today: Cartmel Priory and Furness Abbey.

Before the great boom of the local iron-ore mining industry, the peninsular villages and market towns relied on farming and fishing and, before some of the river estuaries silted up, there was also some import and export trade. The rapid growth of Barrow-in-Furness, which will be forever linked with the shipbuilding industry, changed the face of much of the area, but as the iron industry declined, so too did the town.

The arrival of the railways in the mid-19th century saw the development of genteel resorts such as Grange-over-Sands overlooking the treacherous sands of Morecambe Bay. Grange is still an elegant little town and has been spared the indignity of vast amusement parks and rows of slot machines, retaining its character as a quiet and pleasant holiday centre.

Furness Abbey

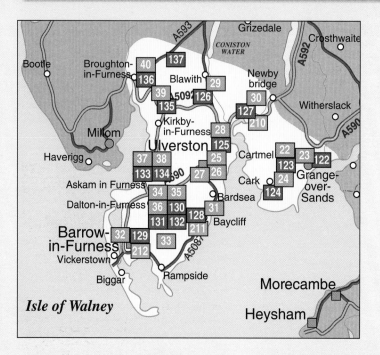

GRANGE-OVER-SANDS

Grange, as it's known locally, is an attractive little town set in a natural sun-trap on the north shore of Morecambe Bay. Much of its Victorian charm can be credited to the **Furness Railway Company** which developed the town after building the Lancaster-to-Whitehaven line in 1857. At that time, the whole of the Cartmel and Furness Peninsulas were part of Lancashire, a detached area whose main link with the rest of the county was the dubious route across Morecambe Sands. The railway provided a safe alternative to this hazardous journey. At Grange the company built an elegant mile-long promenade (now traffic free) and set out the colourful ornamental gardens. Prosperous merchants built grand country homes here, and it wasn't long before local residents began referring to their town as 'the Torquay of the North'.

Though Grange doesn't have a beach to rival that of its neighbour across Morecambe Bay, it does enjoy an exceptionally mild climate, the mildest in the northwest, thanks to the Gulf Stream. It is still a popular place, particularly with people who are looking for a pleasant and quiet place to retire. It was a favourite with Beatrix Potter, who recorded that on one visit to the town she met a 'friendly porker', a meeting that inspired *The Tale of Pigling Bland*. There's no connection, of course, but today the town boasts a butcher's shop, Higginsons, which has been voted the Best Butcher's Shop in England.

The route to Grange, across the sands of **Morecambe Bay**, is a treacherous one, though it was used not only by the Romans but also by

23 AT HOME

Grange-over-Sands

Café and restaurant in the centre of town serving home-made dishes using locally-sourced produce.

see page 143

122 BLACKROCK HOLIDAY FLATS

Grange-over-Sands

Self-catering cottage and flats facing Morecambe Bay; ideal as a base for touring/walking in the Lakes.

see page 185

•

Grange-over-Sands: 'Grange', or 'Graunge', came from the French word meaning 'granary': the monks of nearby Cartmel Priory stored their grain here until Henry VIII dissolved England's monasteries in 1537.

•

Morecambe Bay

•

Grange-over-Sands has a wealth of speciality shops as well as a new family attraction, Berners. The 25 metre pool overlooking Morecambe Bay offers a superb range of water based activities as well as a state-of-the-art fitness centre, sauna and steam room.

•

123 PRIOR'S YEAT

Cartmel

Charming and comfortable accommodation in sight of Cartmel Priory; excellent choice of hearty breakfasts.

⊨ see page 185

the monks of Furness Abbey and, later, even by stage coaches looking to shorten their journey time. Avoiding the quicksands of the bay, which have taken many lives over the centuries, is a difficult task. Back in the 16th century, the Duchy of Lancaster appointed an official guide to escort travellers over the shifting sands, and also provided him with a house at Grange. The town still has an official guide who takes groups on a three-hour walk across the bay. The sands are extremely dangerous since 'the tide comes in with the merciless speed of a galloping horse' – a crossing should never be attempted without the help of a qualified guide.

Away from the hotels, shops and cafés of the town there are some lovely walks, and none is more pleasant than the path behind Grange which climbs through magnificent limestone woodlands rich in wildflowers. The path finally leads to the 727ft **Hampsfell Summit** and **The Hospice**, a little stone tower from which there are unforgettable views over the bay and, in the opposite direction, the craggy peaks of the Lake District. The Hospice was provided by Grange's Vicar, the Reverend Thomas Remington, in 1834 to provide a refuge for travellers who found themselves stranded on the fell overnight. An external flight of stairs leads to a flat roof and, as the Vicar observed in a poem attached to the wall:

The flight of steps requireth care,
The roof will show a prospect rare.

Grange is also the starting point of the **Cistercian Way**, an interesting 33-mile long footpath through Furness to Barrow.

AROUND GRANGE-OVER-SANDS

LINDALE

2 miles NE of Grange-over-Sands off the A590

This small village was the birthplace of a man who defied the scepticism of his contemporaries and built the first successful iron ship. 'Iron Mad' John Wilkinson also built the first cast-iron barges, and later created the castings for the famous Iron Bridge at Coalbrookdale. After his death in 1808 he was buried in an iron coffin (naturally) in an unmarked grave, and the lofty **Wilkinson Obelisk** to his memory that stands near the village crossroads is also cast in iron. The admirers who erected it, however, omitted to provide the iron column with a lightning conductor. A few years later it was struck to the ground by a lightning bolt. The obelisk lay neglected in shrubbery for some years, but has now been restored and towers above the village once again. Just outside Lindale, at **Castle Head**, is the imposing house that Wilkinson built by the River Winster.

CARTMEL

2 miles W of Grange-over-Sands off the B5278

One of the prettiest villages in the Peninsula, Cartmel is a delightful cluster of houses and cottages set around a square from which lead winding streets and arches into back yards. The village is dominated by the famous **Cartmel Priory**, founded in 1188 by Augustinian canons. According to legend, it was originally intended to be sited on nearby Mount Bernard, until St Cuthbert appeared in a vision to the monastic architect and ordered him to build the Priory between two springs of water, one flowing north and the other south. The next morning, water was found to be trickling in two different directions from the foundation stones, and it is here that the church stands today.

Like all monastic institutions, the priory was disbanded with the Dissolution and several of its members were executed for participating in the Pilgrimage of Grace. Today, substantial remains of the 12th-century Gatehouse (National Trust) survive, but the rest of the Priory was cannibalised to build many of the village's cottages and houses. After the Dissolution, only the south aisle of the **Church of St Mary and St Michael** was still standing. In 1620, George Preston of Holker began restoring the entire building; the richly carved black oak screens and stall canopies date from this restoration. St Mary & St Michael's has recently been described as 'the most beautiful church in the northwest'.

Inside, in the southwest corner of the church, is a door known as **Cromwell's Door**. The holes in it are said to have been made by indignant parishioners firing at

Parliamentarian soldiers who had stabled their horses in the nave. Cromwell's troops were certainly in the area in 1643 and, to further establish the story, fragments of lead were found in the wood during restoration work in 1955.

Other features of interest include the glorious 45ft high east window (inspired by York Minster), the 14th-century tomb of Lord and Lady Harrington, a fine Jacobean

22   THE KINGS ARMS

Cartmel

Riverside pub near famous racecourse, with real ales and hearty traditional food.

see page 143

Cartmel Priory

24/124 THE HOPE AND ANCHOR

Flookburgh

Real ales, tasty home-cooked meals and comfortable accommodation in a pristine stonebuilt public house.

see pages 143, 185

screen and some floor tablets referring to people who had drowned trying to cross the sands of Morecambe Bay. By the chancel screen are two sculptures by Josephina de Vasconcellos – one of St Michael, the other depicting the flight to Egypt. Cartmel is also famous for its attractive **Racecourse**, set beside the River Eea, on which meetings are held in May, July and August. Located close to the village, the course must be one of the most picturesque in the country; it is certainly one of the smallest. A holiday atmosphere descends on the village for race days and, though the competition is fierce, it is a wonderful and relaxing day out.

FLOOKBURGH

3 miles SW of Grange-over-Sands on the B5277

An ancient Charter Borough, Flookburgh is still the principal fishing village on Morecambe Bay.

Roads from the square lead down to the shore where fishermen still land their catches of cockle, shrimps and (less often nowadays) flukes, the tasty small flat fish from which the village takes its name. In **Coach House**, Winder Lane, is an unusual attraction in the form of a miniature village. Some 120 buildings made of local Coniston slate are accurate down to the last detail.

New to Flookburgh is Ducky's Farm Park, a fun day out for all the family with a variety of animals to see and stroke as well as a wide range of other activites including donkey rides.

CARK-IN-CARTMEL

3 miles SW of Grange-over-Sands on the B5278

Cumbria's premier stately home, **Holker Hall** is one of many belonging to the Cavendish family, the Dukes of Devonshire. An intriguing blend of 16th-century Georgian and Victorian architecture, a visitor-friendly place with no restraining ropes keeping visitors at a distance, a fire burning in the hearth and a lived-in, family atmosphere. There's an impressive cantilevered staircase, a library with some 3,500 leather-bound books (plus a few dummy covers designed to hide electricity sockets) and an embroidered

Holker Hall

panel said to be the work of Mary, Queen of Scots.

Each year, Holker's 25 acres of award-winning gardens host the **Holker Garden Festival** which has been hailed as the 'Chelsea of the North'. The gardens are the pride of Lord and Lady Cavendish, who developed the present layout from the original 'contrived natural landscape' of Lord George Cavendish over 200 years ago. The Great Holker Lime and the stunning spring display of rhododendrons are among the delights not to be missed. Here, too, are a wonderful rose garden, an azalea walk and a restored Victorian rockery. Lord and Lady Cavendish have put their pride into words: 'If you gain from your visit a small fraction of the pleasure that we ourselves get from them, then the work of generations of gardeners will not have been in vain.' The gardens at Holker Hall have featured in BBC-TV's *An English Country Garden*.

The Holker Hall estate contains a wide variety of other attractions: formal gardens, water features, a 125-acre deer park, picnic and children's play areas, a gift shop and café. Also within the grounds is the **Lakeland Motor Museum**, which as well as boasting a completely restored 1920s garage, has more than 100 vehicles on show among well over 20,000 well-presented exhibits. The cars may hold centre stage, but there's a great deal more, including 'magnificent motorbikes, superb scooters, bygone bicycles and triumphant tractors'. Housed in

a quaint former Shire horse stable and its courtyard, the museum also honours leading figures from the world of motoring, among them Walter Owen Bentley, Frederick Henry Royce, Henry Ford, Colin Chapman and Alec Issigonis. A special exhibit is devoted to the attempts of Sir Malcolm and Donald Campbell to beat the world water speed record on Coniston Water.

ULVERSTON

It was way back in 1280 that Edward I granted Ulverston its market charter. Over 700 years later, colourful stalls still crowd the narrow streets and cobbled market square every Thursday. It's a picturesque scene, but a walk up nearby **Hoad Hill** is rewarded with an even more striking view of the town. The great expanse of Morecambe Bay with a backdrop of the Pennines stretches to the south, the bulk of Ingleborough lies to the east, Coniston Old Man and the Langdale Pikes lie to the west and north.

A famous son of Ulverston was Stanley Jefferson, born at number 3, Argyle Street on June 16th, 1890. Stanley is far better known to the world as Stan Laurel. His 30-year career in more than 100 comedy films with Oliver Hardy is celebrated in the town's **Laurel and Hardy Museum** in Upper Brook Street. The museum was founded in 1976 by the late Bill Cubin, who devoted his life to the famous duo and collected an

25 LAUREL'S BISTRO

Ulverston

Expertly prepared dishes Monday to Saturday in an attractive setting, honouring one of the town's most famous sons, Stan Laurel.

see page 144

26 KINGS CAFÉ WINE BAR

Ulverston

Attractive venue for morning coffee, lunch, afternoon tea and expertly-prepared evening meals.

see page 144

27 OLDE ULVERSTON TEA ROOMS

Ulverston

Word has spread far and wide about the quality of the cuisine and the excellent hospitality on offer here.

see page 144

•

Crowning a hill to the north of Ulverston town centre is the Barrow Monument, *a 100ft-high replica of the Eddystone Lighthouse that was erected in 1850 to commemorate Sir John Barrow. An explorer, diplomat and author, Barrow served as Lord of the Admiralty for more than 40 years, and it was his naval reforms that contributed to England's success in the Napoleonic Wars.*

•

Laurel and Hardy Museum, Ulverston

extraordinary variety of memorabilia, believed to be the largest in the world. Everything is here, including letters, photographs, personal items and even furniture belonging to the two greats of cinema comedy. A large extension has been added to the modest 17th-century house and there is also a small cinema showing films and documentaries throughout the day. The museum is open seven days a week all year round except during January.

Another son of Ulverston was Lord Norman Birkett, who represented Britain at the Nuremberg Trials and Mrs Wallis Simpson when she filed for divorce prior to marrying King Edward VIII.

Yet another great man associated with the town is George Fox, founder of the Quakers. Despite an extremely rough reception from the citizens of Ulverston when he preached here in the 1650s, Fox later married

Margaret, widow of Judge Fell of nearby **Swarthmoor Hall**. This lovely late 16th-century manor house, set in extensive gardens, was the birthplace of the Quaker movement and was for a time George and Margaret's home and the first settled centre of the Quaker movement.

Ulverston itself, with its fascinating alleys and cobbled streets, is a delightful place to wander around. The oldest building in the town is the **Church of St Mary** which dates, in parts, from 1111. Though it was restored and rebuilt in the mid-19th century and the chancel was added in 1903, it has retained its splendid Norman door and some magnificent stained glass, including a window designed by the painter Sir Joshua Reynolds. The present tower dates from the reign of Elizabeth I, as the original steeple was destroyed during a storm in 1540.

Ulverston also boasts England's shortest, widest and deepest **Canal**. Visitors can follow the towpath walk alongside, which runs dead straight for just over a mile to Morecambe Bay. Built by the famous engineer John Rennie and opened in 1796, the canal ushered in a half-century of great prosperity for Ulverston as an inland port. At its peak, some 600 large ships a year berthed here, though those good times came to an abrupt end in 1856 with the arrival of the railway. The railway company's directors bought the canal and promptly closed it.

The town's other attractions

include **The Lakes Glass Centre**, which features the high-quality Heron Glass and Cumbria Crystal. Also at the Centre is the **Gateway to Furness Exhibition**, providing a colourful snapshot of the history of the Furness Peninsula. There's more history at the **Ulverston Heritage Centre**, which also has a gift shop selling souvenirs and crafts made in Cumbria, while modern entertainment is provided at the Coronation Hall theatre complex and the traditional Roxy Cinema.

The open area to the north of Ulverston, known as **The Gill**, is the starting point for the 70-mile Cumbria Way. The route of the Cumbria Way was originally devised by the Lake District area of the Ramblers Association in the mid-1970s, and provides an exhilarating journey through a wonderful mix of natural splendour and fascinating heritage. The first section is the 15-mile walk to Coniston.

AROUND ULVERSTON

HAVERTHWAITE
5 miles NE of Ulverston off the A590

Haverthwaite is the southern terminus of the **Lakeside & Haverthwaite Railway**, a branch of the Furness railway originally built to transport passengers and goods to the steamers on Lake Windermere. It was one of the first attempts at mass tourism in the Lake District. Passenger numbers peaked in the 1920s, but the general decline of rail travel in the 1960s led to the railway's closure in 1967. However, a group of dedicated rail enthusiasts rescued this scenic stretch, restored its engines and rolling stock to working order and now provide a full service of steam trains throughout the season.

SWARTHMOOR
1 mile S of Ulverston off the A590

This small village of whitewashed cottages, now almost entirely incorporated into Ulverston, also has a curious 16th-century hall. **Swarthmoor Hall** stands in well-kept gardens and, although a cement rendering disguises its antiquity, the mullion windows and leaded panes give a clue to its age. It was built in around 1586 by George Fell, a wealthy landowner. It was his son, Judge Thomas Fell, who married Margaret Askew, who, in turn, became a follower of George Fox after hearing him preach in 1652. At that time, many people were suspicious of Fox's beliefs, but Margaret was able to persuade her husband to use his position to give Fox protection and shelter, and the Hall became the first settled centre of the Quaker Movement. Missionaries were organised from here and the library was stocked with both Quaker and anti-Quaker literature. Judge Fell died in 1658 and, 11 years later, Margaret married George Fox. Swarthmoor Hall is open during the summer and offers visitors a fascinating insight into the history of the early Quakers.

30 THE ANGLERS ARMS

Haverthwaite

10 real ales served all day, every day, great food at lunch and dinner in convivial inn close to the Lakeside and Haverthwaite Railway.

see page 145

127 CROOK FARM

Bouth, Haverthwaite

Spacious and well-appointed accommodation in an 18th-century farmhouse.

see page 186

210 THE LAKESIDE & HAVERTHWAITE RAILWAY

Haverthwaite Station

Restored steam railway running through beautiful lakeland scenery.

see page 221

31/128 THE FARMERS ARMS

Baycliff, Ulverston

Superior inn located in the beautiful village of Baycliff just minutes from Morecambe Bay. Great food, drink and accommodation.

❚ ⊨ *see pages 145, 186*

•

Lying between Great Urswick and Bardsea and overlooking Morecambe Bay is Birkrigg Common, *a lovely area of open land. Here, on the east side of the common, is the* Druid's Circle, *with two concentric circles made up of 31 stones up to 3 feet high. The cremated human remains found around the site in 1921 indicate that is was used for burials. There are several other prehistoric sites in the Great Urswick area.*

•

LINDAL-IN-FURNESS

3 miles SW of Ulverston on the A590

The **Colony Country Store** combines the aromatic character of an old-fashioned country general stores with the cost-cutting advantages of a Factory Shop. There's a huge range of textiles, glassware, ceramics and decorative accessories for the home, but the Colony is also Europe's leading manufacturer of scented candles, supplying millions of scented and dinner candles every year to prestigious shops around the world. The 30 fragrances include classic Rose, fruity Fresh Peach and French Vanilla. From a viewing gallery visitors can watch the traditional skills of hand-pouring and dipping being used to create a variety of candle styles. For a small additional fee you can try your hand at dipping your own candle. Open daily all year round, The Colony has a restaurant serving hot meals and snacks, and free parking.

GREAT URSWICK

3 miles S of Ulverston off the A590

The ancient village **Church of St Mary and St Michael** is noted for its unusual and lively woodcarvings that were created by the Chipping Campden Guild of Carvers. As well as the figure of a pilgrim to the left of the chancel arch, there are some smaller carvings in the choir stall of winged children playing musical instruments. Also worthy of a second look is the 9th-century wooden cross which bears a runic inscription.

BARDSEA

2 miles S of Ulverston off the A5087

The village stands on a lovely green knoll overlooking the sea and, as well as having a charming, unhurried air about it, there are some excellent walks from here along the coast either from its Country Park or through the woodland.

Just up the coast, to the north, lies **Conishead Priory**, once the site of a leper colony that was established by Augustinian canons in the 12th century. After the Dissolution, a superb private house was built on the site and the guide service was continued by the Duchy of Lancaster. In 1821, Colonel Braddyll demolished the house and built in its place the ornate Gothic mansion that stands here today. He was also responsible for the atmospheric ruined folly on **Chapel Island** that is clearly visible in the estuary. The monks from Conishead Priory used to act as guides across the dangerous Cartmel Sands to Lancashire.

Latterly, **Conishead Priory** has been a private house, a hydropathic hotel, a military hospital and a rest home for Durham miners; it is now owned by the Tibet Buddhist Manjushri Mahayana Buddhist Centre, who came here in 1977. During the summer months visitors are welcome to the house, which is open for tours, and there is a delightful woodland trail to follow through the grounds. A new Buddhist temple was opened in 1998, based on a traditional design which symbolises the pure world (Mandala) of a Buddha.

BARROW-IN-FURNESS

Undoubtedly the best introduction to Barrow is to pay a visit to the **Dock Museum** (free admission), an impressive glass-and-steel structure which hangs suspended above a Victorian Graving Dock. Audio-visual displays and a series of exhibits describe how Barrow grew from a tiny hamlet in the early 1800s to become the largest iron and steel centre in the world, and also a major shipbuilding force, in just 40 years. The original population of just 200 had, by 1874, increased to over 35,000.

The museum has some spectacular models of ships of every kind, an Art Gallery hosting both permanent and travelling exhibitions, and an interactive film show where characters from Barrow's history come to life to tell the town's story. Other attractions at the museum include a themed adventure playground, a Museum Shop and a coffee shop.

It was James (later Sir James) Ramsden who established the first Barrow Iron Ship Company in 1870, taking advantage of local steel-production skills. In 1896 the firm was acquired by **Vickers**, a name forever linked with Barrow, and for a number of years was the largest armaments works in the world. Sir James was also the General Manager of the Furness Railway and the town's first mayor.

At the Ramsden Square roundabout is a statue to Sir James, and at the next roundabout is a statue of HW Schneider, one of the men who developed the Furness iron mines and was involved in the Barrow Haematite Steel Company.

Today, Barrow is the Peninsula's prime shopping centre, with all the familiar High Street stores mingling with local specialist shops, and the largest indoor market in the area which is open on Mondays, Wednesdays, Fridays and Saturdays. The town also boasts a wide range of entertainment facilities – multiplex cinema, 10-pin bowling, fitness centre and leisure club, and three first-class golf courses all within easy reach.

Barrow is also the western starting point of the **Cistercian Way**, a 33-mile-walk to Grange-over-Sands through wonderfully unspoilt countryside. En route it passes Furness Abbey in the Vale of Deadly Nightshade, prehistoric sites on the hills surrounding Urswick Tarn and many other historical places of interest. The Way is marked on public roads and footpaths, and a fully descriptive leaflet is available from Tourist Information Centres.

AROUND BARROW-IN-FURNESS

GLEASTON

3 miles E of Barrow-in-Furness off the A5087

This village is typical of the small, peaceful villages and hamlets that can be found in this part of the

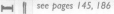

32/129   THE RAMS HEAD HOTEL

Barrow-in-Furness

Large and convivial town-centre pub and hotel with easy access to the many sights and attractions of the region.

see pages 145, 186

212   THE DOCK MUSEUM

Barrow-in-Furness

A modern museum tracing the history of Barrow as it developed from a tiny hamlet to a major iron and steel and shipbuilding centre.

see page 222

33   THE COPPER DOG

Leece, nr Ulverston

Superb free House and restaurant with an excellent menu of freshly prepared dishes at lunch and dinner every day.

see page 146

41

211 GLEASTON WATER MILL

Gleaston, Ulverston

Historic water-driven corn mill, in full working order. Cafe and gallery also on site.

🏛 see page 221

Situated on the Walney Island's long foot, South Walney Nature Reserve is home to the largest nesting ground of herring gulls and lesser black-backed gulls in Europe. It is also the most southerly breeding ground of such species as the oystercatcher, tern and ringed plover. In all, over 250 bird species have been recorded. A stopover for many migratory birds, the reserve has considerable ecological interest with mudflats, sandy beaches, rough pasture and fresh water. There are waymarked trails around the reserve, with a number of hides.

peninsula. Here, standing close by the ruins of **Gleaston Castle**, can be found **Gleaston Water Mill**. The present buildings date from 1774, with the massive original wooden gearing still in place. The machinery is operational most days – an 18ft water-wheel and an 11ft wooden pit wheel serviced by an intriguing water course. Evening tours with supper are available by prior arrangement. To reach Gleaston Water Mill, follow the signs from the A5087. Guided talks, walks and tours can be arranged.

FOULNEY ISLAND

5 miles E of Barrow-in-Furness off the A5087

The island, like its smaller neighbour Roa Island, is joined to the mainland by a causeway. The site of the local lifeboat station, the island is small and sheltered from the Irish Sea by Walney Island.

PIEL ISLAND

5 miles SE of Barrow-in-Furness via foot ferry from Roa island

Though this tiny island was probably visited by both the Celts and the Romans, its first recorded name is Scandinavian – *Fotheray*, from the Old Norse meaning 'fodder island'. In 1127 the islands were given to the Savignac Monks by King Stephen; the order merged with the Cistercian monks in the middle of the 12th century. The monks of Furness Abbey used Piel Island as a warehouse and storage area.

Piel Castle, on the island, was a house fortified in the early part of

the 14th century and at the time it was the largest of its kind in the northwest. Intended to be used as one of the abbey's warehouses and to offer protection from raiders, in later years the castle also proved to be a useful defence against the King's Customs men, and a prosperous trade in smuggling began. The castle has, over many years, been allowed to fall into ruin and now presents a stark outline on the horizon.

One of the most exciting events in Piel's history occurred on 4th June 1487 when a man claiming to be the Earl of Warwick, one of the Princes in the Tower allegedly murdered by Richard III, landed on the island. If true, the Earl was indisputably the true King of England. In reality, this 'Earl of Warwick' was later proved to be Lambert Simnel, the son of a joiner. Supported by an army of German and Irish mercenaries, Simnel set out across Furness to march on London. However, when he arrived in the capital it was as the prisoner of Henry VII, who had defeated Simnel's troops at Stoke.

WALNEY ISLAND

2 miles W of Barrow-in-Furness on the A590

This 10-mile-long island is joined to the Furness Peninsula by a bridge from Barrow docks and is home to two important nature reserves situated at either end of the island. **North Walney National Nature Reserve** covers some 350 acres within which are a great variety of habitats including sand dunes, heath, salt marsh, shingle and scrub. As well as having several species of orchid and over 130 species of bird either living or visiting the reserve, there is also an area for the preservation of the Natterjack toad, Britain's rarest amphibian. Unique to the Reserve is the Walney Geranium, a plant that grows nowhere else in the world. North Walney also boasts a rich prehistoric past, with important archaeological sites from mesolithic, neolithic, Bronze and Iron Age times.

Walney Island's southernmost tip, **Walney Point**, is dominated by a 70ft lighthouse which was built in 1790 and whose light was, originally, an oil lamp.

DALTON-IN-FURNESS

5 miles N of Barrow-in-Furness off the A590

Lying in a narrow valley on the part of Furness that extends deep into Morecambe Bay, it is difficult to imagine that this ancient place was once the leading town of Furness and an important centre for administration and justice. The 14th-century pele tower, **Dalton Castle**, was built with walls 6 feet thick to provide a place of refuge for the monks of Furness Abbey against Scottish raiders and it still looks very formidable. Over the centuries, in its twin role as both prison and court, it has been substantially altered internally although it still retains most of its original external features. It is now owned by the National Trust and houses a small museum with an

interesting display of 16th and 17th-century armour, along with exhibits about iron mining, the Civil War in Furness, and the life and work of George Romney, the 18th-century portrait painter.

Dalton became established as a market town in the 13th century when the Cistercians began to hold fairs and markets in the town. Indeed, the influence of the monks was great here as, before the Dissolution, it was the Abbot who held court and administered justice. Not surprisingly, Dalton's decline coincided with the departure of the monks and also with the growing importance of Ulverston and Greenodd as ports.

The red sandstone **Church of St Mary** was designed by the celebrated Victorian architects Paley and Austin. In the graveyard lies George Romney, best known in his day for his many portraits of Nelson's mistress, Lady Hamilton, with whom he formed a romantic attachment in spite of having a wife in Kendal. His grave is marked with the inscription *pictor celeberrimus*. Also worth seeking out in the graveyard is the plaque which outlines the devastating effect of the bubonic plague which swept through the town in 1662. Of the total population at the time of 612, no fewer than 320 fell victim to the plague.

Visitors to Dalton will find that it is time well spent looking around the many fascinating façades in and close to the market place, such as the unique, cast-iron shop front at No 51, **Market Street**. In the

34/130 CHEQUERS HOTEL & RESTAURANT

Dalton-in-Furness

Distinguished hotel that began life as a school in Victorian times, fully renovated to offer the best in modern comfort and traditional charm.

see pages 147, 187

35/131 CLARENCE HOUSE COUNTRY HOTEL AND RESTAURANT

Skelgate, Dalton-in-Furness

The jewel in the crown of Furness – elegance, quality and comfort are the hallmarks of this superior country house hotel.

see pages 148, 188

36/132 THE RED LION INN

Dalton-in-Furness

Close to the Castle, bar meals and a full menu Tues-Sat 12-2 and 6-9; Sun 12-8. Seven guest bedrooms.

see pages 149, 189

37/133 THE ASKAM HOTEL

Askam-in-Furness

A few hundred yards from the beach, a comfortable and welcoming establishment: accommodation, real ales, food at weekends.

🍴 🛏 see pages 149, 189

38/134 FURNESS TAVERN

Askam-in-Furness

Home-cooked food, secluded beer garden and comfortable accommodation distinguish this traditional tavern from the rest.

🍴 🛏 see pages 149, 189

Furness Abbey

market place itself is an elegant, **Victorian Drinking Fountain** with fluted columns supporting a dome of open iron work above the pedestal fountain. Nearby stand the market cross and the slabs of stone that were used for fish-drying in the 19th century.

From the mostly pedestrianised Tudor Square, visitors can board a bus to the award-winning **South Lakes Wild Animal Park** which has been designated the Region's Official Top Attraction by the Cumbria Tourist Board. It's the only place in Britain where you can see rare Amur and Sumatran tigers (the world's biggest and smallest tigers). At feeding time (14.30 each day) they climb a 20ft vertical tree to 'catch' their food. Ring-tailed lemurs wander freely through the park, visitors can walk with emus and hand-feed the largest collection of kangaroos in Europe. The 17 acres of natural parkland are also home to some of the rarest animals on earth, among them the red panda, maned wolves and tamarin monkeys as well as some 150 other species from around the world, including rhinos, giraffes, tapirs, coatis and the ever-popular

meerkats. Other attractions include a Safari Railway, adventure play area, many picnic spots, a gift shop and café.

To the south of the town lies **Furness Abbey** (English Heritage), a magnificent ruin of eroded red sandstone set in fine parkland, the focal point of south Cumbria's monastic heritage. Among the atmospheric remains can still be seen the canopied seats in the presbytery and the graceful arches overlooking the cloister, testaments to the abbey's former wealth and influence. Furness Abbey stands in the **Vale of Deadly Nightshade**, a shallow valley of sandstone cliffs and rich pastureland. The abbey itself was established in 1123 at Tulketh, near Preston, by King Stephen. Four years later it was moved to its present site and, after 20 years, became absorbed into the Cistercian Order. Despite its remoteness the abbey flourished, with the monks establishing themselves as guides across the treacherous sands of Morecambe Bay. Rich endowments of land, including holdings in Yorkshire and Ireland, led to the development of trade in products such as wool, iron and charcoal. Furness Abbey became the second wealthiest monastery in Britain, after Fountains Abbey in Yorkshire. After the Dissolution in 1537, the abbey became part of Thomas Cromwell's estate and it was allowed to decay into a picturesque and romantic ruin. It is now owned by English Heritage who have a small Interpretative Centre nearby detailing its history. Off the A595 Dalton-to-Askam road, **Sandscale Haws** is one of the most important sand dune systems in Britain, supporting an outstanding variety of fauna.

GRIZEBECK

15 miles N of Barrow-in-Furness on the A595/A5092

This small village on the edge of the Lake District National Park nestles against the flanks of the **Furness Fells**. Although it stands at the junction of roads leading to the Furness Peninsula and the South Cumbria coast, the village and the area around is peaceful and unhurried, offering the visitor an inviting alternative to some of the busier and more crowded Lakeland towns.

BROUGHTON-IN-FURNESS

19 miles N of Barrow-in-Furness on the A595/A593

At the heart of this attractive, unspoilt little town is the **Market Square** with its tall Georgian houses, commemorative obelisk of 1810, village stocks, fish slabs and some venerable chestnut trees. The old Town Hall, occupying the whole of one side, dates back to 1766 and now houses the town's Tourist Information Centre and the Clocktower Gallery, which exhibits paintings, ceramics, mirrors and glassware. On August 1st each year, Broughton's Lord of the Manor comes to the Square to read out the market charter granted by Elizabeth I, while Councillors dispense

pennies to any children in the crowd.

One of the town's famous short-term residents was Branwell Brontë, who was employed here as a tutor at **Broughton House**, a splendid double-fronted, three-storey town house just off the Square. Branwell apparently found time both to enjoy the elegance of the town and to share in whatever revelries were in train. Wordsworth often visited Broughton as a child. Throughout his life he loved this peaceful corner of Lakeland and celebrated its charms in some 150 poems; his 20th-century poetical successor, Norman Nicholson, was similarly enchanted.

Some of the Lake District's finest scenery – the Duddon Valley, Furness Fells, Great Gable and Scafell – are all within easy reach, and about 3 miles west of the town is **Swinside Circle**, a fine prehistoric stone circle, some 60 feet in diameter, containing 52 close-set stones and two outlying 'portal' or gateway stones.

About 3 miles north of the town, the peaceful hamlet of **Broughton Mills** will attract followers of the Coleridge Trail. During the course of his famous 'circumcursion' of Lakeland in August 1802, the poet stopped to refresh himself at the **Blacksmith's Arms** where he 'Dined on Oatcake and Cheese, with a pint of Ale, and 2 glasses of Rum and water sweetened with preserved Gooseberries'. The inn, built in 1748, is still there and barely changed since Coleridge's visit.

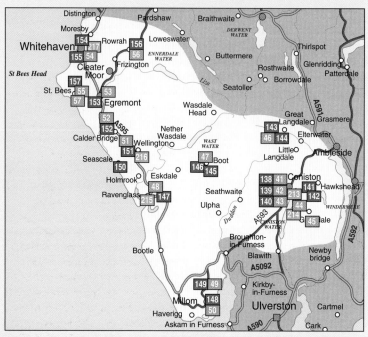

Coniston & South West Cumbria

Three distinct areas lie within the southwest quarter of Cumbria. The enchanting scenery around Coniston Water and its environs is very much on the tourist trail, and also has strong

Esthwaite Water

literary connections. John Ruskin, the 19th-century author, artist and critic, made his home at Brantwood on the shore of Coniston; the lake is also the setting for many of the adventures recounted in *Swallows and Amazons* as told by Arthur Ransome. Wordsworth went to school in Hawkshead, where the desk he defaced with his name can still be seen. But probably the most popular of Coniston's literary denizens is Beatrix Potter, who, after holidaying at Near Sawrey as a child, later bought a house at Hill Top as well as many acres of farms which she bequeathed to the National Trust. Further west is

Cumbria's 'Empty Quarter', a vast terrain of magnificent mountains and desolate fells beloved of climbers and walkers. England's highest mountain, Scafell Pike, rises here; the country's deepest lake, Wast Water, sinks to a depth of some 200 feet and is surrounded by sheer cliffs soaring up to 2,000 feet. The village of Wasdale Head claims to have the smallest church in England.

Bordering this untamed landscape is the narrow coastal strip stretching from Whitehaven down to Millom, which has its own identity as well as a quiet charm. The coastline is dominated by small 18th and 19th century iron-mining communities set between the romantic outline of the Lakeland fells and the grey-blue waters of the Irish Sea. The famous Ravenglass and Eskdale Railway carries many visitors from the coast up one of Cumbria's most picturesque valleys. There are also several genteel Victorian resorts along the coast, including the popular village of Seascale.

Aerial View of Coniston

47

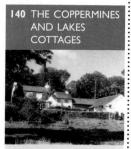
CONISTON

Beatrix Potter, John Ruskin, Arthur Ransome, Sir Donald Campbell – all had strong connections with **Coniston Water**, the third largest and one of the most beautiful of the central Cumbrian lakes. Beatrix Potter lived at Sawrey near Lake Windermere, but she owned the vast **Monk Coniston** estate at the head of Coniston Water. On her death she bequeathed it to the National Trust, a body she had helped to establish and to which she devoted much of her time and fortune.

Ruskin came to Coniston in 1872, moving into a house he had never seen. Brantwood, on the eastern side of the lake, is open to the public and enjoys superb views across the water to the great crumpled hill of the **Old Man of Coniston**, 800 metres high. From its summit there are even more extensive vistas over Scotland, the Isle of Man, and on a clear day as far as Snowdonia.

Arthur Ransome's *Swallows and Amazons* has delighted generations with its tales of children's adventures set in and around the Lake District. As a child he spent his summer holidays near Nibthwaite at the southern end of the lake and recalled that he was always 'half-drowned in tears' when he had to leave. Later he bought a house overlooking Coniston Water and many locations in his books can be recognised today: **Peel Island**, for example, at the southern end of the lake, is the Wildcat Island of his books.

Sir Donald Campbell's associations with the lake were both glorious and tragic. In 1955 he broke the world water speed record here; 12 years later, when he was attempting to beat his own record, his boat, **Bluebird**, struck a log

Coniston Water

Jetty on Coniston Water

42/138   THE CROWN HOTEL

Coniston

Tasteful and stylish hotel within easy reach of Coniston Water; real ales, good food and 12 comfortable bedrooms. 4 Diamonds ETB.

🛏 🍴   see pages 150, 190

43   SPINDLES OF CONISTON

Coniston

On Lake Road, tea rooms and restaurant with expertly-prepared dishes using locally-sourced ingredients.

🍴   see page 150

44   JUMPING JENNY COFFEE HOUSE AND RESTAURANT

Coniston

Excellent home cooking on the grounds of Ruskin's one-time home, Brantwood overlooking Coniston Water.

🍴   see page 151

while travelling at 320 mph. In March 2001 his widow was present as the tailfin of the boat was at last hauled up to the surface. For 34 years the 15ft rear section had lain on a bed of silt, 140 feet down and right in the middle of the lake. Plans are still under way for the boat to be restored and placed on display at the Ruskin Museum, but it could take some time. Sir Donald's body was later recovered and was buried on September 12th, 2001 in the village cemetery – an event that was comparatively little covered by the media, who were obviously concerned with the tragic events in the United States the day before.

Nowadays, boats on Coniston Water are restricted to a 10-mph limit – an ideal speed if you're travelling in the wonderful old steamship, the **Gondola**. So called because of its high prow, which enabled it to come in close to shore to pick up passengers, *Gondola* was commissioned by Sir James Ramsden, General Manager of the Furness Railway Company and first Mayor of Barrow, and was launched on Coniston Water in 1859. She retired in 1936, but found a new career as a houseboat in 1945. Abandoned after a storm in the 1960s, she was saved by a group of National Trust enthusiasts and restored and rebuilt by Vickers Shipbuilding. She was relaunched in 1980. Up to 86 passengers can now travel in opulent comfort on her regular trips around the lake. Coniston Launch also offers lake cruises in its two timber launches, and at the boating centre craft of every kind are available to rent.

Coniston village was once an important copper mining centre, and was also widely known for the

●

The Grizedale Forest Visitor Centre vividly illustrates the story of the forest as well as showing how the combination of wildlife, recreation and commercial timbering can work together hand in hand.

●

beautiful decorative green slate, quarried locally, which is used on so many of the public buildings. The great bulk of the Old Man of Coniston overlooks the village; it was from this mountain, and some of the surrounding hills, that copper was extracted. Mined from the days of the Romans, the industry's heyday in Coniston was in the 18th and 19th centuries but, with the discovery of more accessible deposits, the industry went into decline and the village returned to pre-boom peacefulness. At 2,631 feet, the Old Man of Coniston is a considerable climb, but many make the effort and the summit can be bustling with fell-walkers enjoying the glorious views.

Just south of the village and beside the lake is **Coniston Hall**, the village's oldest building. Dating from the 16th century, it was the home of the Le Fleming family, the largest landowners in the area. Coniston's most famous inhabitant was, however, John Ruskin, the 19th-century author, artist, critic, social commentator and one of the first conservationists. He lies buried in Coniston churchyard and the **Ruskin Museum** nearby contains many of his studies, pictures, letters and photographs as well as his collection of geological specimens. Visitors can also see a pair of his socks, his certificate of matriculation from Oxford, and his funeral pall made of Ruskin lace embroidered with wild flowers. The lace was so called because Ruskin had encouraged the revival of flax hand-spinning in the area. Lace

pieces made to his own designs and based on the sumptuous ruffs worn by sitters in portraits by Titian, Tintoretto and Veronese were attached to plain linen to make decorative cushions, table covers and bedspreads – many of these are on display.

From the jetty at Coniston, a short ferry trip takes you to John Ruskin's home, **Brantwood**, which occupies a beautiful setting on the eastern shores of Coniston Water. It was his home from 1872 until his death in 1900. When he arrived for the first time he described the house, which he had bought for £1,500 without ever seeing it, as 'a mere shed'. He spent the next 20 years extending the house, adding another 12 rooms, and laying out the gardens. The view from the Turret Room he had built was, Ruskin declared, 'the best in all England'.

Visitors today can wander around rooms filled with Ruskin's watercolours, paintings by Turner (who was one of his heroes), see his study which is lined with wallpaper he designed himself, and watch a 20-minute video which provides a useful introduction to his life and works. Every Thursday during the season there are lace-making demonstrations, and readings from Ruskin's works are performed regularly in the study. There's also a well-stocked bookshop, a craft gallery and 250 acres of grounds where there are well-marked nature trails and where a theatre season is held during the summer.

AROUND CONISTON

GRIZEDALE

3 miles SE of Coniston off the B5285

The village lies at the heart of the 9,000-acre **Grizedale Forest** which was acquired by the Forestry Commission in 1934 and is famous for its Sculpture. The Commission's original intention of chiefly cultivating the forest for its timber met with much resistance and, over the years, many pathways have been opened and a variety of recreational activities have been encouraged. The forest, too, is famously the home of some 80 tree sculptures commissioned since 1977. All are created from natural materials found in the forest, and made by some of Britain's best-known contemporary artists, including Andy Goldsworthy, as well as by artists from all over the world. The great beauty of these sculptures is their understated presence: there are no signposts pointing to the exhibits; visitors are left entirely on their own to discover these wonders – though there is a printed map obtainable from the Visitor Centre.

GRIZEDALE

4 miles E of Coniston on the B5285

Though this little village will not be familiar to many visitors to the Lake District, its famous inhabitant, Beatrix Potter, almost certainly will be. After holidaying here in 1896, the authoress fell in love with the place and, with the royalties from her first book, *The Tale of Peter Rabbit*, she purchased **Hill Top** in

Sculpture Trail, Grizedale Forest

1905. After her marriage in 1913 to a local solicitor, she actually lived in another house in the village, Castle Cottage (private), and used the charming 17th-century cottage as her study. Oddly, she wrote very little after the marriage, spending most of her time dealing with the management of the farms she had bought in the area.

Following Beatrix Potter's death in 1943, the house and the land she had bought on the surrounding fells

45 THE EAGLES HEAD

Satterthwaite, nr Ulverston

Excellent 16th-century inn in a picturesque village in the heart of Grizedale Forest, with superb ales, food and hospitality.

see page 151

51

Hill Top, Beatrix Potter's House

141 ESTHWAITE OLD HALL

Hawkshead

Elegant, comfortable accommodation in a refurbished Estate building dating back to the 16th century.

see page 191

•
The only building in Hawkshead to remain from monastic times is the Courthouse, to the north of the village, part of a medieval manor house built by the monks.
•

became the property of the National Trust. In accordance with Beatrix Potter's will, Hill Top has remained exactly as she would have known it.

One of the most popular Lakeland attractions, Hill Top is full of Beatrix Potter memorabilia, including some of her original drawings. The house is very small, so it is best avoided at peak holiday times. **Tarn Hows**, part of the 4,000-acre Monk Coniston estate bought and sold on to the National Trust, was created to resemble a Swiss lake

and is very rich in flora and fauna – it has been designated a Site of Special Scientific Interest.

HAWKSHEAD

3 miles E of Coniston on the B5285

There are more Beatrix Potter connections in the enchanting little village of Hawkshead. Her solicitor husband, William Heelis, worked from an office in the Main Street here, and this has now been transformed into **The Beatrix Potter Gallery**. The gallery features an exhibition of her original drawings and illustrations alongside details of the author's life.

Hawkshead has specific Wordsworth connections, too. **Hawkshead Grammar School** was founded in 1585 by Edwin Sandys, Archbishop of York, and between 1779 and 1787 the young William Wordsworth was a star pupil. The earliest of his surviving poems was written to celebrate the school's 200th year. The school is

Tarn Hows

open from Easter to September, and visitors can inspect the classrooms during the summer holidays, see the desk where William carved his name and have a look around the headmaster's study. Ann Tyson's Cottage, where Wordsworth lodged while he attended the school, has also survived. It stands in Wordsworth Street and is now a guest house.

Hawkshead

Situated at the head of **Esthwaite Water**, enjoying glorious views of Coniston Old Man and Helvellyn, Hawkshead has a history that goes back to Viking times. Its name is Norse in origin, derived from *Haukr*, who built the original settlement. It's a delightful village of narrow cobbled lanes with a pedestrianised main square dominated by the Market House, or Shambles, and another square linked to it by little snickets and arched alleyways which invite exploration. The poet Norman Nicholson observed that 'The whole village could be fitted into the boundaries of a large agricultural show; yet it contains enough corners, angles, alleys and entries to keep the eye happy for hours.'

Hawkshead was once an important market town serving the surrounding area; at that time most of the land here was owned by the monks of Furness Abbey.

The **Church of St Michael & All Angels**, with its massive 15th-century tower, seems rather grand for the village but it too was built at a time when Hawkshead was a wealthy town. Inside, there are some remarkable wall paintings from the late 1600s and also look out for the 'Buried in Woolen' affidavit near the vestry door. In 1666 the Government had decreed that corpses must not be buried in shrouds made from 'flaxe, hempe, silke or hair, or other than what is made of sheeps wool onely'. The idea was to help maintain the local woollen industry, and this was one way of ensuring that even the dead got to help out. The church is the focal point of the annual Lake District Summer Music Festival and a popular venue for concerts and recitals. In the churchyard is a war memorial erected in 1919 and modelled on the ancient runic cross at Gosforth.

142 BORWICK FOLD

Outgate, Ambleside

Excellent self-catering cottages 3 miles southwest of Ambleside off the B5286.

see page 191

46/143 THE OLD DUNGEON GHYLL HOTEL

Great Langdale

14 bedrooms, Hikers Bar & home-made food in a spectacular setting at the head of Great Langdale Valley.

see pages 152, 192

144 MILLBECK FARM & SIDE HOUSE FARM & COTTAGE

Great Langdale

Bed & breakfast and self-catering accommodation amid spectacular countryside near the head of the lovely Langdale Valley.

see page 192

Dungeon Ghyll

Some lovely walks lead from Hawkshead to **Roger Ground** and Esthwaite Water, possibly the least frequented of the Lakes, and also to the nearby hamlet of **Colthouse** where there's an early Quaker Meeting House built around 1690. Esthwaite Water was much loved by Wordsworth, as he shows in his poem

The Prelude: My morning walks were early; oft before the hours of school I travelled round our little lake, five miles Of pleasant wandering. Happy time!

GREAT LANGDALE

9 miles N of Coniston on the B5343

One of the most dramatic of the Lake District waterfalls is **Dungeon Ghyll**, which tumbles 60 feet down the fellside. Nearby is the well known Old Dungeon Ghyll Hotel, which makes an excellent starting point for walks in this spectacularly scenic area where the famous peaks of Crinkle Crags, Bowfell and the Langdale Pikes provide some serious challenges for hikers and ramblers.

The 'dungeon' is actually a natural cave.

SEATHWAITE

5 miles W of Coniston via minor road off the A593

A mere 5 miles or so from Coniston as the crow flies, by road Seathwaite is nearly three times as far. It stands in one of the Lake District's most tranquil and least-known valleys, **Dunnerdale**. Wordsworth captured its natural beauty in a sequence of sonnets. In his poem *The Excursion*, he wrote about the Reverend Robert Walker, the curate of Seathwaite. Nicholas, or 'Wonderful Walker' as Wordsworth referred to him, served the church here for some 67 years though he also filled various other jobs such as farm labourer and nurse as well as spinning wool and making his own clothes. Fell-walkers and hikers who prefer to escape the masses will delight not only in the solitude of this glorious valley but also in the wide variety of plant, animal and birdlife that have made this haven their home.

HARDKNOTT PASS

5 miles W of Coniston off the A593

Surrounded by the fell of the same name, this pass is one of the most treacherous in the Lake District yet it was used by the Romans for the road between their forts at Ambleside (*Galava*) and Ravenglass (*Glannaventa*). Of the remains of Roman occupation, **Hardknott Fort** on a shoulder of the fell, overlooking the Esk Valley, is the most substantial and also provides some of the grandest views in the whole of the Lake District. The walls of the fort, known as

Mediobogdum, still stand up to 2 metres high, and within them the foundations of the commander's house, headquarters building and granary can be seen.

BOOT

8 miles W of Coniston off the A595

Lying at the eastern end of the **Ravenglass and Eskdale Railway**, this is a wonderful place to visit whether arriving by train or car. A gentle walk from the station at Eskdale brings you to this delightful village with its pub, post office, museum, waterfall and nearby St Catherine's Church in its lovely secluded riverside setting. Perhaps because of the rugged walking country to the east, the village is well supplied – with both a campsite and bunkhouse available.

ESKDALE GREEN

10 miles W of Coniston off the A595

One of the few settlements in this beautiful and unspoilt valley, the village lies on the route of the Ravenglass and Eskdale Railway. Further up the valley lies a group of buildings that make up **Eskdale Mill** where cereals have been ground since 1578, when it is recorded that the brothers Henry and Robert Vicars were the tenants, paying an annual rent of eight shillings (40p). The original machinery for grinding oatmeal is in full working order and operated daily. Power for the two waterwheels is provided by Whillan Beck, which surges down from England's highest mountains, the Scafell range. Visitors can enjoy a

Hardknott Fort

picnic in the picturesque mill grounds, browse in the gift shop or explore the Mill's history in the informative exhibition. Eskdale Mill may be reached by crossing a 17th-century packhorse bridge over the beck.

RAVENGLASS

Lying as it does at the estuary of three rivers – the Esk, the Mite, and the Irt – as well as enjoying a sheltered position, it is not surprising that Ravenglass was an important port from prehistoric times. The Romans built a naval base here around AD 78 which served as a supply point for the military zone around Hadrian's Wall. They also constructed a fort, **Glannaventra**, on the cliffs above the town, which was home to around 1,000 soldiers. Little remains of Glannaventra except for the impressively preserved walls of the Bath House. Almost 12 feet high, these walls are believed to be the highest Roman remains in the

145 STANLEY GHYLL HOUSE

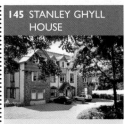

Boot

Excellent accommodation amid stunning scenery just steps from the Ravenglass-to-Eskdale Railway.

see page 193

47/146 BROOK HOUSE INN & RESTAURANT

Boot

Set amid glorious Eskdale Valley countryside, superb inn with real ales, home-cooked dishes and comfortable accommodation.

see pages 152, 193

Originally part of the Muncaster Castle Estate, Muncaster Water Mill can be traced back to 1455, though it is thought that this site may be Roman. The situation is certainly idyllic, with the mill race still turning the huge wooden water wheel and the Ravenglass and Eskdale Railway running alongside. In November 1996, Pam and Ernie Priestley came to the mill and Ernie put his years of engineering experience to use as the miller. Visitors can see the machinery in action, and also enjoy some delicious refreshments in the 17th-century byre tea rooms. Naturally, the organic flour ground here is used in all the cakes, breads and scones, and the flour is also on sale. Muncaster Water Mill is open every day from Easter to the end of October, working just as it has done for hundreds of years.

Ravenglass

country. In the 1700s Ravenglass was a base for smugglers bringing contraband in from coastal ships – tobacco and French brandy.

Today the estuary has silted up but there are still scores of small boats and the village is a charming resort, full of atmosphere. The layout has changed little since the 16th century; the main street is paved with sea pebbles and leads up from a shingle beach. Once, iron-ore was brought to the estuary by narrow-gauge railway from the mines near Boot, in Eskdale, about 8 miles away.

One of the town's major attractions is the 15-inch narrow-gauge **Ravenglass and Eskdale Railway** which runs for 7 miles up the lovely Mite and Esk River valleys. Better known as 'La'al Ratty', it was built in 1875 to transport ore and quarried stone from the Eskdale Valley, and opened the following year for passenger traffic. Since then the railway has survived several threats

of extinction. The most serious occurred at the end of the 1950s when the closure of the Eskdale granite quarries wiped out the railway's freight traffic at a stroke. However, at the auction for the railway in 1960 a band of enthusiasts outbid the scrap dealers and formed a company to keep the little railway running.

Today, the company operates 12 locomotives, both steam and diesel, and 300,000 people a year come from all over the world to ride on what has been described as 'the most beautiful train journey in England'. The La'al Ratty is still the best way to explore Miterdale and Eskdale, and enchants both young and old alike. There are several stops along the journey, and at both termini there is a café and a souvenir shop. At the Ravenglass station there is also a museum which brings to life the history of this remarkable line and the important part it has played in the life of Eskdale.

A mile or so east of Ravenglass stands **Muncaster Castle**, which has been in the ownership of the Pennington family since 1208. In 1464 the Penningtons gave shelter to King Henry VI after his defeat at the Battle of Hexham. On his departure Henry presented them with his enamelled glass drinking bowl, saying that as long as it remained unbroken the Penningtons would survive and thrive at Muncaster. Apart from the many treasures, the stunning Great Hall, Salvin's octagonal library and the barrel ceiling in the drawing room, Muncaster is also famous for its gardens. The collection of species rhododendrons is one of the finest in Europe, gathered primarily from plant-hunting expeditions to Nepal in the 1920s, and there are also fine azaleas, hydrangeas and camellias as well as many unusual trees. For many visitors the chief attraction is the **World Owl Centre**, where many endangered owl species are bred. Snowy owls have become great favourites on the back of the Harry Potter craze, and many visitors have enquired about keeping them as pets. The staff at the Centre have to point out that the snowy owl is a mighty predator with a 5-foot wingspan. Mighty as he is, he is not the mightiest of the owls at the Centre: that honour goes to the Eurasian eagle owl, whose full splendour can be seen at the daily demonstrations. Muncaster's latest attraction is the Meadow Vole Maze (these little creatures are the staple diet of barn owls, and visitors can find out what it's like to be a vole on the run from a hungry owl).

AROUND RAVENGLASS

WABERTHWAITE

4 miles S of Ravenglass on the A595

No visit to west Cumbria is complete without the inclusion of a trip to RG Woodall's shop. Found in the heart of this village, Richard Woodall is world famous for his sausages, in particular for the Waberthwaite Cumberland Sausage, and is the proud possessor of a Royal Warrant from the Queen.

BOOTLE

7 miles S of Ravenglass on the A595

This ancient village is particularly picturesque and quaint. The river Annas flows beside the main road and then dives under the village on its way to the sea. High up on **Bootle Fell**, to the southeast of the village, lies one of the best stone circles in Cumbria. Over the years, many of the 51 stones that make up the **Swinside Stone Circle** have fallen over. When it was originally constructed and all the stones were upright, it is likely, as they were also close together, that the circle was used as an enclosure.

SILECROFT

10 miles S of Ravenglass off the A595

Perhaps of all the villages in this coastal region of the National Park, Silecroft is the perfect example. Just a short walk from the heart of the village is the beach, which extends

215 MUNCASTER CASTLE

Ravenglass

An impressive mansion owned for 800 years by the Pennington family. The house contains a treasure trove of art and antiques. An owl centre located in the grounds is just one of many attractions here.

🏛 *see page 223*

48/147 THE BROWN COW INN

Waberthwaite

Excellent food with local specialities such as Cumberland sausage and Waberthwaite ham grace a superb menu. Accommodation available.

🍴 🛏 *see pages 153, 194*

49/149 UNDERWOOD
COUNTRY
GUEST HOUSE

Millom

Superb restored Victorian vicarage set in 8 acres; elegant, comfortable and renowned for its cuisine and accommodation.

see pages 154, 195

50/148 CAMBRIDGE
HOUSE HOTEL

Millom

Traditional hotel at Millom. Comfortable accommodation and home-cooked meals.Near Railway with links to local attractions

see pages 155, 194

as far as the eye can see. On the horizon lies the distant outline of the Isle of Man. There is also a **Site of Special Scientific Interest** close by, a tract of coastal scrubland which provides the perfect habitat for the rare Natterjack toad.

MILLOM

13 miles S of Ravenglass on the A5093

This small and peaceful town stands at the mouth of the River Duddon with the imposing **Black Combe Fell** providing a dramatic backdrop. Originally called Holborn Hill, the present-day name was taken from nearby **Millom Castle** which is now a private, working farm. Like many neighbouring towns and villages in Furness, Millom was a small fishing village before it too grew with the development of the local iron industry. **Millom Folk Museum**, recently relocated, tells the story of the town's growth and there is also a permanent memorial here to Norman Nicholson (1914-1987) who is generally regarded as the best writer on Lakeland life and customs since Wordsworth himself. Nicholson's book *Provincial Pleasures* records his affectionate memories of Millom, the town where he spent all his life. Other displays include a full-scale reproduction of a drift and cage from nearby Hodbarow mine. South of Millom, at Haverigg, is the **RAF Millom Museum** situated in the former Officers Mess. Visitors to the site will find a fascinating collection of over 2,000 photographs of the

wartime activities of the RAF in the area, various artefacts connected with the period and a number of items recovered from local crash sites. The museum also has a fine collection of aero engines including a Rolls Royce Merlin, a Westland Whirlwind helicopter, the cockpit section of a De Havilland Vampire jet trainer and an example of the HM14 or Flying Flea. The Duddon Estuary is an important site for wildlife, and the RSPB site at **Hodbarrow** is home not only to birds but to many kinds of flora and fauna. **Hodbarrow Beacon**, which still stands, was built in 1879 as a lighthouse to assist vessels taking iron ore from the mines to destinations in Europe.

HOLMROOK

2 miles N of Ravenglass on the A595

Situated on the banks of the River Irt, where it is possible to fish for both salmon and sea trout, this small village also lies on the Ravenglass and Eskdale Railway line. Though the village Church of St Paul is not of particular note, inside there is not only a 9th-century cross of Irish style but also memorials to the Lutwidges, the family of Lewis Carroll.

DRIGG

2 miles N of Ravenglass on the B5343

The main attractions here are the sand dunes and the fine views across to the Lakeland mountains and fells. There is an important nature reserve, **Drigg Dunes**, on the salt marshes that border the

River Irt but – take note, adders are common here. The reserve is home to Europe's largest colony of black-headed gulls.

SANTON BRIDGE

3 miles NE of Ravenglass off the A595

The churchyard of **Irton Church**, reached from Santon Bridge via an unclassified road, from the Holmebrook to Santon Bridge road, offers the visitor not only superb views of the Lakeland fells to the west but also the opportunity to see a beautiful Celtic Cross, in excellent condition, dating from the early 9th centruy. Though the original runic inscription has been eroded away over time, the fine, intricate carving can still be seen. The Bridge Inn here plays host each November to the 'World's Biggest Liar' competition (see Gosforth below).

SEASCALE

4 miles N of Ravenglass on the B5343

One of the most popular seaside villages in Cumbria, Seascale enhanced its resort status in 2000 by restoring the **Victorian Wooden Jetty** to mark Millennium Year. Stretching out into the Irish Sea, it provides the starting point for many walks, including the Cumbrian Coastal Way which passes along the foreshore. This fine sandy beach enjoys views over to the Isle of Man and the Galloway Mountains of Scotland while, behind the village, the entire length of the western Lakeland hills presents an impressive panorama. The Victorian Wooden Jetty at

Seascale is a focal point for fishing, beach-casting, wind-surfing and water-skiing.

Two Victorian buildings stand out: the **Water Tower**, medieval in style and with a conical roof, and the old **Engine Shed** which is now a multi-purpose Sports Hall.

GOSFORTH

5 miles N of Ravenglass on the A595

On the edge of this picturesque village, in the graveyard of **St Mary's Church**, stands the tallest ancient cross in England. Fifteen feet high, the **Viking Cross** towers above the huddled gravestones in the peaceful churchyard. Carved from red sandstone and clearly influenced by both Christian and pagan traditions, the cross depicts the crucifixion, the deeds of Norse gods and Yggdrasil, the World Ash Tree that Norsemen believed supported the universe. The interior of the church also contains some interesting features. There's a **Chinese Bell**, finely decorated with Oriental imagery, which was captured in 1841 at Anunkry, a fort on the River Canton, some delightful carved faces on the chancel arch and a collection of ancient stones the most notable of which dates from Saxon times and depicts the Lamb of God trampling on the serpents of pagan faith.

A major attraction in this appealing village is **Gosforth Pottery**, where Dick and Barbara Wright produce beautifully crafted work and also give pottery lessons.

To the east of Gosforth runs Wasdale, the wildest of the Lake

150 WESTCLIFF HOTEL

Seascale

Superb views over the seafront in tastefully refurbished Victorian residence with nine charming and comfortable guest bedrooms.

see page 196

216 GOSFORTH POTTERY

Gosforth

The skill and craftsmanship of over 20 potters' wares displayed in a handsome setting. Regular lessons, courses and open days.

see page 223

51/151 WESTLAKES HOTEL

Gosforth

Gracious and elegant hotel and restaurant set in mature gardens. Nine bedrooms. Dinner served Mon-Sat from 7 p.m.

see pages 155, 196

District valleys but easily accessible by road. The road leads to **Wast Water**, which is just 3 miles long but is the deepest lake in England. The southern shores are dominated by huge screes some 2,000 ft high that plunge abruptly into the lake; they provide an awesome backdrop to this tranquil stretch of water. A lake less like Windermere would be hard to find, as there are no motorboats ploughing their way up and down the lake. This is very much the country of walkers and climbers, and from here there are many footpaths up to some of the best fells in Cumbria.

Wasdale Head, just to the north of the lake, is a small, close-knit community with a far-famed Inn that has provided a welcome refuge for walkers and climbers since the mid-1800s who have been out discovering Wasdale and the lake. **Wasdale Church** is claimed to be the smallest in England – although this title is hotly disputed by Culbone in Somerset and Dale Abbey in Derbyshire. The church was built in the 14th century and it

Wast Water

is hidden away amidst a tiny copse of evergreen trees. Local legend suggests that the roof beams came from a Viking ship and it is certainly true that until late Victorian times, the church had only an earth floor and few seats.

As well as the deepest lake and the smallest church, Wasdale also boasts the highest mountain, **Scafell Pike** (3,205ft) – and the world's

Scafell Pike

biggest liars. This latter claim goes back to the mid-1800s when Will Ritson, 'a reet good fibber', was the publican at the inn. Will enthralled his patrons with tall stories of how he had crossed foxes with eagles to produce flying foxes and had grown turnips so large he could hollow them out to make a comfortable residence. In the same spirit, the 'World's Biggest Liar' Competition takes place every November, usually at the Bridge Inn at Santon Bridge, when contestants from all over the country vie in telling the most enormous porkies.

Sca Fell, about a mile away, is 'only' 3,162 feet, though getting from one to the other by a direct route isn't straightforward. The easiest routes are either via Lord's Rake on the Wasdale side or by descending and then re-ascending via Foxes Tarn on the Eskdale side.

CALDER BRIDGE

7 miles N of Ravenglass on the A595

From this small 19th-century settlement there is an attractive footpath to **Calder Abbey**. It was founded by monks of Savigny in 1134 but amalgamated with the Cistercians of Furness Abbey when it was ransacked by the Scots a few years later. After the Dissolution the monastery buildings lapsed slowly into the present-day romantic ruin. Part of the tower and west doorway remain, with some of the chancel and transept, but sadly these are unsafe and have to be viewed from the road. To the northeast of the village, the River Calder rises on Caw Fell.

•

Monk's Bridge, the oldest packhorse bridge in Cumbria, was built across the River Calder for the monks of Calder Abbey.

•

61

Beckermet, Egremont

Country inn and hotel in tranquil West Cumbrian village just a mile off the A595.

see pages 156, 197

Egremont

Open all day, every day for ale, tasty meals at lunch and dinner and comfortable accommodation in spacious and newly-refurbished 18th-century inn.

see pages 157, 198

•

Lowes Court Gallery in Egremont, in a listed 18th-century building, holds fine art exhibitions throughout the year and is home to the Tourist Information Centre.

•

EGREMONT

12 miles N of Ravenglass on the A595

This pretty town is dominated by **Egremont Castle** with walls 20 feet high and an 80ft tower. It stands high above the town, overlooking the lovely River Ehen to the south and the marketplace to the north. The castle was built between 1130 and 1140 by William de Meschines on the site of a former Danish fortification. The most complete part still standing is a Norman arch that once guarded the drawbridge entrance. Nearby is an unusual four-sided sundial and the stump of the old market cross dating from the early 13th century.

A legend concerning the castle is related in Wordsworth's poem, *The Horn of Egremont*. Apparently, a great horn hanging in the castle could only be blown by the rightful lord. In the early 1200s the rightful lord, Eustace de Lucy, was on a Crusade to the Holy Land together with his brother Hubert. The dastardly Hubert arranged with local hit men to have Eustace drowned in the Jordan. Hubert returned to Egremont, but during the celebration feast to mark his inheritance a mighty blast on the horn was heard. The hit men had reneged on the deal: Eustace was still alive. Hubert prudently retired to a monastery.

Egremont's prosperity was based on the good quality of its local red iron ore, and jewellery made from it can be bought at the nearby **Florence Mine Heritage Centre**. Visitors to the mine, the last deep working iron-ore mine in Europe, can join an underground tour (by prior arrangement) and discover why the miners became known as the Red Men of Cumbria. The museum here also tells story of the mine, which was worked by the ancient Britons, and there is a re-creation of the conditions that the miners endured at the turn of the 20th century.

In September every year the town celebrates its **Crab Fair**. Held each year on the third Saturday in September, the Fair dates back more than seven centuries – to 1267 in fact, when Henry III granted a Royal Charter for a three-day fair to be held on 'the even, day and the morrow after the Nativity of St Mary the Virgin'. The celebrations include the 'Parade of the Apple Cart' when a wagon loaded with apples is driven along Main Street with men on the back throwing fruit into the crowds. Originally, the throng was pelted with crab apples – hence the name Crab Fair – but these are considered too tart for modern taste, so nowadays more palatable varieties are used. The festivities also feature a greasy pole competition (with a pole 30 feet high), a pipe-smoking contest, wrestling and hound-trailing. The highlight, however, is the **World Gurning Championship** in which contestants place their heads through a braffin, or horse collar, and vie to produce the most grotesque expression. If you're toothless, you start with a great advantage!

WHITEHAVEN

The first impression of Whitehaven is of a handsome Georgian town, but it was already well established in the 12th century as a harbour used by the monks of nearby St Bees Priory. After the Reformation the land was acquired and developed by the Lowther family in order to expand the coal industry. Whitehaven's growth in those years was astonishing by the standards of the time – it mushroomed from a hamlet of just six thatched cottages in 1633 to a sizeable, planned town with a population of more than 2,000 by 1693. Its 'gridiron' pattern of streets, unusual in Cumbria, will be familiar to American visitors,

and the town boasts some 250 listed buildings. By the mid-1700s, Whitehaven had become the third-largest port in Britain, its trade based on coal and other cargo business, including importing tobacco from Virginia, exporting coal to Ireland, and transporting emigrants to the New World. When the large iron steamships arrived, however, the harbour's shallow draught halted expansion and the port declined in favour of Liverpool and Southampton. For that reason much of the attractive harbour area – now full of pleasure craft and fishing smacks – and older parts of the town remain largely unchanged.

The harbour and its environs

54/154 CAP'N SENNYS

Whitehaven

Spacious, welcoming inn with a good range of beers, wines and more. Food at weekends. Late-night opening (til 1 a.m.) Thurs-Sat.

see page 158, 199

Whitehaven Harbour

217 THE BEACON

Whitehaven

Museum tracing the social, industrial and maritime history of the area.

🏛 *see page 223*

155 GLENFIELD GUEST HOUSE

Corkickle, Whitehaven

Six tasteful guest bedrooms in elegant late-Victorian townhouse. Guests stay on B&B or Dinner, B&B basis. 4 Diamonds RAC.

⊨ *see page 199*

•

In Solway Road, Kells, the Haig Colliery Mining Museum features the world's only Bever Dorling Winding Engines, various displays about the mining industry, and exhibits on mining disasters. Haig Colliery was the last deep coal mine worked in the West Cumberland coalfield. Sunk between 1914 and 1918, it closed in 1986 and was later sold for restoration.

•

have been declared a Conservation Area, and here visitors will find **The Beacon**, where, through a series of innovative displays, the history of the town and its harbour are brought to life. Looking a bit like a small lighthouse, the museum deals with the history of the whole of Copeland (the district of Cumbria in which Whitehaven lies) with special emphasis on its mining and maritime past. The displays reflect the many aspects of this harbour borough with a collection that includes paintings, locally-made pottery, ship models, navigational instruments, miners' lamps and surveying equipment. The Beilby 'Slavery' Goblet, part of the museum's collection, is one of the masterpieces of English glass-making and is probably the finest example of its kind in existence. Also here are the **Harbour Gallery**, with an ongoing arts programme, and the **Met Office Gallery**, where visitors can monitor, forecast and broadcast the weather. They can also learn about the 'American Connection' and John Paul Jones' attack on the town in 1778, or settle down in the cinema to watch vintage footage of Whitehaven in times past. John Paul Jones had been an apprentice seaman at Whitehaven before going to the New World, where he became well known in the War of Independence. In 1777 he became Captain of the privateer *The Ranger* and led a raid on Whitehaven with the intention of firing the ships in the harbour. Thwarted by light winds, the party raided the fort and

spiked the guns, then managed to damage only three ships before retreating under fire. The museums at The Beacon trace the social, industrial and maritime heritage of the area.

There's more history at **The Rum Story**, which tells the story of the town's connections with the Caribbean. The display is housed in the original 1785 shop, courtyards, cellars and bonded warehouses of the Jefferson family, the oldest surviving UK family of rum traders. Visitors can learn about the various processes involved in the making of rum, travel through realistic re-creations of far-off villages, and experience the sights, sounds and smells of life on board the trading ships, many of which participated in a trade then considered acceptable but nowadays, of course, abhorrent: the trade in human 'cargo', or slaves.

As well as the elegant Georgian buildings that give the town its air of distinction, there are two fine parish churches that are worth a visit. Dating from 1753, **St James' Church** has Italian ceiling designs and a beautiful Memorial Chapel (dedicated to those who lost their lives in the two World Wars, and also the local people who were killed in mining accidents) while the younger **St Begh's Church**, which was built in the 1860s by EW Pugin, is striking with its sandstone walls. In the graveyard of the parish church of **St Nicholas** is buried Mildred Gale, the grandmother of George Washington. In 1699, this widow and mother of three married George Gale, a merchant who traded from Whitehaven to Maryland and Virginia. Her sons were born in Virginia but went to school in Appleby. When their mother died they returned to Virginia; one of them, Augustin, became the father of George Washington, first President of the United States.

Whitehaven is interesting in other ways. The grid pattern of streets dating back to the 17th century gives substance to its claim to be the first planned town in Britain. Many of the fine Georgian buildings in the centre have been restored and **Lowther Street** is a particularly impressive thoroughfare. Also of note is the **Harbour Pier** built by the canal engineer John Rennie and considered to be one of the finest in Britain. There is a fascinating walk and a nature trail around **Tom Hurd Rock**, above the town.

AROUND WHITEHAVEN

ST BEES

3 miles S of Whitehaven on the B5343

St Bees Head, a red sandstone bluff, forms one of the most dramatic natural features along the entire coast of northwest England. Some 4 miles long and 300 feet high, these towering, precipitous cliffs are formed of St Bees sandstone, the red rock that is so characteristic of Cumbria. Far out to sea, on the horizon, can be seen the grey shadow of the Isle of Man

and, on a clear day, the shimmering outline of the Irish coast. From here the 190-mile **Coast-to-Coast Walk** starts on its long journey across the Pennines to Robin Hood's Bay in North Yorkshire.

Long before the first lighthouse was built in 1822, there was a beacon on the headland to warn and guide passing ships away from the rocks. The present 99ft high lighthouse dates from 1866-7, built after an earlier one was destroyed by fire. St Bees Head is now an important **Nature Reserve** and the cliffs are crowded with guillemots, razorbills, kittiwakes, gulls, gannets, and skuas. Bird watchers are well provided for with observation and information points all along the headland. There is a superb walk of about 8 miles along the coastal footpath around the headland from St Bees to Whitehaven. The route passes Saltam Bay and Saltam Pit, which dates from 1729 and was the world's first undersea mineshaft. The original lamp house for the pit has been restored and is now used by HM Coastguard.

St Bees itself, a short walk from the headland, is a small village which lies huddled in a deep, slanting bowl in the cliffs, fringed by a shingle beach. The village is a delightful place to explore, with its main street winding up the hillside between old farms and cottages. It derives its name from St Bega, daughter of an Irish king who, on the day she was meant to marry a Norse prince, was miraculously transported by an angel to the Cumbrian coast.

•

Whitehaven has a curious literary association with Jonathan Swift, the poet, satirist, journalist and author of Gulliver's Travels. As a sickly infant in a poverty-stricken Dublin home, Swift was wet-nursed by a young girl from Whitehaven named Sarah. She was suddenly called to the deathbed of a relative in Cumbria from whom she expected a legacy. By now Sarah was so attached to the child she could not bear a separation, and carried him off with her to Whitehaven. Later, guilt-stricken, she wrote to Mrs Swift admitting what she had done, and received an answer asking her to continue looking after Jonathan, Mrs Swift being concerned about the effect on the boy's delicate health of another sea crossing. Swift stayed with the girl for three years and was clearly well looked after in every way – by the time he returned to Dublin he was in robust health and 'could read any chapter in the Bible'.

•

55/157 MANOR HOUSE HOTEL & COAST-TO-COAST BAR

St Bees

Charming and welcoming bar and hotel with real ales, lunch and dinner menu and excellent accommodation.

see pages 158, 200

57 HARTLEY'S BEACH SHOP

St Bees

Cakes, coffees, teas, scones, fresh sandwiches and famed ice-creams. Shop with foods, drinks, gifts and camping/ walking gear.

see page 159

According to legend, on Midsummer Night's Eve, St Bega asked the pagan Lord Egremont for some land on which to found a nunnery. Cunningly, he promised her only as much land as was covered by snow the following morning. But on Midsummer's Day, 3 square miles of land were blanketed white with snow, and here she founded her priory. (Incidentally, this 'miracle' snowfall is a not uncommon feature of a Cumbrian summer on the high fells.)

The Priory at St Bees grew in size and importance until it was destroyed by the Danes in the 10th century: the Benedictines later re-established the priory in 1129. **The Priory Church of St Mary and St Bega** is all that is now left, and although it has been substantially altered there is still a magnificent Norman arch and a pre-Conquest,

carved Beowulf Stone on a lintel between the church and the vicarage, showing St Michael killing a dragon. The most stunning feature of all is much more modern, a sumptuous Art Nouveau metalwork screen. In the south aisle is a small museum.

Close by the church are the charming Abbey Cottages and **St Bees School** with its handsome clock-tower. The original red sandstone quadrangle bears his coat-of-arms and the bridge he gave to the village is still in use. Among the school's most famous alumni is the actor and comedian Rowan Atkinson, creator of the ineffable Mr Bean. St Bees School was founded in 1583 by Edmund Grindal, Archbishop of Canterbury under Elizabeth I, and the son of a local farmer.

An anonymous resident of St Bees has also achieved fame of a kind. In 1981, archaeologists excavating a ruined chapel discovered a lead-lined coffin containing one of the best preserved medieval bodies in England. It was the corpse of a local lord who had died during the Crusades. Some of the artefacts including a shroud and hair found with the body can be seen in St Bees Church, together with pictures of the body and the setting in which it was found.

St Bees Head

Research is continuing into his identity and that of a female skeleton found nearby.

CLEATOR MOOR

3 miles SE of Whitehaven on the B5295

The name of this once-industrial town derives from the Norse words for cliff and hill pasture. Cleator developed rapidly in the 19th century because of the insatiable demand during the Industrial Revolution for coal and iron ore. As the Cumbrian poet Norman Nicholson wrote:

From one shaft at Cleator Moor
They mined for coal and iron ore.
This harvest below ground could
show Black and red currants on one tree.

Cleator is surrounded by delightful countryside, and little evidence of the town's industrial past is visible. There is, however, a thriving business nearby – the **Kangol Factory Shop** in Cleator village which stocks a huge range of hats, scarves, bags, caps and golf wear.

ENNERDALE BRIDGE

7 miles E of Whitehaven off the A5086

Wordsworth described Ennerdale's church as 'girt round with a bare ring of mossy wall' – and it still is. The bridge here crosses the River Ehen, which, a couple of miles upstream runs out from **Ennerdale Water**, one of the most secluded and inaccessible of all the Cumbrian lakes. The walks around this tranquil lake and through the quiet woodlands amply repay the slight effort of leaving the car at a distance.

56/156	THE STORK HOTEL

Rowrah

Home-made dishes, Jennings ales and excellent accommodation in pristine country inn.

‖ ⊨ see *page 158, 199*

•

The Coast-to-Coast Walk runs the whole length of Ennerdale, and this section is generally considered to be by far the most beautiful.

•

Ennerdale Water

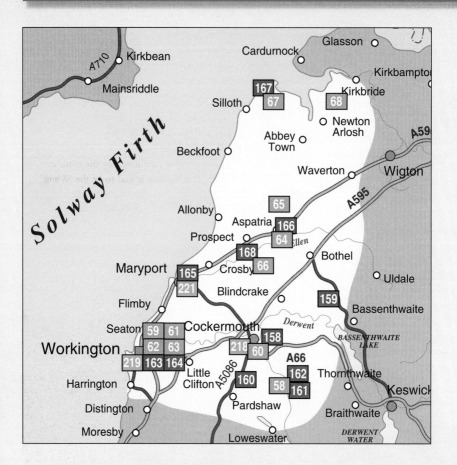

The North Cumbrian Coast

The North Cumbrian coast, from Workington in the south to the Solway Firth in the north, is one of the least-known parts of this beautiful county but it certainly has a lot to offer. It is an area rich in heritage, with a network of quiet country lanes, small villages, old ports, and seaside resorts. The coast's largest town, Workington, on the site of a Roman fort, was once a large port, prospering on coal, iron and shipping. It later became famous for fine-quality steel, and though its importance has declined, it is still the country's largest producer of railway lines. Further up the coast is Maryport, again a port originally built by the Romans.

However, Maryport has not gone down the industrial route to the extent of its neighbour and, as well as being a quaint and picturesque place, it is also home to a fascinating museum dedicated to the town's maritime past. A short distance inland lies Cockermouth on the edge of the Lake District National Park, a pretty market town with some elegant Georgian buildings. However, most visitors will be more interested to see and hear about the town's most famous son, the poet William Wordsworth, who was born here in 1770.

The northernmost stretch of coastline, around the Solway Firth, is an area of tiny villages with fortified towers standing as mute witness to the border struggles of long ago. These villages were the haunt of smugglers, wildfowlers, and half-net fishermen. What is particularly special about this coastline is its rich birdlife. The north Cumbrian coast was also the setting for Sir Walter Scott's novel *Redgauntlet*, and the fortified farmhouse by the roadside beyond Port Carlisle is said to be the 'White Ladies' of the novel.

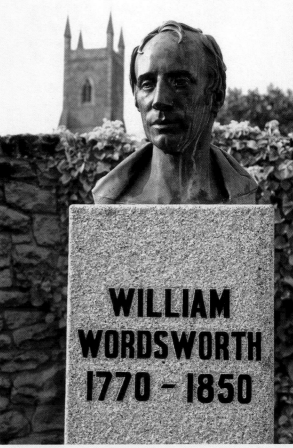

Wordsworth Memorial, Cockermouth

COCKERMOUTH

Cockermouth fully earns its designation as a 'gem town' recommended for preservation by the Department of the Environment. A market town since 1226, Cockermouth has been fortunate in keeping unspoilt its broad main street, lined with trees and handsome Georgian houses, and dominated by a statue to the Earl of Mayo. The Earl was Cockermouth's MP for ten years from 1858 before being appointed Viceroy of India. His brilliant career was brutally cut short when he was stabbed to death by a convict at a prison settlement he was inspecting on the Andaman Islands.

But Cockermouth boasts two far more famous sons. Did they ever meet, one wonders, those two young lads growing up in Cockermouth in the 1770s, both of them destined to become celebrated for very different reasons? The elder boy was Fletcher Christian, who would later lead the mutiny on the *Bounty*; the younger lad was William Wordsworth, born here in 1770 at Lowther House on Main Street, an imposing Georgian house now maintained by the National Trust. Now known as **Wordsworth House**, it was built in 1745 for the Sheriff of Cumberland and then purchased by the Earl of Lowther; he let it to his land agent, John Wordsworth, William's father. All five Wordsworth children were born here, William on 7th April 1770. Many of the building's original features survive, among them the staircase, fireplace, and fine plaster ceilings. A few of the poet's personal effects are still here and the delightful walled garden by the River Cocker has been returned to its Georgian splendour. The garden is referred to in *The Prelude*.

Wordsworth was only eight years old when his mother died and he was sent to school at Hawkshead, but later he fondly recalled walking at Cockermouth with his sister Dorothy, along the banks of the rivers Cocker and Derwent to the

Wordsworth House, Cockermouth

ruined castle on the hill. Built in 1134 by the Earl of Dunbar, **Cockermouth Castle** saw plenty of action against Scottish raiders (Robert the Bruce himself gave it a mauling in 1315), and again during the Wars of the Roses; in the course of the Civil War it was occupied by both sides in turn. Mary, Queen of Scots, took refuge at the castle in 1568 after her defeat at the Battle of Langside. Her fortunes were so low that she was grateful for the gift of 16 ells (about 20 yards) of rich crimson velvet from a wealthy merchant. Part of Cockermouth Castle is still lived in by the Egremont family; the remainder is usually only open to the public during the Cockermouth Festival in July.

Opposite the Castle entrance, **Castlegate House** is a fine Georgian house, built in 1739, which hosts a changing programme of monthly exhibitions of the work of Northern and Scottish artists - paintings, sculptures, ceramics and glass. To the rear of the house is a charming walled garden that is open from time to time during the summer.

Just around the corner from Castlegate House is the **Toy & Model Museum** which exhibits mainly British toys from around 1900 to the present. There are many visitor-operated displays including 0 and 00 gauge vintage tinplate trains, Scalextric cars, Lego models and even a 1950s helicopter to fly. There are prams and dolls houses, and a working railway in a garden shed.

Almost next door, **Jennings Brewery** offers visitors a 90-minute tour which ends with the option of sampling some of their ales – Cumberland Ale, Cocker Hoop or the intriguingly named Sneck Lifter. The last independent brewing company in Cumbria, Jennings have been brewing traditional beers since the 1820s. Today there are more than 100 Jennings pubs across the north of England. In addition to the tours, Jennings has a shop selling gifts and leisure wear, the latter boldly emblazoned with the names of its various brews.

A short walk from the Brewery brings you to the **Kirkgate Centre**, which is housed in a converted Victorian primary school. Run by volunteers, the Centre offers a wide range of events and activities including live music, amateur and professional drama, films, dance, workshops, exhibitions of art and local history.

Two more visitor attractions stand either side of Wordsworth House in the Main Street. The **Printing House Museum** occupies a building dating back to the 16th century and follows the progress of printing from its invention by Johann Gutenberg in 1430 to the end of the letterpress era in the 1960s, when computers took over. On display is a wide range of historical presses and printing equipment, the earliest being a Cogger Press dated 1820. Visitors are offered the opportunity to gain hands-on experience by using some of the presses to produce cards or keepsakes.

218 THE CUMBERLAND TOY & MODEL MUSEUM

Cockermouth

Award winning museum featuring toys and models dating from c.1900 to the present day.

🏛 see *page 223*

•

Located just south of Cockermouth town, the Lakeland Sheep & Wool Centre provides an introduction to life in the Cumbrian countryside with the help of a spectacular visual show, 19 different breeds of live sheep and a wide variety of exhibits. The Centre also hosts indoor sheepdog trials and sheep-shearing displays for which there is a small charge. Open all year round, the Centre has ample free parking, a shop selling woollen goods and gifts, a large café-restaurant and even en suite accommodation.

•

159 IRTON HOUSE FARM

Isel, Cockermouth

High-quality self-catering cottages in 240 acres of pasture and woodland close to many sights and attractions of the northern Lakes.

see page 200

58/161 NEW HOUSE FARM

Lorton, Cockermouth

Superb accommodation amid 17 acres of beautiful grounds. 5 Diamonds AA. Charming tea room next door.

see pages 160, 201

162 THE OLD VICARAGE

Lorton

Small and friendly country house set in wooded grounds in the beautiful Vale of Lorton.

see page 202

AROUND COCKERMOUTH

BRIGHAM

2 miles W of Cockermouth off the A66

St Bridget's Church, which was probably founded as part of a nunnery, contains many interesting features, including pre-Norman carved stones, a rare 'fish window' and a window dedicated to the Reverend John Wordsworth, son of William and vicar of Brigham for 40 years. One of the tombs in the graveyard is that of Charles Christian, the father of Fletcher Christian, the *Bounty* mutineer. Fletcher himself was baptised in the church on the day of his birth, as it was thought unlikely that he would survive.

BRIDEKIRK

2 miles N of Cockermouth off the A595

The village **Church** contains one of the finest pieces of Norman sculpture in the country, a carved font with a runic inscription and a mass of detailed embellishments. It dates from the 12th century and the runic inscription states that:

Richard he me wrought
And to this beauty eagerly me brought.

Richard himself is shown on one side with a chisel and mallet. Not only is this a superb example of early English craftsmanship but it is exceedingly rare to find a signed work. Ancient tombstones stand round the walls of this cruciform church and inside it has unusual reredos of fleur-de-lys patterned tiles.

HIGH & LOW LORTON

5 miles SE of Cockermouth on the B5289

There is a yew tree, pride of Lorton Vale ... wrote Wordsworth in his poem *Yew Trees*, and astonishingly it's still there behind the village hall of High Lorton. It was in the shade of its branches that the Quaker George Fox preached to a large gathering under the watchful eye of Cromwell's soldiers. In its sister village, Low Lorton, set beside the River Cocker, is **Lorton Hall** (private) which is reputed to be home to the ghost of a woman who carries a lighted candle. Less spectral guests in the past have included King Malcolm III of Scotland, who stayed here with his queen while visiting the southern boundaries of his Kingdom of Strathclyde of which this area was a part.

EAGLESFIELD

2 miles SW of Cockermouth off the A5086

This small village was the birthplace of Robert Eaglesfield, who became confessor to Queen Philippa, Edward III's Queen. He was also the founder of Queen's College, Oxford, where he was buried in 1349. Even more famous is **John Dalton**, who was born here in 1766. The son of Quaker parents, Dalton was teaching at the village school by the time he was 12. Despite having had no formal education himself, he became one of the most brilliant scientists, naturalists, and mathematicians of his age and was the originator of the theory that all matter is composed of small indestructible particles called atoms. He was also the first to recognise the existence of colour blindness. He suffered from it himself, and in medical circles it is known as Daltonism.

A memorial to the remarkable John Dalton now marks the house where he lived in Eaglesfield.

WORKINGTON

The largest town on the Cumbrian coast, Workington stands at the mouth of the River Derwent and on the site of the Roman fort of **Gabrosentum**. Its prosperity was founded on the three great Cumbrian industries – coal, iron and shipping. As early as 1650 coal was being mined here and, by the end of the 18th century, Workington was a major port exporting coal as well as smelting iron ore. Many of the underground coal seams extended far out to sea. In later years, Workington became famous for its fine quality steel, especially after Henry Bessemer developed his revolutionary steel-making process here in 1850. The seat of the Curwen family for over 600 years, **Workington Hall** has an interesting history. Originally built around a 14th-century pele tower, the hall was developed over the years with extensive alterations being made in the 18th century by the then-lord of the manor, John Christian Curwen. Now a stabilised ruin, it has several commemorative plaques which give a taste of the hall's history.

John Cristain Curwen travelled throughout Britain and Europe to research and develop a better and more profiatble way of farming. His results were adopted worldwide and are still being used today

The most famous visitor was Mary, Queen of Scots, who sought refuge here when she fled from Scotland in 1568. She stayed for a few days, during which time she wrote the famous letter to her cousin Elizabeth I bemoaning her fate, 'for I am in a pitiable condition ... having nothing in the world but the clothes in which I escaped,' and asking the Queen 'to have compassion on my great misfortunes'. The letter is now in the British Museum. Workington's **Church of St John the Evangelist** is a very grand affair built at enormous expense in 1823 to give thanks for the defeat of Napoleon at Waterloo. It is a copy of St Paul's, Covent Garden, and its walls were built with stones from the local Schoose and Hunday quarries. The interior was splendidly restored by Sir Ninian Comper in 1931. St Michael's is the ancient parish church, restored after a fire in 1994.

The **Helena Thompson Museum**, situated on Park End Road, is a fascinating place to visit with its displays telling the story of Workington's coal-mining, ship-building and iron and steel industries for which the town became internationally renowned. The Georgian Room gives an insight into the variety of decorative styles which were popular between 1714 and 1830,

160 THE HOWE

Mosser, Cockermouth

Charming self-catering accommodation in cosy and comfortable cottages, available all year round. 4 Stars ETC.

see *page 200*

59/164 GREEN DRAGON HOTEL

Workington

Superb food, drink and accommodation in this spacious and elegant traditional hotel, which dates back to the mid-18th century.

see *pages 161, 203*

61/163 THE WESTLANDS HOTEL

Workington

Superb hotel in acres of handsome grounds – comfortable and attractive rooms, hearty meals at lunch and dinner, bar open all day.

see *pages 162, 202*

62 THE TRAVELLERS REST

Workington

Superb dining in traditional setting. Open every day at lunch and dinner.

see page 163

219 HELENA THOMPSON MUSEUM

Workington

Housed in a fine, listed mid-Georgian building, the Helena Thompson Museum is named for the local philanthropist who bequeathed it to the people of Workington in 1940 and has displays of pottery, silver, glass, furniture and costume.

 see page 224

63 THE GALLOPING HORSE

High Harrington, Workington

Great food and drink in a spacious pub just a short drive south of Workington on the A597.

see page 163

with displays of beautiful cut-glass tableware, porcelain from China and period pieces of furniture. Bequeathed to the town by the local philanthropist Miss Helena Thompson, MBE, JP, the museum was opened in 1949 and contains some of her own family heirlooms. One particularly interesting exhibit is the Clifton Dish, a locally-produced 18th-century piece of slipware pottery, while further displays demonstrate the links between this local industry and the famous Staffordshire pottery families. Fashion fans will be interested in the display of women's and children's dresses from the 1700s to the early 1900s, together with accessories and jewellery.

The **Theatre Royal** was built by John Smith in 1845. In the 1920's it became the first cinema. Local people called it "pennymacs". This closed in the 1930's although the "Playgoers" bought the theater and continue giving regular performances.

Workington is at the start of the C2C cycle route that runs to Sunderland and Newcastle. A short distance south of town is **Harrington Reservoir Nature Reserve**, a haven for wildlife with a rich variety of wild flowers, insects, butterflies, birds and animals.

NORTH AND EAST OF WORKINGTON

MARYPORT

6 miles NE of Workington on the A596

Dramatically located on the Solway Firth, Maryport is a charming Cumbrian coastal town rich in interest and maritime history. The old part is full of narrow streets and neoclassical, Georgian architecture that contrast with sudden, surprising views of the sea. Some of the first visitors to Maryport were the Romans, who built a clifftop fort here, **Alauna**, which is now part of the Hadrian's Wall World Heritage Site. The award-winning **Senhouse Roman Museum** tells the story of life in this outpost of the Empire. Housed in the striking Naval Reserve Battery, built in the 1880s, the museum holds the largest collection of Roman altars from a single site in Britain. Other highlights include a reconstruction of the shrine from the fort's headquarters and interpretive panels describing the fort, the Roman coastal defences and the Senhouse family – it was John Senhouse of Netherall who started the collection way back in the 1570s. Modern Maryport dates from the 18th century when another Senhouse, Humphrey, a local landowner, developed the harbour at what was then called Ellenfoot to export coal from his mines, and named the new port after his wife, Mary. Over the next century it became a busy port as well as a ship-building centre; boats had to be launched broadside because of the narrowness of the harbour channel. The town declined, along with the mining industry, from the 1930s onwards. It nevertheless attracted the artist LS Lowry, who was a frequent visitor and loved painting the harbour. Today Maryport is enjoying a well-earned revival, with newly restored Georgian quaysides, clifftop paths, sandy beaches and a harbour with fishing boats.

The town's extensive maritime history is preserved in the vast array of objects, pictures and models on display at the **Maritime Museum** overlooking the harbour. Housed in another of Maryport's more interesting and historic buildings, the former Queen's Head public house, the museum tells of the rise and fall of the harbour and docks. Other exhibits include a brass telescope from the *Cutty Sark* and the town's connections with the ill-fated liner, the *Titanic*, and with Fletcher Christian, instigator of the mutiny on the *Bounty*. The *Titanic* was part of the fleet of the White Star Line, which was founded by a Maryport man, Thomas Henry Ismay. Fletcher Christian was also a local man, being born at Brigham, near Cockermouth in 1764. The Tourist Information Centre is also at the Town Hall.

Close to the Maritime Museum in Maryport is the **Lake District Coast Aquarium** where a series of spectacular living habitat recreations introduce visitors to the profusion of marine life found in the Solway Firth – thornback rays (which can be touched), some small sharks, spider crabs and the comically ugly tompot blenny among them. Open all year, the Aquarium also has a gift shop and a quayside café that enjoys superb views of the harbour and the Solway.

Maryport's other attractions include a fresh fish shop, appropriately named The Catch, and an indoor Karting Centre.

DEARHAM

7 miles NE of Workington off the A594

This village has a very beautiful church with open countryside on three sides. The chancel of **Dearham Church** is 13th century, and the church has a fortress tower built for the protection of men and beasts during the Border raids. There are also some interesting relics within the church including the Adam Stone, dating from AD 900, which depicts the fall of man (with Adam and Eve hand in hand above a serpent), an ancient font carved with mythological beasts, a Kenneth Cross showing the legend of the 6th-century hermit brought up by seagulls, and a magnificent wheel-head cross carved with Yggdrasil, the Norse Tree of the Universe.

ASPATRIA

14 miles NE of Workington on the A596

Lying above the shallow Ellen Valley, Aspatria's main interest for most visitors lies in the elaborate **Memorial Fountain** to 'Watery Wilfred', Sir Wilfred Lawson MP (1829-1906), a lifelong crusader for the Temperance Movement and International Peace. According to one scribe, writing about Sir Wilfred Lawson, 'No man in his day made more people laugh at Temperance meetings.'

Also worth a visit is the much-restored **Norman Church** that is

75

66/168 THE MASONS
ARMS

Gilcrux

Outstanding traditional inn with accommodation. Warm and friendly ambience. Open lunchtime and evenings everyday.

see pages 164, 205

•

A 1730 Government enquiry into contraband trade reported that 'the Solway people were the first working-class folk to drink tea regularly in Britain.'

•

entered through a fine avenue of yew trees. Inside are several ancient relics including a 12th-century font with intricate carvings, a Viking hogback tombstone, and a grave cover with a pagan swastika engraving. Like many other churches in the area, the churchyard contains a holy well in which it is said St Kentigern baptised his converts.

GILCRUX
10 miles NE of Workington off the A596

From this village there are particularly good views across the Solway Firth to Scotland and it is well worth visiting for the 12th-century **Church of St Mary** which is believed to be the oldest building in the district. Standing on a walled mound and with a buttressed exterior, it has a thick-walled chancel. The village is remarkable for the number of its springs, at least five of which have never failed even in the driest summers.

ALLONBY
11 miles N of Workington on the B5300

This traditional Solway village is backed by the Lake District fells and looks out across the Solway Firth to the Scottish hills. Popular with wind-surfers, the village has an attractive shingle and sand beach that received Seaside Awards in 1998 and 2005. The Allerdale Ramble and the Cumbrian Cycle Way both pass close by, and the village is also on the **Smuggler's Route** trail. Smuggling seems to have been a profitable occupation around here.

In the early 1800s, Allonby was a popular sea-bathing resort. The former seawater baths, built in 1835 and now Grade II listed buildings, still stand in the old **Market Square**. In those days, the upper floor was in popular use as a ballroom for the local nobility. Allonby still keeps much of its Georgian and early Victorian charm with cobbled lanes, alleyways and some interesting old houses. It was also an important centre for herring fishing, and some of the old kippering houses can still be seen. Allonby was the birthplace of Joseph Huddart, hydrographer and inventor of various ships' safety measures. He is buried at St Martin's in the Fields, London.

HOLME ST CUTHBERT
14 miles N of Workington off the B5300

This inland hamlet is also known as Rowks because, in the Middle Ages, there was a chapel here dedicated to St Roche. The present church dates from 1845 but it contains an interesting torso of a medieval knight wearing chain mail. Found by schoolboys on a nearby farm, the hollowed-out centre of the torso was being used as a trough. It seems to be a 14th-century piece and could be a representation of Robert the Bruce's father, who died at Holm Cultram Abbey.

Northeast of the hamlet, and enveloped among low hills, is a lovely 30-acre lake known as **Tarns Dub**, which is a haven for birdlife. A couple of miles to the southwest, the headland of **Dubmill Point** is popular with sea anglers. When the tide is high and driven by a fresh westerly wind, the sea covers the road with lashing waves.

BECKFOOT

16 miles N of Workington on the B5300

At certain times and tides, the remains of a prehistoric forest can be seen on the sand beds here and, to the south of the village, is the site of a 2nd-century Roman fort known as **Bibra**. According to an inscribed stone found here, it was once occupied by an Auxiliary Cohort of 500 Pannonians (Spaniards) and surrounded by a large civilian settlement. The small stream flowing into the sea was used in World War I as a fresh water supply by German U-boats.

SILLOTH

18 miles N of Workington on the B5300

This charming old port and Victorian seaside resort is well worth exploring. With the coming of the railways in the 1850s, Silloth developed as a port and railhead for Carlisle. The Railway Company helped to develop the town and had grey granite shipped over in its own vessels from Ireland to build the handsome church which is such a prominent landmark. The town's name is derived from 'Sea Lath' – sea because of its position and lath being a grain store, used by monks from nearby Holm Cultram Abbey.

The region's bracing air and low rainfall helped to make Silloth a popular seaside resort. Visitors today will appreciate the invigorating but mild climate, the leisurely atmosphere, and the glorious sunsets over the sea that inspired Turner to record them for posterity. The town remains a delightful place to stroll, to admire the sunken rose garden and the pinewoods and 2 miles of promenades.

One of the most popular attractions is the **Solway Coast Discovery Centre**, where Auld Michael the Monk and Oyk the Oystercatcher guide visitors through 10,000 years of Solway Coast history.

WIGTON

The pleasant market town of Wigton has adopted the title 'The Throstle Nest of all England' – throstle being the northern term for a thrush. The story is that a Wigton man returning home from the trenches of the Great War crested the hill and on seeing the familiar cluster of houses, churches, farms and the maze of streets, yards and alleys, exclaimed 'Awa' lads, it's the throstle's nest of England.'

For centuries Wigton has been the centre of the business and social life of the Solway coast and plain, its prosperity being based on the weaving of cotton and linen. It has enjoyed the benefits of a Royal Charter since 1262 and the market is still held on Tuesdays. Horse sales are held every April (riding horses and ponies) and October (Clydesdales, heavy horses and ponies). Today, most of the old town is a Conservation Area and, particularly along the **Main Street**,

Silloth's 2-mile-long promenade provides wonderful views of the Solway Firth and the coast of Scotland.

Silloth's 18-hole golf course was the 'home course' where Miss Cecil Leitch (1891-1978), the most celebrated woman golfer of her day, used to play. Another keen woman golfer was the great contralto, Kathleen Ferrier, who stayed in the town for part of her tragically short life. She lived on Eden Street, above the bank where her husband was the manager. A plaque on the wall records her stay here between 1936 and 1941.

67/167 THE
SKINBURNESS
LEISURE HOTEL

Skinburness

Impressive coastal hotel with full facilities including swimming pool, sauna and fitness suite. 26 en suite rooms. Licensed bar and spacious restaurant.

🛏 🍴 *see pages 165, 204*

the upper storeys of the houses have survived in an almost unaltered state. On street corners, metal guards to prevent heavy horse-drawn wagons damaging the walls can also still be seen.

One feature of the town that should not be missed is the magnificent **Memorial Fountain** in the Market Place. Its gilded, floriate panels are set against Shap granite and surmounted with a golden cross. It was erected in 1872 by the philanthropist George Moore in memory of his wife, Eliza Flint Ray, with whom he fell in love when he was a penniless apprentice. Bronze reliefs show four of her favourite charities – giving clothes to the naked, feeding the hungry, instructing the ignorant, and sheltering the homeless. The bronzes were created by Thomas Woolner, the pre-Raphaelite sculptor.

Wigton boasts a couple of interesting literary connections. Charles Dickens and Wilkie Collins stayed at The King's Arms Hotel in 1857, during the trip described in *The Lazy Tour of Two Idle Apprentices*, and the author and broadcaster Melvyn Bragg (now Lord Bragg) was born here. The town, often disguised as Thurston, features in several of his novels, and sequences for the television dramatisation of *A Time to Dance* were set and filmed in Wigton.

One mile south of Wigton are the scant remains of the Roman fort of **Olenacum**; most of its stones were removed to rebuild Wigton in the 18th and 19th centuries.

AROUND WIGTON

SKINBURNESS

11 miles W of Wigton off the B5302

A lively market town, in the Middle Ages Skinburness was used by Edward I in 1299 as a base for his navy when attacking the Scots. A few years later a terrible storm destroyed the town; what survived became a small fishing hamlet. From nearby **Grune Point**, the start of the **Allerdale Ramble**, there are some tremendous views over the Solway Firth and the beautiful, desolate expanse of marshland and sandbank. Grune Point, which was once the site of a Roman fort, now forms part of a designated Site of Special Scientific Interest notable for the variety of its birdlife and marsh plants.

ABBEYTOWN

5 miles W of Wigton on the B5302

As its name suggests, Abbeytown grew up around the 12th-century **Abbey of Holm Cultram** on the River Waver and many of the town's buildings are constructed of stone taken from the Abbey when it fell into ruins. Founded by Cistercians in 1150, the Abbey bore the brunt of the constant feuds between the English and the Scots. In times of peace the community prospered and soon became one of the largest suppliers of wool in the North. Edward I stayed here in 1300 and again, in 1307, when he made Abbot Robert De Keldsik a member of his Council. After Edward's death the Scots returned with a vengeance and in 1319

Robert the Bruce sacked the Abbey, even though his own father, the Earl of Carrick, had been buried there 15 years earlier.

The final blow came in 1536 when Abbot Carter joined the Pilgrimage of Grace, the ill-fated rebellion against Henry VIII's seizure of Church lands and property. The rebellion was put down with ruthless brutality and the red sandstone **Church of St Mary** only survived because local people pointed out that the building was necessary to provide protection against Scottish raiders. It is still the parish church and was restored in 1883, a strange yet impressive building with the original nave shorn of its tower, transepts and chancel. The east and west walls are heavily buttressed, and a porch with a new roof protects the original Norman arch of the west door. Within the church buildings is a room, opened by Princess Margaret in 1973, which contains the gravestones of Robert the Bruce's father and that of Mathias and Juliana De Keldsik, relations of Abbot Robert.

NEWTON ARLOSH

5 miles NW of Wigton on the B5307

Situated on the **Solway marshes**, the village was first established by the monks of Holm Cultram Abbey in 1307 after the old port at Skinburness had been destroyed by the sea. The village's name means 'the new town on the marsh'. Work on the church did not begin until 1393, but the result is one of the most delightful examples of a Cumbrian fortified **Church**. In the Middle Ages there was no castle nearby to protect the local population from the border raids and so a pele tower was added to the church. As an additional defensive measure, the builders created what is believed to be narrowest church doorway in the country, barely 2 ft 7 inches across and a little over 5 ft high. The 12-inch arrow-slot east window is also the smallest in England. After the Reformation, the church became derelict but was finally restored in the 19th century. Inside there is a particularly fine eagle lectern carved out of bog oak.

• *Near Abbeytown's Church of St Mary there are some lovely walks along the River Waver, which is especially rich in wildlife.* •

68 JOINERS ARMS COUNTRY INN

Newton Arlosh

Picture-postcard inn with excellent cuisine at lunch and dinner seven days a week. Real ales.

see page 165

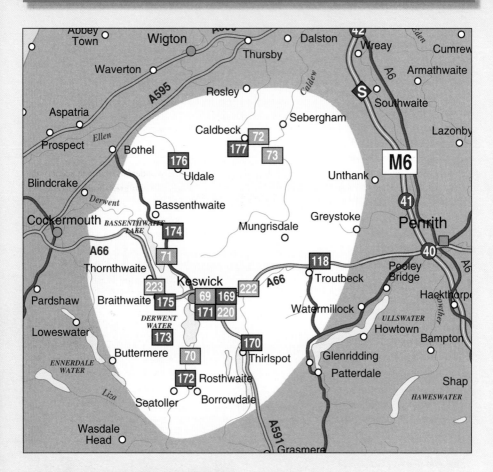

Keswick & The Northern Lakes

For many visitors this part of the county is classic Lakeland, the scenery dominated by the rounded, heather-clad slopes of the Skiddaw range to the north of Keswick, and the wild, craggy mountains of Borrowdale, to the south. Yet, despite this area's popularity, there are still

Derwent Water

many hidden places to discover and many opportunities to leave the beaten track.

The major town, Keswick, on the shores of Derwent Water, is a pleasant Lakeland town that has much to offer the visitor. The lake too, is interesting as, not only is it in a near perfect setting, but it is unusual in having some islands – in this case four. It was the view over the lake, from Friar's Crag, that formed one of John Ruskin's early childhood memories.

However, there is much more to this part of Cumbria than scenic appeal. The area is rich in history and there is frequent and significant evidence of

Roman occupation. Castlerigg Stone Circle can be found here. The industrial heritage is also important, and many of the villages in the region relied on coal mining and mineral extraction for their livelihood.

But it is the wonderful, dramatic scenery that makes this area of the Lake District so special. Not only are there several charming and isolated lakes within easy reach of Keswick, but Buttermere, considered by connoisseurs to be the best of all, lies only a few miles away. Not all the lakes, however, are what they first appear to be: Thirlmere, for example, is a 19th-century reservoir constructed to supply Manchester's growing thirst.

The Lakeland Fells are home to Herdwick sheep, one of the country's hardiest breeds. Their coarse fleece cannot be dyed, but Herdwick sheep of various ages yield wool in a variety of subtle shades of grey and black which produces an unusual and very durable tweed-like weave.

Ashness Bridge, Keswick

81

69 GINGER & PICKLES COFFEE SHOP

Keswick

Truly scrumptious cakes, biscuits, sandwiches and savouries at charming coffee shop open seven days a week for morning coffee, lunch and afternoon tea.

see page 166

169 BROOKFIELD GUEST HOUSE

Keswick

Victorian house with four en suite rooms a scenic walk to the town centre.

see page 206

KESWICK

'Above it rises Skiddaw, majestic and famous, and at its door is Derwentwater, the lake beyond compare.'

For generations, visitors to Keswick have been impressed by the town's stunningly beautiful setting, surrounded by the great fells of Saddleback, Helvellyn and Grizedale Pike.

Tourism, now the town's major industry, actually began in the mid-1700s and was given a huge boost, first by local clergyman Dr John Brown, and then by the Lakeland Poets in the early 1800s. By the 1780s the area was the most fashionable tourist destination in Europe, and the arrival of the railway in 1865 firmly established Keswick as the undisputed 'capital' of the Lake District with most of the area's notable attractions within easy reach. In a letter of 1752 Dr Brown wrote, 'The perfection of Keswick rests on three

circumstances: beauty, horror and immensity.'

The grandeur of the lakeland scenery is of course the greatest draw but, among the man-made features, one not to be missed is the well-preserved **Castlerigg Stone Circle**. About a mile to the east of the town, the 38 standing stones, some of them 8 feet high, form a circle 100 feet in diameter. They are believed to have been put in place some 4,000 years ago and occupy a hauntingly beautiful position. Beautiful, but forbidding, as evoked by Keats in his poem *Hyperion*:

A dismal cirque of Druid stones, upon a
forlorn moor,
When the chill rain begins at shut of eve,
In dull November, and their chancel vault,
The Heaven itself, is blinded throughout
night.

Keswick old town developed along the banks of the broad River Greta, with a wide main street leading up to the attractive **Moot Hall**. Built in 1813, the Hall has been at various times a buttermarket, courthouse and prison, Town Hall and now houses the Tourist Information Centre. A little further south, in **St John's Street**, the church of that name was built in the very same year as the Moot Hall and its elegant spire provides a point of reference from all around the town. In the churchyard is the grave of Sir Hugh Walpole,

Castlerigg Stone Circle

whose once hugely popular series of novels, *The Herries Chronicle* (1930-33), is set in this part of the Lake District.

In the riverside Fitz Park is the town's **Museum & Art Gallery** which is well worth a visit not just to see original manuscripts by Wordsworth and other Lakeland poets but also for the astonishing 'Rock, Bell and Steel Band' created by Joseph Richardson of Skiddaw in the 19th century. It's a kind of xylophone made of 60 stones (some a metre long), 60 steel bars and 40 bells. Four musicians are required to play this extraordinary instrument.

Surrounded by a loop of the River Greta to the northwest of the town is a museum which must be pencilled in on any visit to Keswick. This is the **Cumberland Pencil Museum**, which boasts the 6-foot long 'Largest Pencil in the World'. The 'lead' used in pencils (not lead at all but actually an allotrope of carbon) was accidentally discovered by a Borrowdale shepherd in the 16th century, and Keswick eventually became the world centre for the manufacture of lead pencils. The pencil mill here, established in 1832, is still operating – though the wadd, or lead, is now imported.

Other attractions in the town centre include the **Cars of the Stars Museum**, ideal for movie buffs since it contains such gems as Laurel and Hardy's Model T Ford, James Bond's Aston Martin, Chitty Chitty Bang Bang, Batman's

Keswick Town Centre

Batmobile, Lady Penelope's pink Rolls-Royce FAB 1, the Mad Max car, and Mr Bean's Mini. There are film set displays and vehicles from series such as *The Saint*, *Knightrider*, *Bergerac* and *Postman Pat*, and Del Boy's 3-wheel Reliant from *Only Fools and Horses* is here, too. **The Teapottery** makes and sells a bizarre range of practical teapots in the shape of anything from an upright piano to an Aga stove.

A short walk from the town centre, along Lake Road, leads visitors to the popular **Theatre by the Lake**, which hosts a year-round programme of plays, concerts, exhibitions, readings and talks. Close by is the pier from which there are regular departures for cruises around Derwentwater and ferries across the lake to Nichol End where you can hire just about every kind of water craft, including your own private cruise boat. One trip is to the National Trust's **Derwent Island House**, an Italianate house of the 1840s on a wooded island.

171 GRASSMOOR GUEST HOUSE

Keswick

Friendly early 19th-century guest house with four en suite guest bedrooms. 4 Diamonds ETC.

⊨ see page 206

220 CARS OF THE STARS MUSEUM

Keswick

A fascinating collection of vehicles from both the small and the big screen including James Bond's Aston Martin and the Batmobile.

🏛 see page 224

In 1778 Father Thomas West produced A Guide to the Lakes, which began the era of true tourism. In his book West stated that the intention was: to encourage the taste of visiting the lakes by furnishing the traveller with a Guide; and for that purpose, the writer has here collected and laid before him, all the select stations and points of view, noticed by those authors who have last made the tour of the lakes, verified by his own repeated observations. These 21 spots around four lakes – the first 'station' being Derwent Water – were followed religiously by 18th-century tourists.

Another short walk will bring the visitor to **Friar's Crag**. This famous view of Derwent Water and its islands, now National Trust property, formed one of John Ruskin's early childhood memories, inspiring in him 'intense joy, mingled with awe'. Inscribed on his memorial here are these words: 'The first thing which I remember as an event in life was being taken by my nurse to the brow of Friar's Crag on Derwentwater.' The Crag is dedicated to the memory of Canon Rawnsley, the local vicar, who was one of the founder members of the National Trust, which he helped to set up in 1895. Hardwicke Drummond Rawnsley, born at Shiplake, Oxfordshire in 1851, was a man of many parts – noted athlete at Balliol, writer, poet, traveller, vicar of Crosthwaite, Canon Carlisle, campaigner for the protection of footpaths. Keswick is host to several annual festivals, covering films, Cumbrian literature, jazz and beer. And on the first Sunday in December a colourful 'Christmassy' Fayre is held in the Market Place.

AROUND KESWICK

THRELKELD

3 miles E of Keswick off the A66

From Keswick there's a delightful walk along the track bed of the old railway line to the charming village of Threlkeld, set in a plain at the foot of mighty **Blencathra**. The village is the ideal starting point for a number of mountain walks, including an ascent of Blencathra, one of the most exciting of all the Lake District mountains. Also known as Saddleback and a smaller sister of Skiddaw to the west, the steep sides ensure that it looks every inch a mountain. Threlkeld is famous for its annual sheepdog trials, though its economy was built upon the several mines in the area and the granite quarry to the south. At **Threlkeld Quarry & Mining Museum** visitors can browse through the collection of vintage excavators, old quarry machinery and other mining artefacts, wander through the locomotive shed and machine shop, or join the 40-minute tour through a re-created mine. The museum has interpretive displays of Lakeland geology and quarrying, and is used as a teaching facility by several university geology departments.

Derwent Water

Threkleld Mining Museum has perhaps the finest collection of small mining and quarrying artefacts – everything from wedges, chisels and drills to candles, clogs and kibbles (large iron buckets used to transport ore).

MATTERDALE END

8 miles E of Keswick on the A5091

This tiny hamlet lies at one end of Matterdale, a valley that an essential stop on any Wordsworth trail – for it was here, on April 15th 1802, that he and his sister saw that immortal

host of golden daffodils,
Beside the lake,
beneath the trees,
Fluttering and dancing in the
breeze.

THIRLMERE

4 miles S of Keswick off the A591

This attractive, tree-lined lake, one of the few in the Lakes that can be driven around as well as walked around, was created in the 1890s by the Manchester Corporation. More than 100 miles of pipes and tunnels still supply the city with water from Thirlmere. At first there was no public access to the lake shore, but today these have been opened up for recreational use with car parks, walking trails and picnic places.

The creation of the huge **Thirlmere Reservoir**, 5 miles long, flooded the two hamlets of **Armboth** and **Wythburn**. All that remains of these places today is Wythburn chapel towards the southern end. Overlooking the narrow lake is **Helvellyn**,

Wordsworth's favourite mountain and one that is also very popular with walkers and climbers today. At 3,116 feet, it is one of the four Lakeland fells over 3,000 feet high, and the walk to the summit should not be undertaken lightly – but those reaching the summit will be rewarded with some spectacular views. The eastern aspect of the mountain is markedly different from the western, as it was here that the Ice Age glaciers were sheltered from the mild, west winds.

BORROWDALE

Runs S from Keswick via the B5289

'The Mountains of Borrowdale are perhaps as fine as anything we have seen,' wrote John Keats in 1818. Six miles long, this brooding, mysterious valley, steep and narrow with towering crags and deep woods, is generally regarded as the most beautiful in the Lake District. Just to the south of Derwent Water are the **Lodore Falls**, where the Watendlath Beck drops some 120 feet before reaching the lake. Further along the dale, in woodland owned by the National Trust, lies the extraordinary **Bowder Stone** which provides an irresistible photo-opportunity for most visitors. A massive 50 feet square and weighing almost 2,000 tons, it stands precariously on one corner, apparently defying gravity. A wooden staircase on one side provides easy access to the top. South of Grange village, the valley narrows into the 'Jaws of Borrowdale'. Castle Crag, the

222 THRELKELD MINING MUSEUM

Threlkeld, Keswick
The industrial heritage of the area is told here through artefacts, locomotives and a tour through a re-created mine.

🏛 *see page 225*

170 STYBECK FARM

Thirlmere
Picture-postcard farmhouse or self-catering accommodation in ideal touring spot.

🛏 *see page 206*

70 GRANGE BRIDGE COTTAGE TEASHOP

Grange-in-Borrowdale, Keswick
Home baking in spacious and attractive setting at the side of the River Derwent, just off the B5289.

🍴 *see page 166*

172 HAZEL BANK COUNTRY HOUSE

Rosthwaite, Borrowdale
Eight superb guest bedrooms and a self-catering cottage in four acres of marvellous grounds.

🛏 *see page 206*

•

Just south of Rosthwaite the road turns westwards to the village of Seatoller where there's a National Park Information Centre, and a minor road turns off to Seathwaite, which enjoys the unenviable reputation of being the wettest place in England with an average of 131 inches of rain a year. Seathwaite is the starting point for many fell walks and climbing expeditions, particularly to the Scafells and Great Gable.

•

western mandible of the Jaws, has on its summit the remains of the defensive ditches of a Romano-British fort.

From Seatoller, the B5289 slices through the spectacular **Honister Pass**, overlooked by the dramatic 1,000-foot-high Honister Crag. At the top of the pass, the 18th-century **Honister Slate Mine** has been re-opened and is once again producing the beautiful green slate that adorns so many Lakeland houses and is famous throughout the world. Buckingham Palace, The Ritz Hotel, New Scotland Yard and RAF Cranwell are among the prestigious buildings donned with this stone. Helmets and lights are provided for a guided tour through great caverns of the mine to show how a mixture of modern and traditional methods is still

extracting the slate which was formed here some 400 million years ago. The monks of Furness Abbey are thought to have been the first to avail themselves of the mine's resources, about 500 years ago. After the tour, complimentary tea or coffee is served in the Bait Cabin beside a warm fire, and the complex also has an informative Visitor Centre (honoured as the friendliest in the North of England) and a gift shop selling the ornamental green slate.

BUTTERMERE

8 miles SW of Keswick on the B5289

Half the size of its neighbour, Crummock Water, Buttermere is a beautiful lake set in a dramatic landscape. To many connoisseurs of the Lake District landscape, this is the most splendid of them all. The walk around Buttermere gives superb views of the eastern towers of **Fleetwith Pike** and the great fell wall made up of High Crag, High Stile and Red Pike.

In the early 1800s the village became involved in one of the great scandals of the age. Mary Robinson, the daughter of a local innkeeper, had been described as a maiden of surpassing beauty in J Budworth's book *A Fortnight's Ramble in the Lakes*. She became something of a local attraction, with people flocking to the inn to admire her beauty, among them Wordsworth and Coleridge. Another was a smooth-tongued gentleman who introduced himself as Alexander Augustus Colonel Hope, MP, brother of the Earl of

Borrowdale

86

Hopetoun. Mary fell for his charms and married him, only to discover that her husband was really John Hatfield, a bankrupt impostor and a bigamist to boot. Hatfield was tried at Carlisle for fraud, a capital offence in those days, and Coleridge supplemented his meagre income by reporting the sensational trial for the *Morning Post*. Hatfield was found guilty and was hanged at Carlisle gaol in 1802; Mary later married a local farmer and went on to live an uneventful and happy life.

The author, broadcaster and great supporter of Cumbria, Melvyn (Lord) Bragg, tells the story of Mary Robinson in his novel, *The Maid of Buttermere*.

Standing above the village is the small, picturesque **Church of St James**, where the special features of interest include an antique organ and a memorial to Alfred Wainwright.

Buttermere

LOWESWATER

10 miles W of Keswick off the B5289

Reached by narrow winding lanes, Loweswater is one of the smaller lakes, framed in an enchanting fellside and forest setting. The name, appropriately, means 'leafy lake', and eons ago it was just part of a vast body of water that included what is now Crummock Water and Buttermere. Because it is so shallow, never more than 60 feet deep, Loweswater provides an ideal habitat for wildfowl, which also benefit from the fact that this is perhaps the least-visited lake in the whole of Cumbria. To the east of the lake lies the small village of the same name, while to

Scenery near Loweswater

173 LITTLETOWN FARM

Newlands, Keswick

Magnificent farmhouse set amid a 90-acre mixed farm, licensed bar and guests' lounge, eight comfortable and attractive bedrooms available all year round.

see page 206

175 BRAITHWAITE FARM

Braithwaite

Comfortable farmhouse bed-and-breakfast or self-catering accommodation amid glorious scenery in tranquil village.

see page 208

223 WHINLATTER FOREST PARK

Braithwaite, Keswick

The only mountain forest park in England, Whinlatter Forest Park offers a whole range of outdoor activities including walking, cycling and orienteering.

see page 225

•

Which is the only lake in the Lake District? Answer: Bassenthwaite, because all the others are either Waters or Meres.

•

the north stretches one of the quietest and least-known parts of the National Park, a landscape of low fells through which there are few roads or even paths.

CRUMMOCK WATER

9 miles SW of Keswick on the B5289

Fed by both Buttermere and Loweswater, this is by far the largest of the three lakes. In this less-frequented part of western Cumbria, where there are few roads, the attractions of Crummock Water can usually be enjoyed in solitude. Best seen from the top of Rannerdale Knotts, to the east, the lake has a footpath running around it – though, in places, the going gets a little strenuous.

BRAITHWAITE

3 miles W of Keswick on the B5292

This small village lies at the foot of the **Whinlatter Pass**, another of Cumbria's dramatic routes. The summit of this steep road, the B5292, is some 1,043 feet above sea level and, on the westerly descent, there are magnificent views over Bassenthwaite Lake. The road runs through the **Whinlatter Forest Park**, the only Mountain Forest in England and one of the Forestry Commission's oldest woodlands. The park offers a wide range of activities for all ages and fitness levels, from waymarked trails to cycling, orienteering or just strolling along and admiring the views. Whinlatter Forest Park boasts a Visitor Centre, adventure playground, viewpoints, gift shop and a tearoom with a terrace

overlooking the woodlands and valley. Whinlatter Forest Park is the starting point for several trails suitable for the whole family.

Many of the record numbers who visit the centre come to see live footage of the Lake District ospreys, beamed to a special viewing facility, or to see the birds through high-powered telescopes at the Dodd Wood viewing point. **The Lake District Osprey Project** is a partnership of the Forestry Commission, the Lake District National Park Authority and the RSPB, whose aim is to protect the nesting ospreys and to encourage other ospreys to settle and breed in other suitable locations.

BASSENTHWAITE LAKE

4 miles NW of Keswick on the A66

Only 70 feet deep and with borders rich in vegetation, Bassenthwaite Lake provides an ideal habitat for birds – more than 70 species have been recorded around the lake. Successful breeding is encouraged by the fact that no powerboats are allowed on the lake, and some areas are off limits to boats of any kind. Also, most of the shoreline is privately owned, with public access restricted mostly to the eastern shore where the Allerdale Ramble follows the lakeside for a couple of miles or so.

At the northern end of the lake, at Coalbeck Farm, **Trotters World of Animals** is home to many hundreds of animals – rare breeds, traditional farm favourites, endangered species, birds of prey and reptiles. In addition to the ring-tailed lemurs, wallabies, racoons and gibbons, 2002 saw the arrival of rough-coated lemurs, lechwe antelope, red, fallow and sika deer and guanaco. Visitors to the 25-acre site can bottle-feed baby animals, cuddle bunnies, meet Monty the python, take a tractor trailer ride, watch the birds of prey demonstrations, find a quiet picnic spot or sample the fare on offer in Trotters Tea Room. And for the smaller children there's an indoor soft play climbing centre. Winner of the Good Britain Guide Cumbria Family Attraction of the Year, as a member of the National Association of Farms for Schools the farm can cater for school groups either for an informal day out or for a structured programme based on National Curriculum requirements.

Rising grandly above Bassenthwaite's eastern shore is **Skiddaw** which, ever since the Lake District was opened up to tourists by the arrival of the railway in the 19th century, has been one of the most popular peaks to climb. Although it rises to some 3,054 feet, the climb is both safe and manageable, if a little unattractive lower down, and typically takes around two hours. From the summit, on a clear day, there are spectacular views to Scotland in the north, the Isle of Man in the west, the Pennines to the east, and to the south the greater part of the Lake District.

Also on the eastern shore is the secluded, originally Norman,

Church of St Bridget & St Bega which Tennyson had in mind when, in his poem *Morte d'Arthur*, he describes Sir Bedivere carrying the dead King Arthur:

to a chapel in the fields,
A broken chancel with a broken cross,
That stood on a dark strait of barren land.

This, then, would make Bassenthwaite Lake the resting place of Excalibur but, as yet, no one has reported seeing a lady's arm, 'clothed in white samite, mystic, wonderful', rising from the waters and holding aloft the legendary sword.

Set back from the lakeside, **Mirehouse** is a 17th-century building which has been home to the Spedding family since 1688. Literary visitors to the house included Tennyson, Thomas Carlyle, and Edward Fitzgerald, the poet and translator of *The Rubaiyat of Omar Khayyam*. As well as some manuscripts by these family friends, there is also a fine collection of furniture and visitors can wander

174 RAVENSTONE LODGE

Bassenthwaite
Superb accommodation in spacious and elegant stonebuilt Victorian former stables surrounded by magnificent scenery. 4 Diamonds VB and RAC.

see page 207

71 THE OLD SAWMILL TEAROOM

Mirehouse, Keswick
Specialities include sticky gingerbread, Cumberland sausage, fresh sandwiches and soups, all home-made and very tasty.

see page 166

Winter in the Lake District

176 PONDEROSA GUEST HOUSE

Uldale

Comfortable accommodation (B&B or self-catering) in picturesque village. Open all year round.

see *page 208*

72 THE OLD SMITHY CRAFTS, GIFTS AND TEAROOM

Caldbeck

Superb choice of delicious cakes and light meals, and a wide range of locally-produced craftware. Open seven days a week 9.30-6.

see *page 166*

177 SWALEDALE WATCH

Whelpo, Caldbeck

Comfortable accommodation on working farm surrounded by glorious countryside within the Lake District National Park.

see *page 208*

around the wildflower meadow, the walled garden and the lakeside walk. The gardens are open daily from April to October but the house, because it is still a family home, is open only on Sunday and Wednesday afternoons during the season, and also on Friday afternoons during August.

ULDALE

11 miles N of Keswick off the A591

To the northeast of Bassenthwaite Lake stretches the area known locally as the 'Land Back of Skidda', a crescent of fells and valleys constituting the most northerly part of the Lake District National Park. This peaceful region is well off the tourist track and offers visitors a delightful landscape of gently undulating bare-backed fells and valleys sheltering unspoilt villages such as Uldale. Horace Walpole featured Uldale and its moorland surroundings in two of his *Herries Chronicle* novels, *Judith Paris* and *The Fortress*. The village boasts a friendly traditional pub, The Snooty Fox, and a Victorian school which now houses the **Northern Fells Gallery** where a wide range of work by Cumbrian artists – watercolours, jewellery, copperwork, ceramics, knitwear and woodcarvings – can be seen, all available to buy. This tranquil village has one additional claim to fame: it was the daughter of an Uldale farmer who eloped with and married the legendary huntsman, John Peel (see Caldbeck).

CALDBECK

13 miles N of Keswick on the B5299

Caldbeck is perhaps the best-known village in the northern Lakes because of its associations with **John Peel**, the famous huntsman who died in 1854 after falling from his horse. He is buried in the churchyard here. His ornate tombstone is decorated with depictions of hunting horns and his favourite hound. Also buried here are John Peel's wife Mary and their four children. John Peel was Master of Hounds for over 50 years, and was immortalised by his friend John Woodcutt Graves, who worked in a Caldbeck mill making the grey woollen cloth mentioned in the song, 'D'ye ken John Peel with his coat so grey?' The tune itself is based on an old Cumbrian folk song adapted by William Metcalfe, a chorister and organist at Carlisle Cathedral.

A few paces from Peel's tomb lies 'The Fair Maid of Buttermere', mentioned earlier, whose grave bears her married name, Mary Harrison. With its picturesque church, village green, cricket pitch, pond and blacksmith's forge, Caldbeck has all the ingredients of a picture-postcard village. There has been a **Church** here since the 12th century, one of only eight in England to be dedicated to St Kentigern. The other seven are also to be found in the north of Cumbria, where Kentigern, a bishop in the Strathclyde area of Scotland who was also known as Mungo, spent his time in exile.

Some 200 years ago Caldbeck was an industrial village, with corn mills, woollen mills and a paper mill all powered by the fast-flowing 'cold stream' – the Caldbeck. **Priest's Mill**, built in 1702 by the Rector of Caldbeck, next to his church, was a stone-grinding corn mill, powered by a waterwheel which has now been restored to working order. It is open to the public and has an accompanying Mining Museum and a collection of old rural implements. The Priest's Mill buildings are also home to a gift shop and craft workshops.

About a quarter of a mile outside the village is the limestone gorge known as **The Howk**, a popular beauty spot where the Caldbeck rushes past the restored ruins of one of the old bobbin mills.

HESKET NEWMARKET
13 miles N of Keswick off the B5305

Set around a well-kept village green, this pleasing little village used to have its own market, as the name suggests, and much earlier there was probably also a racecourse here, since that is what 'Hesket' meant in Old Scandinavian. It could well be the reason why the village's main street is so wide. Although the market is no longer held, Hesket hosts two important agricultural events each year: an Agricultural Show and Sheepdog Trials. There's also a vintage motor cycle rally in May.

Charles Dickens and Wilkie Collins stayed at Hesket Newmarket in the 1850s and wrote about it in their *Lazy Tour of Two Idle Apprentices*.

MUNGRISDALE
7 miles NE of Keswick off the A66

The name of the village comes from Mungo, the name by which St Kentigern was known by those close to him, and the village church, not surprisingly, is dedicated to him. Though **St Kentigern's Church** is believed to have been established here as early as AD552, the present building dates from 1756 and contains a fine example of a 17th-century triple-decker pulpit. A memorial on the church wall reveals an intriguing connection with Wordsworth. The tablet commemorates Raisley Calvert whose son, also called Raisley, was 'nursed by Wordsworth'. The younger Raisley was a sculptor and friend of the poet, but fell ill of consumption (tuberculosis). Wordsworth spent many hours by his bedside in Penrith hospital but Raisley passed away in 1795, leaving in his will the huge sum of £900 to his friend. The bequest was timely and enabled the poet to complete, with his friend Coleridge, the seminal poems that were published in 1798 as the *Lyrical Ballads*.

73 THE OLD CROWN
Hesket Newmarket

Real ales brewed at rear of pub, indian curries and traditional food on offer (Weds-Sun).

see page 167

118 GREENAH CRAG
Troutbeck

Excellent B&B in old farmhouse plus self-catering cottage in lovely quiet but accessible countryside.

see page 183

•

In a converted barn at the back of the Old Crown pub, Hesket Newmarket Brewery was set up in 1988, and beer sales, which at first were limited to the pub, soon spread across Cumbria. Many awards have come the way of Hesket Newmarket beers, which include Skiddaw Special Bitter, the nearly black Great Cockup Porter and the pale but potent Catbells Pale Ale. On Wednesday and Thursday evenings brewery tours, followed by a meal at the Old Crown, can (must) be booked in advance – Tel: 016974 78288.

•

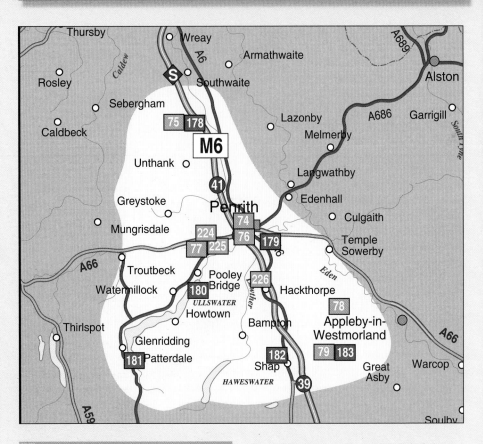

In and Around Penrith

Penrith is the most historic of Lakeland towns and was almost certainly settled long before the Romans arrived. They quickly appreciated its

Ullswater

strategic position on the main west coast artery linking England and Scotland, and built a fort nearby, although nothing visible of it remains today. Most of the town's oldest buildings have also disappeared, victims of the incessant Border conflicts down the centuries. Penrith today is a busy place, its location close to the M6 and within easy reach not only of the Lakes but also the Border Country and the Yorkshire Dales making it a hub of this northwestern corner of England.

Only a few miles from the town, Ullswater, 8 miles long and the second longest lake in Cumbria, is also one of its most beautiful. The area around Penrith has some interesting old buildings, notably Shap Abbey and Brougham Castle, as well as two outstanding stately homes, Hutton-in-the-Forest where the Inglewood family have lived since 1605, and Dalemain, a fine mixture of medieval, Tudor and Georgian architecture which has also been inhabited by the same family for more than 300 years. Sadly, Greystoke Castle, which according to Edgar Rice Burroughs was the ancestral home of Tarzan, is not open to the public.

The Lake District

93

74 THREE CROWNS TEA SHOP

Penrith

Charming and welcoming tea rooms in the heart of Penrith.

❙❙ see *page 167*

76 PURPLE SAGE RESTAURANT

Penrith

Expertly prepared traditional English cuisine in handsome 18th-century surroundings. Morning coffee and lunchtime bar menu with local specialities.

❙❙ see *page 167*

PENRITH

In Saxon times Penrith was the capital of the Kingdom of Cumbria, but after the Normans arrived the town seems to have been rather neglected – it was sacked several times by the Scots before **Penrith Castle** was finally built in the 1390s. The much-maligned Richard, Duke of Gloucester (later Richard III) strengthened the castle's defences when he was Lord Warden of the Western Marches and was responsible for keeping the peace along the border with Scotland. By the time of the Civil War, however, the castle was in a state of ruin. The Cromwellian General Lambert demolished much of what was left and the townspeople helped themselves to the fallen stones to build their own houses. Nevertheless, the ruins remain impressive, standing high above a steep-sided moat.

A short walk from the castle leads to the centre of this lively town with its charming mixture of narrow streets and wide-open spaces, such as **Great Dockray** and **Sandgate**, into which cattle were herded during the raids. Later they became market places; a market is still held every Tuesday.

Penrith has a splendid Georgian church in a very attractive churchyard, surrounded by a number of interesting buildings. The oldest part of **St Andrew's Church** dates from Norman times but the most recent part, the nave, was rebuilt between 1719 and 1772, possibly to a design by Nicholas Hawksmoor. Pevsner described it as 'the stateliest church of its time in the county'. Of particular interest is the three-sided gallery and the two chandeliers which were a gift from the Duke of Portland in 1745 – a reward for the town's loyalty during the Jacobite Rising. A tablet on the wall records the deaths of 2,260 citizens of Penrith in the plague of 1597.

The church's most interesting feature, however, is to be found in the churchyard, in the curious group of gravestones known as **Giant's Grave** – two ancient cross-shafts, each 11 feet high, and four 10th-century hogback tombstones which have arched tops and sharply sloping sides. They have clearly been deliberately arranged, but their original purpose is no longer known. According to a local legend the stones mark the burial place of a 5th-century King of Cumbria, Owen Caesarius. Also buried somewhere in the churchyard is Wordsworth's mother, but her grave is not marked.

Overlooking the churchyard is a splendid Tudor house, bearing the date 1563, which is now a restaurant but was, at one time, Dame Birkett's School. The school's most illustrious pupils were William Wordsworth, his sister Dorothy, and his future wife, Mary Hutchinson. William is also commemorated by a plaque on the wall of the Robin Hood Inn stating that he was a guest there in 1794 and again in 1795.

Other notable buildings in the

town include the **Town Hall**; this is the result of a 1905 conversion of two former Adam-style houses, one of which was known as Wordsworth House as it was the home of the poet's cousin, Captain John Wordsworth.

Penrith's most spectacular visitor attraction, **Rheged Discovery Centre**, opened in Easter 2000 and dedicates itself to 'a celebration of 2,000 years of Cumbria's history, mystery and magic – as never seen before'. Named after Cumbria's Celtic Kingdom, this extraordinary grass-covered building is also home to Britain's only exhibition dedicated to mountains and mountain adventure. It also has a giant cinema screen, speciality shops, pottery demonstrations, artists' exhibitions, restaurants and a children's play area.

The town is dominated by **Beacon Hill Pike**, which stands amidst wooded slopes high above Penrith. The tower was built in 1719 and marks the place where, from 1296, beacons were lit to warn the townsfolk of an impending attack. The beacon was last lit during the Napoleonic wars in 1804 and was seen by the author Sir Walter Scott, who was visiting Cumberland at the time. Seeing it prompted Scott to hasten home to rejoin his local volunteer regiment.

It is well worth the climb from the Beacon Edge, along the footpath to the summit, to enjoy a magnificent view of the Lakeland fells. It was on top of this hill, in 1767, that Thomas Nicholson, a murderer, was hanged. The gibbet was left on the summit and so, it is said, was Nicholson's ghost, seen in the form of a skeleton hanging from the noose.

The red sandstone from which many of Penrith's Victorian houses were built was quarried along the escarpments of Beacon Edge, and one of the old quarries, at **Cowraik**, is now a local nature reserve. In addition to the interesting variety of wildlife established down the years, it is a Site of Special Scientific Interest for the geological interest of the quarry faces. The rocks are the remnants of sand dunes formed 250 million years ago when the Eden Valley was part of a dry, sandy desert that started just north of the Equator.

AROUND PENRITH

HUTTON-IN-THE-FOREST

6 miles N of Penrith on the B5305

The home of the Inglewood family since 1605, **Hutton-in-the-Forest Historic House** was originally a medieval stronghold and the **Pele Tower** still exists. Among the notable features are the 17th-century Gallery, the Hall dominated by a Cupid staircase, and a room decorated in the Arts and Crafts style. The splendid grounds include a beautiful walled garden built in the 1730s, topiary terraces that were originally laid out in the 17th century, and fine specimen trees and a 17th-century dovecote that form part of the Woodland Walk.

75/178 THE GLOBE INN

Calthwaite

Beautiful traditional family-run 17th-century coaching inn with home-made food, real ale and comfortable accommodation.

🍴 ⇤ *see pages 167, 209*

224 RHEGED DISCOVERY CENTRE

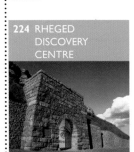

Redhills, Stainton

A spectacular visitor attraction detailing the last 2000 years of Cumbrian history. A 6 storey high cinema screen shows a specially commisioned film

🏛 *see page 226*

•

Hutton-in-the-Forest Historic house has been added to and altered by successive generations, with the result that an unusual number of architectural and decorative styles can be seen.

•

Beautiful Grade II listed country house with seven guest bedrooms. Packed lunches and evening meals by arrangement.

⊨ *see page 209*

•

About 100 yards from the church stands the Plague Stone where, during medieval times, coins were left in vinegar in exchange for food for the plague victims. An ancient Sanctuary Stone, now concealed behind a grille, marks the point beyond which fugitives could claim sanctuary.

•

•

The Greystoke Castle Estate is open throughout the year, offering a wide variety of outdoor activities, from falconry and fly-casting to clay target-shooting, off-road driving and quad-bike safaris.

•

GREYSTOKE

5 miles W of Penrith on the B5288

According to Edgar Rice Burroughs, **Greystoke Castle** was the ancestral home of Tarzan, Lord of the Apes, a fiction which was perpetuated in the 1984 film *Greystoke*. Tarzan's aristocratic credentials would have come as something of a surprise to the dignified Barons of Greystoke, whose effigies are preserved in **St Andrew's Church**. As imposing and spacious as a cathedral, St Andrew's boasts a wonderful east window with much 13th-century glass and, in the Lady Chapel, a figure of the Madonna and Child carved by a German prisoner-of-war.

Around the time of the American War of Independence, Greystoke Castle was bought by the 11th Duke of Norfolk, a staunch Whig who delighted in annoying his dyed-in-the-wool Tory neighbour, the Duke of Portland. Portland of course detested the American rebels, so Norfolk built two curious castle/farmhouses close to Portland's estate, and named them Fort Putnam and Bunkers Hill after the two battles in which the British had been trounced. Norfolk displayed a similarly elegant disdain for one of his tenants, a religious bore who maintained that church buildings were an abomination. The Duke built a medieval-looking farmhouse for him and crowned it with a very ecclesiastical spire.

Greystoke village itself is a gem, its attractive houses grouped around a trimly maintained village

green. Nearby are the stables where Gordon Richards trained his two Grand National winners, *Lucius* and *Hello Dandy*.

BROUGHAM

1 mile SE of Penrith off the A66

About a mile southeast of Penrith, the substantial and imposing remains of **Brougham Castle** (English Heritage) stand on the foundations of a Roman fort. The castle was inherited in the 1640s by the redoubtable and immensely rich Lady Anne Clifford, whose patrimony as Countess of Pembroke, Dorset and Montgomery also included another six northern castles. She spent a fortune restoring them all in medieval style and, when told that Cromwell had threatened to destroy them, replied 'As often as he destroys them I will rebuild them while he leaves me a shilling in my pocket.' Brougham was Lady Anne's favourite castle and she died here in 1676 at the age of 86.

From the castle there's a delightful riverside walk to **Eamont Bridge** and the circular **Mayburgh Henge**, which dates from prehistoric times. On the huge embankment, more than 100 yards across, stands a single, large stone about 10 feet high. Close to the village, on the banks of the River Eamont, is **Giant's Cave**, the supposed lair of a man-eating giant called Isir. This local tale is linked with the legend of Tarquin, a giant knight who imprisoned 64 men in his cave and was eventually killed by Sir Lancelot. Some people also claim that Uther Pendragon, King Arthur's father, lived here and that he too ate human flesh. A nearby prehistoric earthwork has been known as **King Arthur's Round Table** for many centuries. Lady Anne also rebuilt the chapel that stands on a hill above the castle, next to Brougham Hall. The Hall's colourful history goes back 500 years and its fame reached its height in the Victorian age, when, with its splendid appearance and its royal associations, it was dubbed 'the Windsor of the North'. The Hall today is home to a number of shops, craft workshops and even a brewery. The chapel, dedicated to St Wilfred, contains a remarkable collection of items acquired by William Brougham, later the 2nd Baron Brougham and Vaux; notable among them are French and Flemish stalls from the 16th and 17th centuries. The old parish church of Brougham is the remotely located **St Ninian's**, also known as Ninekirks, which contains some family box pews that are screened so that they look almost like cages.

STAINTON

2 miles W of Penrith off the A66 or A592

At Stainton, off the A592, **The Alpaca Centre** was set up in 1997 and has become a focal point for the development and expanding knowledge of the alpaca. The Centre is a working farm: breeding, rearing and selling alpacas, and welcomes visits at any time of the year. Visitors can see the alpacas in their paddocks and browse through the goods in the Spirit of the Andes shop, mostly made from the exceptional alpaca fibre. Also at the centre are a tea room and a gallery with a collection of furniture and ornamental pieces in wood.

TIRRIL

2 miles SW of Penrith on the B5320

Like its neighbour, Yanwath, Tirril has connections with the Quaker Movement. At Tirril there is an old **Quaker Meeting House** (now in private ownership), while **Yanwath Hall**, reputed to be the finest manorial hall in England, was the birthplace of the Quaker Thomas Wilkinson. Modern Yanwath also boasts an interesting gallery, located in a cottage garden setting.

DALEMAIN

3 miles SW of Penrith off the A592

Dalemain House is one of the area's most popular attractions – an impressive house with a medieval and Tudor core fronted by an imposing Georgian façade. The house has been home to the same family since 1679 – Sir Edward Hasell bought the property in that year – and over the years they have accumulated fine collections of china, furniture and family portraits. The grand drawing rooms boast some very fine oak panelling and in the Chinese Room is some beautifully preserved 18th-century Chinese wallpaper and a rococo chimneypiece by Nathaniel Hedges in Chinese Chippendale style; visitors also have access to the Nursery (furnished with toys from all ages) and Housekeeper's Room.

77 KINGS ARMS

Stainton

Spacious and traditional early 18th-century inn with great food, drink and hospitality at lunch and dinner every day.

¶ see page 168

225 DALEMAIN HISTORIC HOUSE & GARDENS

Dalemain

Dating back in parts to Tudor times, this splendid house holds an amazing collection of furniture, paintings and ceramics. Superb gardens, refreshments and gift shop.

🏛 see page 226

A *14th-century pele tower, Dacre Castle (in private hands) is a typical example of the fortified house or small castle that was common in northern England during the Middle Ages. This was the seat of the Dacre family, Catholic Earls of Cumberland, and its turrets and battlements have walls that are 8 feet thick. Leonard Dacre took part in the ill-fated Rising of the North in 1589 and, some time later, the estate passed to the Earls of Sussex who restored the castle in 1675 and whose coat of arms can still be seen.*

•

180 PARK FOOT CARAVAN AND CAMPING PARK

Pooley Bridge

Camping, caravan berths, B&B and self-catering accommodation amid breathtaking scenery with full facilities and a range of activities.

see *page 209*

The Norman pele tower at Dalemain House displays the regimental collection of the Westmorland and Cumberland Yeomanry, a troop of mounted infantry usually led by the Hasell family itself.

The 16th-century Great Barn contains an interesting assortment of agricultural bygones. The extensive grounds include a medieval herb garden, a Tudor-walled knot garden with a fine early Roman fountain, a wild garden alongside Dacre Beck, a deer park, Fell Pony Museum and woodland and riverside walks.

DACRE

4 miles SW of Penrith off the A66

There is much of historic interest in this village. The **Church** occupies a site of a former monastery which was mentioned by the Venerable Bede in his accounts of Cumberland in the 8th century. A later reference shows that in AD 926 the Peace of Dacre was signed between Athelstan of England and Constantine of Scotland. Fragments of masonry are reputed to have come from the monastery and the four weather-beaten carvings of bears in the churchyard are probably of Anglo-Viking origin. The bears are shown, respectively, sleeping, being attacked by a cat, shaking off the cat and eating the cat.

POOLEY BRIDGE

5 miles SW of Penrith on the B5320

Wordsworth noted the curious fact that the lake creates a sextuple echo, a natural phenomenon that

the Duke of Portland exploited in the mid-1700s by keeping a boat on the lake equipped 'with brass guns, for the purpose of exciting echoes'. In Wordsworth's opinion Ullswater provides 'the happiest combination of beauty and grandeur, which any of the Lakes affords' – a view with which most visitors concur.

The charming village of Pooley Bridge stands at the northern tip of **Ullswater**, and there are regular cruise departures from here during the season, stopping at Glenridding and Howton. Rowing and powered boats are available for hire, and since Ullswater is in effect a public highway, private boats can also be launched. A speed limit of 10mph applies over the whole of the 8-mile-long serpentine lake. Also, the greater part of the shoreline is privately owned and landing is not permitted.

The oldest building in Pooley Bridge is part of **Holly House**, which dates back to 1691, while the Bridge of the village's name dates from 1763 when the elegant structure over the River Eamont was built at a cost of £400. At that time a regular fresh fish market was held in the village square. Before Bridge was added, the name Pooley meant 'pool by the hill' and was derived from the pond which existed behind **Dunmallard**, the cone-shaped hill on the other side of the River Eamont. Above the village, on the summit of Dunmallard, are the remains of an Iron Age fort and, of course, splendid views southwards over Ullswater.

WATERMILLOCK

7 miles SW of Penrith on the A592

This small village, perfectly situated on the shores of Ullswater, is hidden amongst the woodland which occupies much of the lake's western shores. About 4 miles southwest of the village, there are a series of waterfalls which tumble down through a wooded gorge and then into Ullswater. The name of the largest fall is **Aira Force** (70 feet high) and the second largest is **High Force**. They can easily be reached on foot through the woodlands of **Gowbarrow Estate**, which is owned by the National Trust. This famous waterfall, which can be viewed from stone bridges at top and bottom, was the setting for the romantic and tragic story of Emma, who fell in love with a renowned knight called Sir Eglamore. He had to leave her to follow the Crusades. As the months lengthened into years and he had not returned, Emma became so distraught that she started to sleepwalk to Aira Force, where she eventually met her tragic death. On his return, the grief-stricken Sir Eglamore became a hermit and lived by the waterfall for the rest of his days.

GLENRIDDING

14 miles SW of Penrith on the A592

A popular base for walkers about to tackle the daunting challenge of **Helvellyn** (3,115ft), Glenridding is the largest and busiest of Ullswater's lakeside villages. Lake cruises depart from here, rowing

Ullswater

boats are available for hire and there's plenty of room for waterside picnics.

PATTERDALE

15 miles SW of Penrith on the A592

It is this village's magnificent setting that makes it such a popular tourist destination. Close to the head of Ullswater and with a series of fells

181 OLD WATER VIEW

Patterdale

Handsome Victorian country house offering first-class accommodation, with a range of individual touches that make any stay memorable.

see page 209

Patterdale

99

226 LAKELAND BIRD OF PREY CENTRE

Lowther, Nr Penrith

A sanctuary for birds of prey set within the grounds of Lowther Castle.

🏛 *see page 227*

framing the views, the scenery is indeed splendid. On the north side of the village is **St Patrick's Well**, which was thought to have healing properties. The medieval chapel dedicated to the saint was rebuilt in the 1850s.

CLIFTON

3 miles S of Penrith on the A6

One of the last battles to be fought on English soil took place at nearby **Clifton Moor** in December 1745. Bonnie Prince Charlie was in retreat and his exhausted troops were easily routed by the English forces. Eleven soldiers were killed and are buried in Clifton churchyard, but some of the wounded Highlanders were hanged from the Rebels' Tree on the outskirts of the village. The tree is a sorry sight nowadays with its gaunt, dead branches, but it is still a place of pilgrimage for the Scots.

To the southeast of the village is **Wetheriggs Country Pottery**, which was founded in 1855. Visitors can try their hand at the often messy business of throwing a pot, or they can paint a pot, paint on glass and make a candle, and also take a conducted tour of the steam-powered pottery, the only one of its kind in the UK. The pottery was designated an Industrial Monument in 1973, and has a tearoom, several shops and a pond that is home to three types of newt.

The steam engine at Wetheriggs Country Potter was restored by none other than Fred Dibnah, the famous steeplejack.

ASKHAM

3 miles S of Penrith off the A6

Askham is a pleasant village set around two greens. In the centre of the village is one of its most interesting shops, the **Toy Works**, which combines a traditional toy shop with a toymaker's workshop. Special services include advice on restoring rocking horses and a repair service 'for ailing and worn old teddy bears'. **Askham Fell**, which rises to the west, is dotted with prehistoric monuments including one known as the Copt (or Cop) Stone, said to mark the burial site of a Celtic chieftain. On the edge of the village is **Askham Hall** (private), now the home of the head of the Lonsdale family, who abandoned Lowther Castle in 1936 and moved here.

LOWTHER

4 miles S of Penrith off the A6

Lowther Castle is now only a shell, most of it having been demolished in 1957, but it was clearly once a grand place: after one visit Queen Victoria is reputed to have said that she would not return to the castle as it was too grand for her. The ancestral owners of the castle were the illustrious Earls of Lonsdale, a family of statesmen and sportsmen. The most famous is perhaps the 5th Earl (1857-1944), known as the Yellow Earl because of the colour of the livery used on his private carriage. He was the first President of the Automobile Association and permitted his family colours to be used by that organisation. The yellow flag of the Lonsdales can be seen in Lowther Church. The grounds include the **Lakeland Bird of Prey Centre**, whose aim is to conserve birds of prey through education, breeding and caring for injured or orphaned birds before releasing them back into the wild.

The 5th Earl was a patron of amateur boxing; the famous Lonsdale Belt attests to his patronage and interest.

Lowther village itself was built in the 1680s by Sir John Lowther,

View Towards Haweswater

who moved his tenants here to improve the view from the new house he was building. He also built **St Michael's Church** where several generations of the Lowthers are buried in a series of magnificent tombs beginning with a medieval style alabaster monument to Sir Richard, who died in 1608. Fashions in funerary sculpture continue through the obligatory skull of the late 17th century to the grandiose representation of the 1st Viscount Lonsdale, who sits nonchalantly with his viscount's coronet. Later monuments show a moustachioed Henry, Earl of Lonsdale, in military garb, and a charming Pre-Raphaelite plaque to Emily, wife of the 3rd Earl, who is depicted with her favourite dog at her feet.

BAMPTON

8 miles S of Penrith off the A6

For several hundred years this small village was well known for its **Grammar School**, two of whose pupils rose swiftly in the church hierarchy. One was Hugh Curwen, who as a Protestant became Chaplain to Henry VIII, as a Catholic under Queen Mary was elevated to the Archbishopric of Dublin, and then prudently re-embraced Protestantism when Elizabeth took the throne. Another Bampton boy was less pliable: Edmund Gibson was baptised in the church here in 1669 and later became a fiery Bishop of London who repeatedly denounced the degenerate morals of the age – with little apparent effect.

A couple of miles south of Bampton, **Haweswater** is the most easterly of the lakes. It is actually a reservoir, created in the late 1930s to supply the growing needs of industrial Manchester. Beneath the water lies the village of **Mardale** and several dairy farms for which Haweswater Valley was once famous. By 1940 the lake had reached its present extent of 4 miles, and Manchester Corporation set about planting its shores with conifers. Today the area is managed

101

182 THE HERMITAGE

Shap

Impressive and comfortable bed-and-breakfast accommodation in traditional 17th-century home with 19th-century additions.

see page 210

as a nature reserve. Walkers have a good chance of seeing woodpeckers and sparrowhawks, buzzards and peregrine falcons, and with luck may even catch sight of golden eagles gliding on the thermals rising above Riggindale. An observation is manned throughout the breeding season if the eagles are nesting.

Above Haweswater runs the **High Street**, actually a Roman road, which is now one of the most popular fell walks in the Lake District. It overlooks the remote and lovely Blea Tarn and the lonely valley of Martindale, a cul-de-sac valley to the south of Ullswater, where England's last remaining herd of wild red deer can often be seen.

SHAP

10 miles S of Penrith on the A6

This small village on the once-congested A6 enjoys some grand views of the hills. In coaching days Shap was an important staging post for the coaches before they tackled the daunting climb up **Shap Fell** to its summit some 850 feet above sea level. Much earlier, in medieval times, the village was even more significant because of nearby **Shap Abbey**, constructed in the local Shap granite which has been used in many well-known buildings, St Pancras Station and the Albert Memorial in London among them.

The Abbey stands about a mile to the west of the village, just inside the National Park, and it's well worth seeking it out to see the imposing remains of the only abbey

founded in Westmorland. It was also the only one in the Lake District mountains, the last abbey to be consecrated in England (around 1199) and the last to be dissolved, in 1540. Henry VIII's Commissioners seem to have been especially thorough in their demolition of the Abbey, and local builders continued the depredations. But the mighty west tower and some of the walls remain, and they enjoy a lovely setting – secluded, tranquil and timeless.

From the Abbey there's a pleasant walk of well under a mile to **Keld**, a tiny village of just 17 houses. So quiet today, in medieval times Keld was a busy little place servicing the monks of Shap Abbey nearby. It was the monks of Shap Abbey who built the village's oldest building, the early 16th-century **Keld Chapel** (National Trust). After the closure of the Abbey, the chapel fell on hard times and for 200 years was used as a dwelling house – that's when the incongruous chimney was added. In 1860 it was 'serving as a cow-house' but was saved from this ignominious role in 1918 by the National Trust. A service is held in the tiny chapel once a year in August; at other times, a notice on the chapel door tells you where you can obtain the key.

MAULDS MEABURN

11 miles SE of Penrith off the A6

This charming village in the Lyvennet Valley has a large green through which the river flows, crossed by footbridges and stepping stones. As well as a fine collection of 17th and 18th-century cottages, there is also an early 17th-century Hall.

ORTON

15 miles S of Penrith on the B6260

By far the best approach to Orton is along the B6290 from Appleby to Tebay. This scenic route climbs up onto the moors, passing **Thunder Stone**, some mighty limestone bluffs and the pavements of **Great Asby Scar**, the setting for BBC-TV's *The Tenant of Wildfell Hall*. As motorists descend the side of Orton Scar, grand views open up of the Howgills and the Lune Gorge with the Shap Fells looming on the horizon.

A village now ('one of the prettiest in Westmorland' according to one writer), for centuries Orton was a market town of some consequence. There are reminders of Orton's former importance in the noble church tower, completed in 1504, in the attractive proportions of **Petty Hall**, an Elizabethan house at the lower end of the village (a private residence) and the grandeur of **Orton Hall**, built in 1662 and now converted into holiday apartments.

Orton's most famous visitor was Bonnie Prince Charlie, on his way northwards after the crushing defeat of his troops at Derby. He was followed soon afterwards by the Duke of Cumberland, 'Butcher' Cumberland, the victor of the Battle of Culloden. The Duke may

have stayed in the village at an inn that was later re-named the Cumberland Hotel. The Inn, dating from 1632, still stands in the centre of the village, although it is now a private house.

The village church, in common with many in the Eden Valley, has a massive 16th-century tower built for defensive purposes and, presumably, was one place that the villagers sought shelter. Its features include an ancient oak parish chest and a stained glass window by Beatrice Whistler, wife of the American artist James McNeill Whistler. Orton was the birthplace of George Whitehead (1636-1723) who, along with George Fox, was one of the founders of the Quaker Movement.

TEBAY

17 miles S of Penrith, by Exit 38 of the M6

At one time a sheep-farming area and a railway settlement, this long rambling village now owes its importance to the arrival of the M6 motorway, Cumbria's main thoroughfare. The village was the home of Mary Baynes, the **Witch of Tebay**, who died in 1811 at the age of 90. She is said to have foretold the coming of fiery horseless carriages speeding across Loups Fell where, today, the London-to-Glasgow railway line runs. Greatly feared by the people of Tebay, she is said to have withered and died at the same time as some eggs on which she had placed a curse were fried in boiling fat.

78 WHITE HORSE INN

Kings Meaburn

Excellent food and drink in peaceful village found off the A66 or A6. Annual beer festival held in late July.

see page 168

79/183 MEABURN B&B AND RESTAURANT

Maulds Meaburn

Characterful and elegant restaurant and comfortable accommodation in picturesque location. 4 Diamonds AA.

see pages 168, 210

•

To the north of Orton there is some superb limestone scenery, and the village stands below Orton Scar, on which a beacon was lit to warn people to seek safety from advancing Scottish raiders.

•

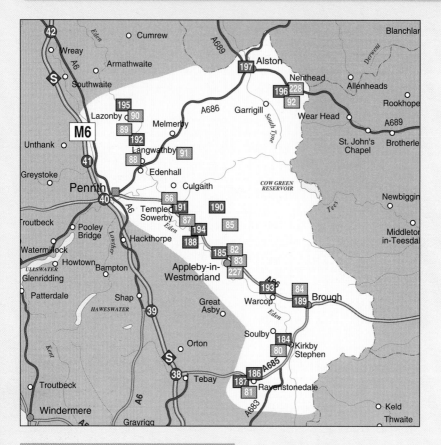

The Eden Valley & East Cumbria

The River Eden is entirely Cumbrian and is one of the few large rivers in England that flows northwards. The source of the river is on the high limestone fells above Mallerstang

Warcop Fell, Appleby

Common, near the North Yorkshire border, and it runs to the outskirts of Carlisle where it turns sharply east and flows into the Solway Firth. For much of its course, the river is accompanied by the famous Settle-Carlisle Railway, a spectacularly scenic route saved from extinction in the 1960s by the efforts of local enthusiasts.

Carved through boulder clay and red sandstone and sandwiched between the Lakeland fells and the northern Pennines, the Eden Valley is green and fertile – in every sense another Eden. But the valley was vulnerable to Scottish raids in medieval times and the number of pele towers and castles in the area are testament to a turbulent and often violent past.

This, too, is farming country and many of the ancient towns and villages have a market place. Appleby-in-Westmorland, the old county town of Westmorland, had an important market and also an annual horse fair that continues today and has gained a large following.

An attractive man-made feature of the valley is the collection of specially commissioned stone sculptures known as Eden Benchmarks dotted along its length. Each created by a different sculptor, they have been located beside public paths and, since they also function as seats, provide the perfect setting in which to enjoy the valley's unspoilt scenery. There are 10 of them in all, beginning with Mary Bourne's *Water Cut*, an intriguing limestone sculpture, shaped rather like a tombstone riven from top to bottom by a serpentine space representing the river. It stands on Lady Anne's Way, a public path along the eastern ridge of the Mallerstang Fells.

The Eden Valley

105

KIRKBY STEPHEN

There are many delightful walks from the Kirkby Stephen, to Croglam Earthworks for example, a prehistoric fort, or to nearby Stenkrith Park where the second of the Eden Benchmarks can be found. Created by Laura White in Ancaster limestone and titled Passage, the sculpture is deceptively simple, suggesting perhaps the course of a river bed. There are also some pleasant strolls along the riverside to a fine waterfall where the River Eden cascades into Coop Karnel Hole. One interesting path is the Poetry Path, where 12 short poems, written by Meg Peacocke have been carved into stone blocks placed at intervals along a circular route of path either side of the River Eden. For more strenuous exercise, walkers could tackle a stretch of the Coast-to-Coast long-distance footpath, which passes through the town. Look out for the unusual shapes of the weathered limestone rock along the riverside at Coop Karnel Hole.

Surrounded by spectacular scenery, the old market town of Kirkby Stephen lies at the head of the beautiful Eden Valley. It was the Vikings who first established a village here and they named it 'Kirke and Bye'. Although essentially part of the Eden Valley, Kirkby Stephen has a strong Yorkshire Dales feel about it. Indeed, the church, with its long, elegant nave, has been called the Cathedral of the Dales.

Dating from Saxon times, rebuilt in 1220 and with a 16th-century tower, **St Stephen's Church** is one of the finest in the eastern fells, dominating the northern end of the town from its elevated position. Until the last century the **Trupp Stone** in the churchyard received money from local people every Easter Monday in payment of church tithes and, at 8 o'clock, the curfew is still sounded by the **Taggy Bell**, once regarded by local children as a demon. Inside the church are a number of pre-Conquest stones, some of which show Norse influence. The most remarkable is the 10th-century **Loki Stone**, one of only two such carvings in Europe

to have survived. Loki was a Norse God; presumably the Viking settlers brought their belief in Loki to Kirkby Stephen. The carving of Loki shows a figure resembling the Devil with sheep's horns, whose legs and arms are bound by heavy irons, an image symbolising the overpowering of paganism by Christian beliefs. For many years the stone lay undiscovered, reused as a building stone. The church also boasts some interesting memorials, among them the Elizabethan tomb of Thomas, Lord Wharton and his two wives, and the earlier memorial to Sir Richard de Musgrave of Hartley Castle, who died in the early 1400s. Sir Richard was the man reputed to have killed that last boar upon Wild Boar Fell, and the

Cycling near Kirkby Stephen

story was given credence when, some years ago, the tomb was opened to reveal the bones of a man and woman alongside two tusks from a boar. The splendid pulpit, given by the town in memory of a much-loved vicar, is made of Shap granite and Italian marble.

Between the church and the market square stand the cloisters, which served for a long time as a butter market. The **Market Square** is surrounded by an ancient collar of cobblestones which marked out an area used for bull-baiting – a 'sport' that ceased here in 1820 after a disaster when a bull broke loose. The market, still held every Monday, has existed since 1351 and has always been a commercial focus for the surrounding countryside. In the 18th century, knitting – mostly of stockings – was the most important product of the town. A restored spinning gallery reflects the importance of the woollen industry.

AROUND KIRKBY STEPHEN

OUTHGILL

5 miles S of Kirkby Stephen on the B6259

This remote village has close links with the Clifford family of Skipton Castle, North Yorkshire. The village **Church of St Mary**, first built in 1311, was repaired by Lady Anne Clifford who, from 1643 when she finally obtained possession of the Clifford estates, devoted her life to restoring her many properties and lived in each

of them for varying periods of time. Her estates included six castles – Skipton and Barden in Yorkshire, and Appleby, Brough, Brougham and Pendragon in Westmorland. Lady Anne's zeal for restoration didn't stop at castles: she also repaired the Roman road between Wensleydale and the Eden Valley, a route she often travelled (along with a huge retinue) between her castles and her birthplace at Skipton. The route is now known as Lady Anne's Way but in times past it was aptly called the **High Way** since it was a regular place of employment for highwaymen such as Dick Turpin and William 'Swift' Nevison.

To the south is **Wild Boar Fell**, a brooding, flat-topped peak

80/184 THE PENNINE HOTEL

Kirkby Stephen

Real ales, hearty and delicious meals and six guest bedrooms.

⊪ ⊨ see pages 168, 210

Wild Boar Fell

107

187 STOUPHILL GATE

Ravenstonedale

Lovely property in scenic
location offering
comfortable and attractive
B&B and self-catering
accommodation.

see page 212

81/186 THE KINGS
HEAD HOTEL

Ravenstonedale

Superb village inn with food,
drink and accommodation in
an area of outstanding
natural beauty.

see pages 169, 211

where the last wild boar in England
was reputedly killed, while tucked
down in the valley are the romantic
ruins of Lammerside and
Pendragon Castles.

Pendragon Castle, about a
mile north of the village, is
shrouded in legend but there are
claims that it was the fortress of
Uther Pendragon, father of King
Arthur. If so, nothing remains of
that 6th-century wooden castle.
The present structure dates from
the 1100s and was built by Hugh de
Morville, one of the four knights
who murdered Thomas à Becket, to
guard the narrow pass of
Mallerstang. Twice it was burned
by the Scots and twice restored, on
the latter occasion by the
formidable Lady Anne Clifford in
1660. Another mile or so
downstream, **Lammerside Castle**
dates from the 12th century, though
only the remains of the keep
survive. They can be found along a
bridle path between Pendragon and
Wharton Hall.

RAVENSTONEDALE

5 miles SW of Kirkby Stephen on the A685

Known locally as Rissendale, this
pretty village of stone-built cottages
clustered along the banks of
Scandal Beck lies on the edge of
the Howgill Fells. The parish
Church of St Oswald dates to
1738 and is especially interesting.
An earlier church, built on the same
site, had a separate bell tower that
rested on pillars; at its centre hung
a refuge bell. Anyone guilty of a
capital offence who managed to
escaped to Ravenstonedale and

sound the bell was free from arrest
by the King's officials. This custom
was finally abolished during the
reign of James I.

Ravenstondale's Church of St
Oswald is one of the few Georgian
churches in Cumbria. The present
church, surrounded by yew trees, is
well worth a visit. It features bow
pews facing one another, a three-
decker pulpit complete with a
sounding board and, at the back of
the third deck, a seat for the
parson's wife. The window at the
east end commemorates the last
woman in England to be put to
death for her Protestant faith.
Elizabeth Gaunt was sentenced in
1685 by the notorious Judge
Jeffreys to be burnt at the stake for
sheltering a fugitive rebel. She met
her end at Tyburn in London.

NATEBY

2 miles S of Kirkby Stephen on the B6269

Now a quiet hamlet of houses
standing alongside a beck, for
centuries Nateby was dominated by
Hartley Castle. Believed to have
been built in the 13th century, the
castle was the home of Sir Andrew
de Harcala, a renowned soldier
during the reign of Edward II.
Harcala was one of the first men to
fight on a pony and he was made
Earl of Carlisle in recognition of
his services to the Crown.
However, his failure to prevent
Robert the Bruce invading the
north of England led him to be
accused of treason and he was
executed in 1325. His castle was
finally demolished by the Musgrave
family, who used the stone to build

their manor house at Edenhall near Penrith.

CROSBY GARRETT

4 miles W of Kirkby Stephen off the A685

Local legend has it that the Devil, seeing all the stones lying ready to build **Crosby Garrett Church**, carried them in his leather apron to the top of a nearby hill. He reasoned that, as people grew old, they would be unable to climb the hill and attend church and thus would come to him rather than go to Heaven. Such tales apart, the church itself is said to be of Anglo-Saxon origin though the visible fabric is 12th century. Inside there are some superb carvings, particularly near the font. The church is also famous for its hagioscope, cut through the wall to allow people in the north aisle to see the altar. Near the church gates is a tithe barn, built in the 18th century to store farm produce given to the church as a religious tax.

WINTON

3 miles N of Kirkby Stephen off the A685

This is a quiet and picturesque hamlet whose name, in old English, means 'pasture farmland'. It is built on a spring line and, like many other Cumbrian villages of medieval origin, once followed the runrig, or two-field system of agriculture. The evidence is still visible in long, thin fields to the north of the village. These would have been individual strips in medieval times: the open fields were enclosed in the 17th and 18th centuries.

In the centre of the village is the manor house, built in 1726. It was formerly a boys' school where, apparently, the boys were treated like prisoners and not allowed to return home until the end of their education in case they told of their life at the school. The oldest building is **Winton Hall**, built of stone and dated 1665, but looking older with its stone buttresses and mullion windows with iron bars.

Those taking a walk on **Winton Fell** are likely to see red grouse lifting off from the large tracts of heather on the fellside. Indeed, the wildlife is much more prolific around this area where the limestone provides more plentiful food than on the fells around the lakes.

KABER

4 miles N of Kirkby Stephen off the A685

In 1663, this small village was the improbable focus of the **Kaber Rigg Plot**, a rebellion against Charles II led by Captain Robert Atkinson of Watergate Farm in Mallerstang. The rising failed and Atkinson was hanged, drawn, and quartered at Appleby; tragically, a messenger carrying his reprieve was delayed on Stainmore and arrived too late to save Atkinson from his gruesome fate.

APPLEBY-IN-WESTMORLAND

The old county town of Westmorland, Appleby is one of the most delightful small towns in England. It was originally built by

To the west of the village of Crosby Garrett, the splendid viaduct of the Settle-Carlisle Railway dominates Crosby Garrett.

the Norman Ranulph de Meschines, who set it within a broad loop of the River Eden which protects it on three sides. The fourth side is guarded by **Castle Hill**. The town's uniquely attractive main street, **Boroughgate**, has been described as the finest in England. A broad, tree-lined avenue, it slopes down the hillside to the river, its sides lined with a pleasing variety of buildings, some dating back to the 17ᵗʰ century. At its foot stands the 16ᵗʰ-century **Moot Hall**; at its head rises the great Norman Keep of **Appleby Castle** which is protected by one of the most impressive curtain walls in northern England. Attractions here include the dramatic view from the top of the five-storey keep and the attractive grounds which are home to a wide variety of animals and include a **Rare Breeds Survival Centre**.

During the mid-1600s, Appleby Castle was the home of Lady Anne Clifford, the remarkable woman

who has already been mentioned several times and to whom Appleby has good cause to be grateful. The last of the Clifford line, the diminutive Lady Anne (she was just 4 ft 10 inches tall) inherited vast wealth and estates, among them no fewer than six northern castles. She lavished her fortune on rebuilding or restoring them all. Churches and chapels in the area also benefited from her munificence and at Appleby, in 1651, she also founded the almshouses known as the Hospital of St Anne, for '12 sisters and a Mother'. Set around a cobbled square, the picturesque cottages and minuscule chapel still serve their original function, maintained by the trust endowed by Lady Anne; visitors are welcome.

Lady Anne died in 1676 and was buried with her mother, Margaret Countess of Cumberland, in **St Lawrence's Church**. The church is well worth visiting to see their magnificent tombs and also the historic organ, purchased from Carlisle Cathedral in 1684, which is said to be oldest still in use in Britain.

Just a few years after Lady Anne's death, James II granted the town the right to hold a Fair during the week leading to the second Wednesday in June. More than 300 years later, the **Gypsy Horse Fair** is still thriving, with hundreds flooding into the little town (population 1,800) with caravans and horse-drawn carts. The trade, principally in horses, and the trotting races provide a picturesque and colourful spectacle.

Boroughgate

Fells near Appleby

188 TARKA HOUSE

Bolton, Appleby-in-Westmorland

Lovely accommodation just four miles northwest of Appleby-in-Westmoreland off the A66.

⊨ see page 212

84/189 THE CASTLE HOTEL

Brough

Inn with good menu and daily specials, range of ales and 14 comfortable rooms.

⊨ ∦ see pages 170, 212

AROUND APPLEBY-IN-WESTMORLAND

BROUGH

8 miles SE of Appleby-in-Westmorland on the A66/A685

This small town, standing at the point where the **Stainmore Pass** opens into the Vale of Eden, is, in fact, two settlements: **Church Brough** and **Market Brough**. Church Brough is a group of neat houses and cottages clustered around a little market square in which a maypole stands on the site of the former market cross. **Brough Castle**, built within the ramparts of the Roman camp of *Verterae*, was constructed to protect the Roman road over Stainmore Pass. The building of this Norman castle was begun by William Rufus in 1095 but it was largely destroyed in 1174 by William the Lion of Scotland. Many times Scottish raiders laid siege to Brough Castle and fierce battles were fought. An ancient ballad tells of the legendary bravery of one knight from the town who defended the tower alone after his comrades had fallen. He was finally vanquished when the Scottish army set fire to his hiding place but the incident was so dramatic that it became a part of local folklore and was remembered in the ballad of the Valiant Knight of Brough. Another fortification restored by the remarkable Lady Anne Clifford, the castle, with its tall keep 60 feet high is well worth visiting, if only for the superb panorama of the surrounding fells seen from the battlements.

Market Brough is also an ancient settlement and was particularly important in the 18th and 19th centuries when it became a major coaching town on the stagecoach routes between England and Scotland. It was on the junction of several routes and boasted more than 10 inns. The width and breadth of its High

•

One custom still celebrated in Brough is the Twelfth Night Holly Burning, a unique festival with pagan origins.

•

The Eden Valley

193 HAYBERGILL CENTRE

Warcop

Unique Centre offering a venue and catered or self-catering accommodation for groups in a spacious and environmentally-friendly timber building.

see page 213

Street also indicates its importance as a market town. Brough was granted a charter in 1330 enabling it to hold a weekly market as well as four cattle markets and an annual fair.

The distinctive, low hills that lie to the west of Brough are drumlins – heaps of material deposited by Ice Age glaciers. In this area many drumlins are marked by broad, grassy ridges, remains of ancient lynchets or ploughing strips.

NORTH STAINMORE

10 miles SE of Appleby-in-Westmorland on the A66

The village lies on the Stainmore Pass which carries the old Roman road, now the A66, through a remote area of the North Pennines which David Bellamy has described as 'England's last wilderness'. Near Stainmore summit are the foundations of **Maiden Castle**, a Roman fort built to guard the pass against marauders. A few yards over the Cumbrian border, into County Durham, is the stump of

the ancient **Rey Cross** which was erected before AD 946 and which, until 1092, marked the boundary between England and Scotland. It is thought to be the site of the battle at which the last Viking King of York and North England, Eric Bloodaxe, was killed following his expulsion from the city.

WARCOP

5 miles SE of Appleby-in-Westmorland on the B6259

The largest village in this part of the Eden Valley, Warcop grew up as a crossing point of the river. The bridge, the oldest to cross the river, dates from the 16th century and the red sandstone buildings surrounding the village green, with its central maypole, make this a charming place to visit.

The **Church of St Columba** is built outside the village on the site of a Roman camp. An interesting building in its own right, it is particularly famous for the rush-bearing ceremony which takes place in late June each year. Warcop is surrounded by Ministry of Defence tank-firing ranges from which the public are understandably excluded, but on the hills above the village are stones, cairns and the remains of what is claimed to be a **Druid Temple**.

GREAT ORMSIDE

2 miles SE of Appleby-in-Westmorland off the B6260

This was once an important fort guarded by a pele tower, and the ancient **Church of St James**, which dates from the 11th century, occupies a site on the steep-sided defence mound. Relics of pre-Christian burials have been found in the mound, as well as a Viking sword (now in the Tullie Museum in Carlisle). A silver gilt and enamel bowl from the 7th century has also been found and is regarded as one of the most important pieces of Anglo-Saxon metalware to survive. A particularly beautiful piece, richly decorated with vine scrolls, birds and animals, it is now on permanent display in the Yorkshire Museum in York.

From the village a path leads across fields to the village of **Little Ormside**, with its large cedar tree said to have been brought back from Lebanon as a sapling by General Whitehead. On the voyage home he grew it in his hat, and shared with it his daily ration of one pint of water.

GREAT ASBY

4 miles S of Appleby-in-Westmorland off the B6260

———

This pretty village is set in a wooded hollow, its houses separated by **Hoff Beck**. Alongside the beck is **St Helen's Well**, and nearby are the splendid almshouses of St Helen's, built between 1811 and 1820. Across a footbridge is **Asby Hall** (in private hands), built in 1670. It was once the home of the Musgrave family of Edenhall, whose crest and coat of arms can still be seen above the door.

BRAMPTON

2 miles N of Appleby-in-Westmorland off the A66

———

This village, along with the surrounding area, was said to be

haunted by the ghost of Elizabeth Sleddall, the wife of a 17th-century owner of nearby Crackenthorpe Hall. Elizabeth died believing that she had been cheated out of her share of the estate, so to shame the false inheritors her spirit was seen being driven around the countryside in a coach drawn by four black horses. Her ghost became so troublesome that the local people exhumed her body and reburied the remains under a larger boulder. Her ghost, while no longer troubling the local people, is said still to visit the Hall.

DUFTON

3 miles N of Appleby-in-Westmorland off the A66

———

Behind this delightful hamlet lies **Dufton Gill**, a beautiful, secluded wooded valley through which runs a footpath. Also from Dufton there is a track carrying the Pennine Way up to High Cup Nick, a great horseshoe precipice at the edge of the northern Pennine escarpment that was formed by a glacial lake during the Ice Age.

LONG MARTON

3 miles N of Appleby-in-Westmorland off the A66

———

Visitors to this village can experience two very different forms of architecture, both of them equally impressive. The village church, with its carvings of knights and monsters over the doorway, is remarkably unspoilt and Norman, while nearby the Settle-Carlisle Railway sweeps across a grand viaduct.

---

85 THE STAG INN

Dufton, Appleby-in-Westmorland

Real ales, fresh home-made food and nearby holiday cottage in picturesque village 3 miles north of Appleby off the A66.

see page 170

---

190 MILBURN GRANGE

Knock, Appleby-in-Westmorland

Outstanding self-catering cottages in countryside 4 miles northeast of Appleby. 15 mins M6 junction 40.

see page 212

86/191 THE KINGS ARMS HOTEL

Temple Sowerby

Food, drink and year-round accommodation in a tranquil rural village setting.

🍴 ⊨ see pages 170, 212

87/194 THE BRIDGE END INN

Kirkby Thore, Penrith

Convivial and spacious inn with changing guest ale, food from lunch through to late.

🍴 ⊨ see pages 171, 214

•

Evidence of a Stone Age settlement has been found at Temple Sowerby, and a Roman milestone just outside the village marks the route of the old Imperial highway, now the A66.

•

TEMPLE SOWERBY

7 miles NW of Appleby-in-Westmorland on the A66

Temple Sowerby prides itself on the title 'Queen of Westmorland villages', an accolade justified by its lovely setting in the Eden valley. (Here's a bonus: the average rainfall here is half that recorded in the Lake District National Park to the west.) To the north, the massive bulk of **Cross Fell**, the highest point in the Pennines, swells skywards to provide a spectacular backdrop. The village itself, picturesquely grouped around a sloping green and an 18th-century red sandstone church, takes its name from the medieval Knights Templar who owned the manor of Sowerby until their Order was suppressed in 1308.

From Temple Sowerby there are delightful walks through the Eden valley or, if you prefer a gentle stroll, it's only a mile to the National Trust gardens at **Acorn Bank** where **Crowdundle Beck** splashes beneath an elegant 18th-century bridge. The 16th-century manor house is now a Sue Ryder Home and not open to the public, but visitors are welcome to explore the attractive gardens planted with a collection of some 250 medicinal and culinary herbs. A circular woodland walk runs along the beck to a watermill that was first mentioned on the site as far back as the 14th century. At different times it has been a saw mill, a corn mill and a source of power for the local gypsum mines; now restored, it is open for visits.

NORTHEAST OF PENRITH

EDENHALL

3 miles NE of Penrith off the A686

An old tradition asserts that in the 8th century the monks of Jarrow, fleeing from Viking invaders with the body of St Cuthbert, stopped here briefly. As a result the village church is dedicated to the saint. Part of the **Church of St Cuthbert** appears to be pre-Norman but most of the structure dates from the 1100s. Close to the church is the **Plague Cross** which stands where there was once a basin filled with vinegar. This acted as a disinfectant into which plague victims put their money to pay for food from the people of Penrith. The plague of the 16th century killed a quarter of the village's inhabitants.

Edenhall is particularly famous for the story of the 'Luck of Eden Hall', a priceless glass cup which, according to legend, was stolen from some fairies dancing round the garden wall by a butler in the service of the Musgrave family back in the 15th century. Despite the fairies' entreaties, the butler refused to return the 6-inch high glass to them. As he departed with the precious goblet, the fairies laid a curse upon it: 'If ever this cup shall break or fall, Farewell the luck of Eden Hall.' On inspection, the glass was identified as a 13th-century chalice of enamelled and gilded glass that is thought to have come from Syria and may well have been brought back by a Crusader.

It was a treasured heirloom of the Musgraves for many generations and is now in the Victoria & Albert Museum in London. The goblet is still intact, but Eden Hall has long since disappeared.

LANGWATHBY

4 miles NE of Penrith on the A686

Located on the opposite bank of the River Eden from Edenhall, Langwathby's name means 'the settlement by the long ford' and, though there are two prehistoric pathways crossing here, the name of the village and of its neighbouring settlements suggests a Viking past. Langwathby has a huge village green that still hosts maypole dancing on the third Saturday in May. The green is medieval in origin and would once have been surrounded by wood and mud houses, perhaps to protect cattle but also for defence against border raids. After the Civil War and the growth in prosperity in the late 17th century, these wattle-and-daub cottages were replaced by stone buildings. The drovers from Scotland passed through here to the market towns of England.

LITTLE SALKELD

6 miles NE of Penrith off the A686

A lane from the village leads to **Long Meg** and her Daughters, a most impressive prehistoric site and second only to Stonehenge in size. Local legend claims that Long Meg was a witch who, with her daughters, was turned to stone for profaning the Sabbath, as they danced wildly on the moor. The circle is supposedly endowed with magic so that it is impossible to count the same number of stones twice. Another superstition is that Long Meg will bleed if the stone is chipped or broken. The actual name, Long Meg, has been the subject of debate. It has been suggested that Meg may be a corruption of the word 'magus' meaning a magician.

There are more than 60 stones in the Circle (actually an oval), which is approximately 300 ft across. The tallest, Long Meg, is a 15ft column of Penrith sandstone, the corners of which face the four points of the compass. Cup and ring symbols and spirals are carved on this stone, which is over 3,500 years old. The circle is now known to belong to the Bronze Age, but no one is certain of its purpose. It may have been used for rituals connected with the changing seasons, since the midwinter sun sets in alignment with the centre of the circle and Long Meg herself. The brooding majesty of the site was perfectly evoked by Wordsworth:

A weight of awe, not easy to be borne,
Fell suddenly upon my spirit – cast
From the dread bosom of the unknown past,
When first I saw that family forlorn.

In 1725 an attempt was made by Colonel Samuel Lacy of Salkeld Hall to use the stones for mileposts. However, as work began, a great storm blew up and the workmen fled in terror, believing that the Druids were angry at the desecration of their temple.

88 BRIEF ENCOUNTER

Langwathby, Penrith

Café and restaurant in elegantly restored station building on the famous Settle-Carlisle line. Delicious food from 9-5 every day.

see page 171

•

West of the village of Langwathby , at Langwathby Hall Farm, Eden Ostrich World offers visitors the chance to see these splendid birds in a farm setting in the heart of the Eden Valley. The farm is also home to rare breed sheep, cattle and pigs, donkeys, deer, wallabies, alpacas and many other creatures from around the world. A giant maze was opened in 2001, and the farm has a tea room, gift shop, picnic areas and adventure play areas.

•

89/192 THE HIGHLAND DROVE INN

Great Salkeld

Superb menu, real ales, great hospitality and five en suite guest bedrooms in friendly and welcoming atmosphere.

🍽 🛏 see pages 172, 212

•

The Helm Winds are a curious meteorological feature: localised gusts which sweep through the Eden Valley with the force of a gale while the surrounding countryside remains perfectly calm.

•

195 HOWSCALES

Kirkoswald

Charming and comfortable accommodation in five traditional cottages.

🛏 see page 214

It was the same Colonel Lacy who gave his name to the **Lacy Caves**, a mile or so downstream from Little Salkeld. The Colonel had the five chambers carved out of the soft red sandstone, possibly as a copy of St Constantine's Caves further down the river at Wetheral, as at that time it was fashionable to have romantic ruins and grottoes on large estates. Colonel Lacy is said to have employed a man to live in his caves, acting the part of a hermit.

Alternatively, the caves may have been intended to provide a wine store: Colonel Lacy used to entertain his guests here, and there were probably gardens around the caves. The rhododendrons and laburnums still flower every spring.

GREAT SALKELD

6 miles NE of Penrith on the B6412

The River Eden formed the boundary between the two old counties of Westmorland and Cumberland, so while Little Salkeld was in Westmorland, its larger namesake stood in Cumberland. The village is a picturesque collection of 18th-century cottages and farmhouses built in red sandstone which are typical of this area. Great Salkeld is best known for the impressive **Church** with its massive, battlemented pele tower built in the 14th century and complete with a dungeon. The Norman doorway in the porch is less than a yard wide and its arch has three rows of deeply cut zig-zags with five heads, one with a crown.

KIRKOSWALD

8 miles NE of Penrith on the B6413

The village derives its name from the **Church of St Oswald**: Oswald was the King of Northumbria who, according to legend, toured the pagan north with St Aidan in the 7th century. The church is unusual in having a detached bell tower standing on top of a grassy hill some 200 yards from the main building (this is in a valley, so the bells could not be heard by the villagers).

This once thriving market town still retains its small cobbled market place and some very fine Georgian buildings. There's also a striking ruined 12th-century **Castle**, formerly the home of the Featherstonehaugh family which, although not open to the public, can be seen from the road and footpath. In 1210 a licence was received from King John to fortify the original structure and enclose the extensive park. The castle was later destroyed by Robert the Bruce in 1314 but was rebuilt and extended in the late 15th century. The whole site covered 3 acres, with the courtyard surrounded by a massive wall and a main gate with a drawbridge over the moat. The castle's splendour was due to the efforts of Thomas, Lord Dacre but, after his death in 1525, the panelling, stained glass and beamed ceilings were transferred to Naworth and the castle became a quarry. Today it is still protected by a wide moat, and the great turreted tower rises 65 feet above the remains of the vaulted dungeons. One of Kirkoswald's most splendid buildings is the **College**, its name recalling the days when St Oswald's was a collegiate church. The two-storey house with its sloping-ended roof was originally built as a pele tower and converted into the college for priests in the 1520s. The manor house opposite has a particularly attractive entrance front in sandstone, which was added in 1696.

ARMATHWAITE
10 miles NE of Penrith off the A6

Set on the western bank of the River Eden, the village has a particularly fine sandstone bridge from which there is a lovely view of **Armathwaite Castle** (private), the home of the Skelton family, one of whose forebears was Poet Laureate to Henry VIII. Close by, visitors to the **Eden Valley Woollen Mill** can see traditional looms rattling away and browse through a huge range of knitwear produced from the finest wools and mohair. The Mill offers an inexpensive making-up service and accepts commissions for pile and rag rugs. It is open daily during the season but times vary during the winter months. Also worth seeking out in **Coombs Wood** to the south is another of the Eden Benchmarks. Entitled *Vista* and created by Graeme Mitchison, this remarkable sculpture seems to make the Lazenby Sandstone flow into liquid shapes. North of Armathwaite, the River Eden approaches Carlisle and the Solway

Firth; these lower stretches of the river are surveyed in the next chapter.

MELMERBY
9 miles NE of Penrith on the A686

Melmerby nestles at the foot of **Hartside Pass**, its spacious village green dissected by three becks. Even today, every householder in Melmerby has grazing rights on the green. Horses are grazed more commonly now, but in the past it would have been more usual to see flocks of geese – indeed, there was once a cottage industry here making pillows and mattresses from goose feathers. Overlooking the 13-acre village green is **Melmerby Hall**, a defensive tower that was extended in the 17th and 18th centuries. The village church, with its tower, is a Victorian building, but the first known rector of the church on the site came here in 1332.

From Melmerby the main road climbs out of the Eden Valley to the east and the landscape changes suddenly. The road passes Fiend's Fell, close to the highest point in the Pennine Chain, the summit of Cross Fell. Early Christians erected a cross on the highest point of the fell to protect travellers from the demons who haunted the moors. Today, a cairn marks the spot where the cross once stood.

ALSTON
18 miles NE of Penrith on the A689/A686

For a few weeks in 1999 the small town of Alston, 1,000 feet up in the Pennines, became transformed

Just to the northwest of Kirkoswald are the Nunnery Walks which start at a Georgian house built in 1715 on the site of a Benedictine Nunnery founded during the reign of William Rufus. Narrow footpaths have been cut into the sandstone cliffs along the deep gorge of Croglin Beck and they pass through beautiful woodland to reveal exciting waterfalls. The Nunnery Walks are open to the public during the summer months.

90 THE JOINERS ARMS

Lazonby

Real ales and great food in refurbished 18th-century inn found 6 miles north of Penrith on the B6413.

❙❙ see page 172

91 THE FOX INN

Ousby, Penrith

Real ale, great food and a friendly welcome in this spacious traditional country inn.

❙❙ see page 172

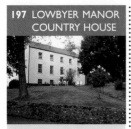

197 LOWBYER MANOR COUNTRY HOUSE

Alston

Superb country house with beautifully well-tended grounds surrounded by lovely countryside and boasting nine luxurious and welcoming bedrooms.

see page 215

92/196 THE MINERS ARMS

Nenthead, Alston

Home-made dishes, good ales, and excellent accommodation along the Coast-to-Coast cycle path and Pennine Way.

see page 173, 214

into Bruntmarsh, the fishing village in which the fictional Oliver Twist spent his early years. To re-create the squalid conditions of the poor in early 19th-century England, production designers 'dressed down' the town, so much so that anxious visitors noticing the soot-blackened buildings enquired whether there had been a major fire.

One of the many strengths of Alan Bleasdale's re-working of the Dickens classic was the authenticity of the locations. Alston proved to be ideal, since the town centre has changed little since the late 1700s and there are many buildings even older than this.

The town has a cobbled main street and, from the picturesque **Market Cross**, narrow lanes radiating out with courtyards enclosing old houses. Many of the older buildings still have the outside staircase leading to the first floor –

a relic from the days when animals were kept below while the family's living accommodation was upstairs. This ancient part of Alston is known as **The Butts**, a title acquired by the need of the townspeople to be proficient in archery during the times of the border raids.

The tall spire of **St Augustine's Church** is a well-known local landmark and its churchyard contains a number of interesting epitaphs, as well as affording wonderful views of the South Tyne Valley.

Considering its small population, Alston supports an astonishing diversity of shops and pubs. In addition, the town is home to a wide variety of craftspeople, ranging from blacksmiths to candlemakers, wood-turners to potters, and also boasts an outstanding art and crafts centre in the **Gossipgate Gallery**. Housed in

Alston

118

a converted congregational church built 200 years ago and with its original gaslights still intact, this gallery is the premier centre in the North Pennines for contemporary art and craft. A programme of exhibitions runs non-stop from February to December, and in the gallery shop a huge range of artefacts is for sale, including original watercolours and prints, jewellery, glass, ceramics, sculpture and striking turned wooden bowls made from native woods.

Another popular attraction in Alston is the **South Tynedale Railway**. This narrow-gauge (2ft) steam railway runs regular services during the summer months and at the northern terminus of the 2½-mile long track travellers can join a stretch of the Pennine Way that runs alongside the River South Tyne. In between the station and the A686, is the **HUB Exhibition** of historic vehicles, a wealth of local images and the stories that bring them alive.

Alston Moor, to the south of the town, was once the centre of an extremely important lead mining region, one of the richest in Britain. Lead and silver were probably mined on the moor by the Romans, but the industry reached its peak in the early 19th century when vast quantities of iron, silver, copper and zinc were extracted by the London Lead Company. A Quaker company, it was a pioneer of industrial welfare and also built the model village of Nenthead to house the miners. Here, not only were the workers and their families provided with a home, but education was compulsory and there were some public baths.

Nenthead Mines Heritage Centre is a 200-acre site high in the hills that tells the story of the lead and zinc mining industry. One of the main visitor attractions is 'The Power of Water', an impressive interactive area that looks at the technology used, including three working water wheels that drive model machinery. Another is the Brewery Shaft with its 328ft drop and amazing virtual stone feature.

228 NORTH PENNINES HERITAGE TRUST

Nenthead, Alston

A 200-acre site which offers an insight into the mining heritage of the Pennines, told through exhibitions and interactive displays

🏛 see page 227

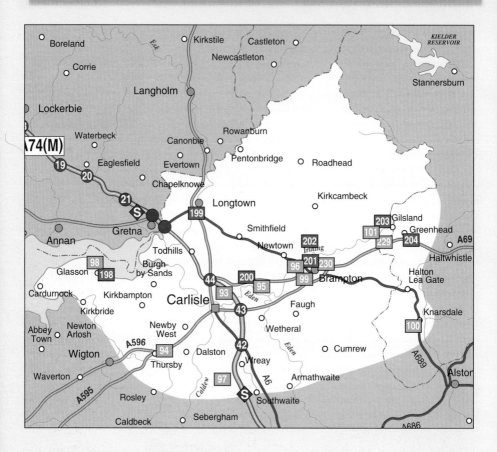

Carlisle & The Scottish Borders

For more than 350 years the area around Carlisle was known as the Debatable Lands, a lawless region where the feared Border Reivers sacked and plundered at will. Every winter, when their own food stocks were almost depleted, armed gangs from across the border would ride southwards to seize the cattle and sheep of their more prosperous neighbours. Stealing and murdering, they wreaked havoc in this area and almost every village would have had a fortified structure, usually a pele tower, where the inhabitants and their animals could hide safely. There are some 77 names on record as belonging to these disreputable Reiver families – among them the names Trotter and Maxwell – and anyone who wishes to find out if their family was involved should go to Carlisle's Tullie House Museum.

This is, too, the country of Hadrian's Wall, the most important monument built in Britain by the Romans; many stretches of the wall are still visible, and Birdoswald and other centres give an excellent insight into Roman border life. The wall was built as a great military barrier across the narrowest part of Britain, from the mouth of the River Tyne, in the east, to Bowness-on-Solway, in the west.

Guarded by forts at regular intervals, it was built between AD 122 and AD 128 following a visit by the Emperor Hadrian, who saw the then military infrastructure as insufficient to withstand the combined attacks of northern barbarians. Originally, much of the western side was built from turf, but by AD 163 this had been replaced by stone. The wall was finally abandoned in the late 4th century, and in later centuries many of the stones were used for local buildings and field walls.

There are many ways of exploring the Wall (including the bus number AD 122!), and for those with the energy to walk from end to end the newly opened Hadrian's Wall National Trail passes some of the country's greatest archaeological monuments.

The Citadel, Carlisle

CARLISLE

Carlisle's castle, cathedral, many other historic buildings, parks, thriving traditional market, shopping centres and leisure facilities all combine to endow Carlisle with the true feel of a major city. Carlisle is the largest settlement in Cumbria, with a population of around 130,000, and is also its county town. The city stands at the junction of three rivers, the Eden, the Caldew and the Petteril, and was already fortified in Celtic times when it was named Caer Lue, the 'hill fort'. It became a major Roman centre: it was the military base for the Petriana regiment, *Luguvallum*, guarding the western end of Hadrian's Wall, and also an important civilian settlement with fountains, mosaics, statues and centrally-heated homes.

According to a recent survey, if you are born in Carlisle you are more likely to stay here than the inhabitants of any other place in England.

Today, the squat outline of **Carlisle Castle** (English Heritage) dominates the skyline of this fascinating city. There has been a castle at Carlisle since 1092 when William Rufus first built a palisaded fort. The Norman Castle was originally built of wood, but, during the Scottish occupation in the 12th century, King David I laid out a new castle with stones taken from Hadrian's Wall. The 12th-century keep can still be seen enclosed by massive inner and outer walls. Entry is through a great 14th-century gatehouse, complete with portcullis, and with a maze of vaulted passages, chambers, staircases, towers and dismal dungeons. Children, especially, enjoy the legendary 'licking stones' from which parched Jacobite prisoners tried to find enough moisture to stay alive. Archaeologists working outside the castle walls unearthed the remains of three Roman forts, and many of

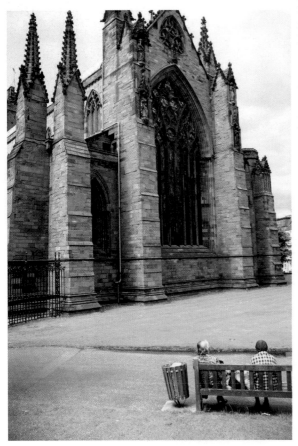

Carlisle Cathedral

the finds are on display in a special exhibition at the castle. Carlisle Castle is everything a real castle should be and is still the headquarters of the King's Own Royal Border Regiment, whose **Regimental Museum** is located within the castle walls. Two floors of displays include uniforms, weapons, medals, pictures, photographs and archives. During the Civil War the castle was besieged for eight months by the Parliamentarians under General Leslie. When the Royalists finally capitulated, Leslie began repairing the castle and the city walls. The Puritans were no respecters of Britain's ecclesiastical heritage: stones from six of the eight bays of the cathedral were used for the repairs and the building of block-houses for the Puritan troops.

Partly for this reason, **Carlisle Cathedral** is now one of the smallest cathedrals in England – yet it retains many interesting features, including an exquisite east window that is considered to be one of the finest in Europe. Below the beautifully painted wooden ceiling of the choir, with its gold star shimmering against deep blue, are the carved, canopied choir-stalls with their medieval misericords. These wonderful carved beasts and birds include two dragons joined by the ears, a fox killing a goose, pelicans feeding their young, and a mermaid with a looking glass. In St Wilfrid's Chapel is the superb 16th-century Flemish Brougham Triptych, which was originally in Cologne Cathedral. In the 19th

Fisher Street, Carlisle

century it was brought to Brougham Chapel near Penrith. The altar piece was later restored by the Victoria & Albert Museum in London and is now on permanent loan to Carlisle. It is a beautiful, intricate piece with delicately carved figures depicting scenes from the life of Christ.

It is hard to believe that it was here that Edward I solemnly used bell, book and candle to excommunicate Robert the Bruce. It was here also that the church

Town Hall Square, Carlisle

The Old Town Hall in Carlisle, now an excellent Tourist Information Centre, dates from the 17th century and once housed the Muckle Bell, an alarm bell which, it was claimed, could be heard 11 miles away. The bell is now housed in the Tullie House Museum.

---

bells were rung to welcome Bonnie Prince Charlie in 1745. It is claimed that after the suppression of the Jacobite rebellion the bells were removed for their 'treason' and only replaced in the 19th century.

Carlisle Cathedral is one of the few where visitors can enjoy refreshments actually within the precincts, in this case in the Prior's Kitchen Restaurant situated in the Fratry Undercroft. Seated beneath superb fan vaulting, customers have a good choice of home-made soups, cakes and pastries, as well as morning coffee, lunches and afternoon teas.

Although an appointment is usually necessary, a visit to the nearby **Prior's Tower** is a must. On the first floor of this 15th-century pele tower is a wonderful 45-panel ceiling incorporating the popinjay crest and arms of the Prior Senhouse. The 16th-century Prior's gatehouse leads to a narrow lane called Paternoster which is named after the prayer the monks would recite during their offices.

Like many great medieval cities, Carlisle was surrounded by walls. Guided walks and tours are available and the best view is to be found in a little street called **West Walls** at the bottom of Sally Port Steps, near the Tithe Barn. The walls date from around the 11th century and they remained virtually intact until the 1800s.

When the castle was under siege, the **Sally Port** allowed an individual to 'sally forth'. It was later used for access to the **Tithe Barn** to avoid paying city tolls. It is unusual to find a Tithe Barn within a city wall, but this exception was probably made because of the Border raids. The barn dates from the 15th century and was used to collect and store taxes, or tithes, destined for the Priory.

Close by is **St Cuthbert's Church**, the official city church of Carlisle and where the Lord Mayor's pew can be found. Although the present building dates from 1778, there has been a church on this site since the 7th century. St Cuthbert was Bishop of Carlisle in AD 680. It is a charming Georgian building with several interesting features including a moveable pulpit on rails.

The award-winning **Tullie House Museum & Art Gallery**, in the centre of the city close to the cathedral, is certainly another place not to be missed. Through skilful and interpretive techniques the fascinating, and often dark, history of the Debatable Lands, as this border region was called, is told. The museum's centrepiece is its story of the Border Reivers who occupied the lands from the 14th to the 17th century. These lawless, unruly people raged interfamily warfare with each other, destroying or threatening the lives of the local people with their bloodthirsty raids. Their treacherous deeds have also added such words as 'bereave' and 'blackmail' to the English language. The horrific stories of the Reivers have been passed down through the generations in the Border Ballads, and many of the Reivers family names are still known – the museum even offers a genealogy service, so that visitors can find out if their ancestry includes any infamous forebears. What is perhaps the definitive Reiving story has been told in *The Steel Bonnets* by George MacDonald Fraser, author of the Flashman books.

The city of Carlisle dates back far beyond those desperate days, however, and Tullie House also has an extensive collection of Roman remains from both the city and the Cumbrian section of Hadrian's Wall. The Art Gallery features contemporary arts and crafts, and the spectacular underground Millennium Gallery has a stunning collection of local minerals, archaeological finds of wood and leather, artist-made glass and interactive exhibits. Old Tullie House showcases paintings and drawings by renowned Pre-Raphaelite artists, as well as other artworks and a selection of fine English porcelain.

A short walk from the Museum leads to the **Linton Visitor Centre** in Shaddongate which provides an insight into the city's industrial heritage. Standing next to a 280ft high chimney built in 1836 as part of what was once one of the largest cotton mills in Britain, the Centre has displays of hand-weaving on original looms, informative displays and a selection of world-famous fabrics and designer knitwear for sale.

The **Guildhall Museum** is housed in an unspoilt medieval building constructed by Richard of Redeness in 1407. Originally a town house, it provides an ideal setting for illustrating the history of both the Guilds and the City. Several rooms are devoted to creating the atmosphere of trade Guilds such as the shoemakers, the butchers, the weavers and the glovers. There is a splendid early 19th-century banner of the Weavers Guild and an impressive collection of 17thm and 18th-century Guild silver. One of the silver bells on show is thought to be the earliest horse-racing trophy in the country. Displays also feature other items relating to the history of Carlisle and include medieval stocks and a magnificent ironbound Muniment Chest dating from the 14th century. Conducted tours of this remarkable Guildhall are available.

Across the road from the Citadel is the railway station. The first railway to Carlisle opened in July 1836 and Citadel Station, which opened in 1850, was built to serve seven different railway companies whose coats of arms are still displayed on the façade. So

Not far from the Guildhall Museum is the Citadel, which is often mistaken for the castle. In fact, this intimidating fortress with its well-preserved circular tower was built in 1543 on the orders of Henry VIII to strengthen the city's defences. Much of it was demolished in the early 1800s to improve access to the city centre, but what remains is mightily impressive.

elegant was its interior – and much of it remains – that Carlisle was known as the 'top hat' station. Today it is still an important centre of communications; InterCity trains from Glasgow and London now link with lines to Dumfries, Tyneside, West Cumbria and Yorkshire, and it is, of course, the northern terminus of the famous **Settle-Carlisle Railway** line.

One of the last great mainline railways to be built in Britain – it was completed in 1876 – the Settle-Carlisle line takes in some of the most dramatic scenery that the north of England has to offer. Scenic it may be, but the terrain caused the Victorian engineers many problems. It is only thanks to their ingenuity and skill that the line was ever finished. During the course of its 72 miles, the line crosses 20 viaducts and passes through 12 tunnels, each of which was constructed by an army of navvies who had little in the way of resources besides their strength and some dynamite to remove the rock.

Located on the northwestern edge of the city, **Kingmoor Nature Reserve** occupies an area of moorland given to the city in 1352 by Edward III. Citizens enjoyed the right to graze sheep on the moors and to cut peat for fuel. Later, Carlisle's first racecourse was established here with annual Guild races being held up until 1850. A half-mile circular path wanders through the woodland with gentle gradients of 1 in 20 making it fully accessible to wheelchairs and pushchairs, and with seats every 100 yards or so providing plenty of resting places. Another path links the reserve to **Kingmoor Sidings**, which since the old railway sheds closed has been colonised by a wide variety of wildlife. In 1913 Kingmoor became one of the first bird sanctuaries in England, and today provides a peaceful retreat away from the bustle of the city centre.

AROUND CARLISLE

WREAY

5 miles S of Carlisle off the A6

This little village is known for its extraordinary **Church of St Mary**, designed by a local woman, Sarah Losh, in memory of her sister and her parents. It was built in 1835 and incorporates many Italian Romanesque features. The church is full of beautiful touches, including the carvings, mostly by Sarah herself, on the font.

DALSTON

4 miles SW of Carlisle on the B5299

Lying on the banks of the **River Caldew**, Dalston became a thriving centre of the cotton industry in the late 18th century, thanks to George Hodgson of Manchester, who used the river as a source of power for the flax mill and four cotton mills that were established here. The local economy was sustained still further by the creation of a forge and two corn mills.

At the eastern end of the village square stands **St Michael's Church**, believed to date back to Norman times, which can be approached via a memorial lychgate. One of the few red-brick buildings to be found in the village is the **Victorian Chapel**, which stands somewhat hidden between several Georgian houses along the village green.

There's a pleasant 2-mile circular walk along the banks of the River Caldew at Dalston.

BURGH BY SANDS

5 miles W of Carlisle off the B5307

On 7th July 1307, the body of King Edward I was laid out in the village church: he was already a dying man when he left Carlisle to march against his old enemy, Robert the Bruce. A monument to Edward was erected on the marshes and a later monument still marks the spot. At the time of the king's death, the **Church of St Michael** was already well over a century old and is possibly the earliest surviving example of a fortified church. Dating from 1181 and constructed entirely of stones from a fort on the Roman wall, the church was designed for protection against Border raids, which is why its tower has walls seven feet thick. The tower can only be entered through a strong iron grille.

PORT CARLISLE

12 miles W of Carlisle off the B5307

At one time sailing boats could make their way by canal from Port Carlisle to the heart of the city of Carlisle. Boats were towed there, a journey that took about 1 hour 40 minutes, enabling Carlisle to be reached within a day by sea from

Liverpool. The canal was later replaced by a railway which brought many Scandinavian emigrants through the village on their way to the United States and Canada. But the building of the Bowness railway viaduct altered the deep-water channels, causing Port Carlisle to silt up. The railway was eventually dismantled but its old course can still be traced and stretches of it form part of the Cumbrian Cycle Way.

BOWNESS-ON-SOLWAY

14 miles W of Carlisle off the B5307

Hadrian's Wall continues along the Solway coast to Bowness, and many of the sandstone cottages around here contain stones from the Wall. Some of these stones can easily be identified, such as the small inscribed altar let into a barn near the King's Arms. The Roman fort of **Maia** once covered a 7-acre site, but today there is only a plaque explaining where it used to be. Bowness is sometimes said to be the end of the Wall, but in fact the Wall just turned a corner here and continued south along the coast for another 40 miles.

One local story tells that, in 1626, some Scotsmen crossed the Solway and stole the Bowness church bells. The thieves were spotted, chased and forced to lighten their boats by throwing the bells overboard. Later, the men of Bowness crossed the Firth and, in retaliation, seized the bells of Middlebie, Dumfries. Two miles south of the village lies **Glasson Moss National Nature Reserve**,

---

98/198   THE HOPE AND ANCHOR INN

Port Carlisle

Early 19th-century inn with great food, drink and accommodation in scenic location overlooking the Solway Firth.

see *pages 175, 215*

•

The stretch of the Solway coastline from Point Carlisle provided the setting for Sir Walter Scott's novel Redgauntlet, and the fortified farmhouse by the roadside at nearby Drumburgh is said to be the 'White Ladies' of the novel.

•

199 HOME FROM
HOME

Longtown

Handsome Victorian
premises offering
comfortable and superbly-
appointed accommodation.

see page 215

*An impressive survival
dominates the village
churchyard in Bewcastle.
Here stands the
Bewcastle Cross, erected
around AD 670 and one
of the oldest and finest
stone crosses in Europe.
Standing over 13 feet in
height, its intricate Celtic
carvings have survived
the centuries of
weathering and much of
the runic inscription can
still be made out in the
yellow sandstone. One of
the carvings, a semicircle
with 13 radiating lines,
three of which have
crossbars, is believed to
be a sophisticated sundial
which not only indicated
the 12 hours of the
Roman clock but also the
three 'tides' of the Saxon
day – morning, noon and
eventide.*

a lowland raised mire extending to
93 hectares. Many species of
sphagnum moss are to be found
here, and the birdlife includes red
grouse, curlew, sparrowhawk and
snipe.

LONGTOWN

9 miles N of Carlisle on the A7

Situated on the north side of
Hadrian's Wall, only a couple of
miles from the Scottish border, this
is the last town in England. The
Romans occupied this land, and
they were followed by other
conquerors. The legendary King
Arthur attempted to organise the
Northern Britons against the pagan
hordes who tried to settle and
control this territory. In AD 573
the mighty battle of Ardderyd was
fought here and, according to
legend, 80,000 men were slain.

Longtown's position on the
River Esk, so close to the Scottish
border, has influenced its history
from earliest times.

Until 1750 Longtown was a
small hamlet of mud dwellings. Dr
Robert Graham, an 18th-century
clergyman, proposed the building of
the Esk bridge which was completed
in 1756, and it was this venture that
led to Longtown's establishment as a
bustling border town. These days it
has some fine individual buildings
and broad, tree-lined terraces of
colour-washed houses.

On the outskirts of Longtown
is **Arthuret Church**. The earliest
records of the church date from
1150 and it was originally served by
the monks of Jedburgh. But it is
thought that the earliest church

here may have been founded by St
Kentigern in the 6th century;
recent research has led some to
believe that King Arthur was
actually interred here after his last
battle, Camboglanna, was fought a
few miles east of Longtown at
Gilsland. The present church,
dedicated to **St Michael and All
Angels**, was built in 1609, financed
by a general collection throughout
the realm which James I ordered
after a report that the people of
Arthuret Church were without faith
or religion. The people that he
referred to, of course, were the
infamous Reivers, ungoverned by
either English or Scottish laws.

Archie Armstrong, favourite
Court Jester to James I and later to
Charles I, is buried in the
churchyard, which also contains an
unusual stone cross. It consists of
two parts of an early medieval
wheel-head cross clamped together
onto a tapering shaft with 19th-
century decorations.

BEWCASTLE

14 miles NE of Carlisle off the B6318

Roman legionaries assigned to the
fort at what is now Bewcastle must
certainly have felt that they had
drawn the short straw. The fort
stood all on its own, about 9 miles
north of Hadrian's Wall, guarding a
crossing over the Kirk Beck. The
site covered around 6 acres and
most of it is now occupied by the
ruins of a **Norman Castle**. Most
of the south wall is still standing
but little else remains and the castle
is best admired for its setting rather
than its architecture.

WETHERAL

4 miles E of Carlisle off the A69

Wetheral stands above the **River Eden**, over which runs an impressive railway viaduct, carrying the **Tyne Valley Line**, which was built by Francis Giles in 1830. Wetheral **Parish Church** lies below the village beside the river and contains a poignant sculpture by Joseph Nollekens of the dying Lady Mary Howard clasping her dead baby. Nearby, occupying a lovely riverside setting, is another of the **Eden Benchmarks**, a sculptured bench in St Bee's sandstone by Tim Shutter, entitled *Flight of Fancy*.

St Constantine was the local patron and the church is dedicated to the Holy Trinity, St Constantine and St Mary. Constantine is said to have lived in caves in what are now National Trust woodlands alongside the river, a location known as **Constantine's Caves**. (The caves were also used later by the nearby Priory to conceal their valuables during the Reiver raids.) Constantine died as a martyr in AD 657 and a life-sized statue of him can be seen in the grounds of **Corby Castle** to the south of the village. The castle also boasts an impressive 13th-century keep and terraced gardens overlooking the Eden. Corby Castle is usually open during the summer months.

During the reign of William Rufus, one of his barons, Ranulph de Meschines, founded a priory for Benedictine monks at Wetheral above a red-rock gorge of the River Eden. It was a dependency of the Abbey of St Mary at York, and the prior and the monastery served the church and domestic chapel of Corby Castle. All that remains now is the imposing three-storey gatehouse.

WARWICK

4 miles E of Carlisle on the A69

It is well worth visiting the village's remarkable Norman **Church of St Leonard**, which consists of a restored nave and chancel with a curiously buttressed apse and a splendid arch leading into a modern vestibule. Warwick's other church, St Paul's, is reputed to have been commissioned by a wealthy Carlisle man who took umbrage at a sermon preached at St Leonard's.

CROSBY-ON-EDEN

4 miles NE of Carlisle off the A689

The tiny hamlet of **High Crosby** stands on the hillside overlooking the River Eden; the small village of **Low Crosby** sits beside the river, clustered around a Victorian sandstone church. Inside the church there's a modern square pulpit, intricately carved with pomegranates, wheat and vines. Apparently, it was carved from one half of a tree felled nearby; the other half was used to create a second pulpit which was installed in the newly-built Liverpool Cathedral.

A couple of miles east of Crosby, The **Solway Aviation Museum** is one of only a few museums located on a 'live' airfield, in this case Carlisle Airport.

95/200 CROSBY LODGE COUNTRY HOUSE HOTEL & RESTAURANT

Crosby-on-Eden, Carlisle

A gracious, elegant and romantic country mansion with modern comforts and traditional service.

see pages 174, 216

96/201 FARLAM HALL HOTEL

Brampton

Truly elegant accommodation and dining at one of the region's finest country house hotels.

⚟ ∥ see pages 174, 216

99 THE CAPON TREE

Brampton

Justly popular café serving fresh and tasty dishes from breakfast to high tea.

∥ see page 175

230 BORDER HERITAGE TRAIL

Brampton

A trail which encompasses historic sites and spectacular scenery.

🏛 see page 228

Opened in 1997, the museum is home to several British jet aircraft of the 1950s and 1960s, among them the mighty Vulcan and the Canberra. Other exhibits include a wartime air-raid shelter where a video presentation explains the story behind the museum, displays of the Blue Streak rocket programme, testing for which took place only a few miles from here, and a very impressive engine room which houses one of Frank Whittle's first development jet engines. Testing for the Blue Streak rocket programme took place just a few miles from Crosby-on-Eden.

BRAMPTON

Nestling in the heart of the lovely Irthing Valley, Brampton is a delightful little town where the Wednesday market has been held since 1252, authorised by a charter granted by Henry III. Overlooking the Market Place is the town's most striking building, the octagonal **Moot Hall** topped by a handsome clock tower. There has been a Moot Hall here since 1648, though the present Hall was built in 1817 by Lord Carlisle. The iron stocks at the foot of a double flight of external stairs were last used in 1836.

Just around the corner, in **High Cross Street**, is the house (now a shop) which once witnessed one of the high-points in Bonnie Prince Charles' rebellion of 1745. It was here that the Prince stayed during the siege of Carlisle and it

was here, on November 17, 1745 that the Mayor and Aldermen presented him with the keys to the city. A few months later, following the Prince's defeat, six of his supporters were hanged on the Capon Tree on the south side of the town and in sight of the Scottish hills. The tree survived until the last century; in its place there now stands a monument commemorating the event.

Just off the Market Place is **St Martin's Church**, which was built anew in 1874 and contains one of the undiscovered secrets of the area – some magnificent stained glass windows designed by one of the founder members of the pre-Raphaelite brotherhood, Edward Burne-Jones. It was his fellow-member of the brotherhood, Philip Webb, William Morris's associate, who designed the church and insisted that contemporary stained glass should be installed.

AROUND BRAMPTON

LOW ROW

3 miles E of Brampton off the A69

Within easy reach of the town is **Hadrian's Wall**, just 3 miles to the north. If you've ever wondered where the Wall's missing masonry went to, look no further than the fabric of **Lanercost Priory** (English Heritage). An impressive red sandstone ruin set in secluded woodland, the priory was founded in 1166 by Robert de Vaux. In 1306, Edward I spent six months at the Priory recuperating after his skirmishes with the Scots. Lanercost is well preserved, and its scale is a reminder that it was a grand complex in its heyday. However, the Priory suffered greatly in the border raids of the 13th and 14th centuries. One such raid is known to have been led by William Wallace, an early campaigner for Scottish independence. When the Priory was closed in 1536, the sandstone blocks were recycled once again for houses in the town. But much of the Priory's great north aisle remains intact, set in a romantic and hauntingly beautiful position in the valley of the River Irthing. The Priory is well signposted and lies only 3 miles off the A69 (leave at Brampton).

Also most impressive is **Naworth Castle**, built around 1335 in its present form by Lord Dacre as an important border stronghold. The castle passed through the female line to the Howard family after the last Lord Dacre was killed as a child – improbably as it might seem, by falling off his rocking horse. Now owned by the Howard family, Earls of Carlisle, the Castle is private but there are good views from the minor road off the A69 that passes in front of it – the scene is particularly attractive in spring when the lawns are ablaze with daffodils. Pre-booked parties are welcome all year round and the Castle has become a popular venue for weddings and corporate events.

The Castle's supreme glory is the Great Hall, hung with French tapestries and guarded by four unique heraldic beasts holding aloft their family pennants. The Long Gallery extends for 116 feet and was used as a guardroom. It now houses an interesting collection of paintings, many brought together by the 9th Earl, George Howard. He entertained many pre-Raphaelite painters here, but the only surviving example of their work is Burne-Jones's *Battle of Flodden* – the rest were destroyed by a fire in 1844. In the courtyard there are some intriguing medieval latrines!

The area around Brampton had good reason to be grateful to the Dacres of Naworth, who as Wardens of the Northern Marches protected it against marauding Scots. However, the townspeople of Brampton in Victorian times must have had mixed feelings about a later descendant, Rosalind, wife of the 9th Earl of Carlisle. An enthusiastic supporter of total abstinence, she contrived to get most of the small town's 40 public houses and drinking rooms closed.

South of Brampton are **Gelt Woods**, lying in a deep sandstone ravine carved by the fast-flowing River Gelt. By the River Gelt is an inscribed rock called **Written Rock** which is thought to have been carved by a Roman standard-bearer in AD 207. Access is discouraged however, as the path can be dangerous.

TALKIN

2 miles S of Brampton off the B6413

Talkin Tarn, now the focus of a 120-acre country park, has been a

202 WALTON HIGH RIGG FARM

Walton, Brampton
Farmhouse B&B accommodation on 144-acre mixed farm. 18th-century listed farmhouse with panoramic views. 3 Diamonds ETC.

see page 217

100 KIRKSTYLE INN

Knarsdale, Brampton
Hidden away off the A689 between Brampton and Alston, a beautiful and welcoming inn with real ales and excellent food.

see page 175

101/203 SAMSON INN

Gilsland

Superb inn adjacent to the Trans-Pennine railway. Real ales, home-cooked food and two guest bedrooms.

🍴 🛏 *see pages 175, 217*

204 HOLMHEAD GUESTHOUSE

Greenhead, Brampton

Licensed premises with excellent accommodation within a stone's throw of Hadrian's Wall.

🛏 *see page 217*

229 BIRDOSWALD ROMAN FORT

Gilsland

One of the best preserved Roman remains along the length of Hadrian's Wall

🏛 *see page 228*

popular place for watersports for over 100 years. Glacial in origin, the Tarn was formed some 10,000 years ago and is continually replenished by underground springs. Modern-day visitors can sail, windsurf, canoe or hire a rowing boat. Talkin Tarn Rowing Club has been rowing on the tarn for 130 years, and holds its annual regatta in July. Fishing licences are available, there's a nature trail and an orienteering course, a play area for children under 8, a tea room and a gift shop; guided walks with a warden are also available for organised groups. The park is a peaceful place but, according to legend, beneath the surface of the lake there is a submerged village destroyed by a wrathful god, the ruins of which can still be seen below the water's surface in a certain light.

GILSLAND

7 miles E of Brampton on the B6318

Located in one of the most picturesque settings along the whole length of Hadrian's Wall and overlooking the River Irthing, **Birdoswald Roman Fort** (English

Heritage) is one of the best-preserved mile-castles along the Wall and unique in that all the components of the Roman frontier system can be found here. Set high on a plateau with magnificent views over the surrounding countryside, the early turf wall, built in AD 122, can be seen along with the fort. Originally, Birdoswald Roman Fort would have covered 5 acres and may have been the base for up to 500 cavalry and 1,000 foot soldiers.

Gilsland village is also known for its sulphur spring; there was once a convalescent home for miners and shipyard workers here. Now a hotel, it is owned by the Co-operative Society and people still drink the waters as a cure for arthritis and rheumatism. Near the spring is the **Popping Stone**, traditionally the place where a man 'popped the question' to his lover. It was here that Sir Walter Scott successfully 'popped' to Charlotte Carpenter, daughter of a French refugee, after just three weeks' courtship. In spite of his family's early disquiet, the two were happily married for 30 years and had four children.

Advertisements

Food and Drink in Cumbria

The selection of establishments serving food and drink featured in this section includes restaurants, cafés, hotels, pubs, inns and tea & coffee shops. Each establishment has an entry number which is used to identify its location on the map below and its name and short address in the list below the map. The entry number can also be used to find more information and contact details for the establishment in the ensuing pages. In addition full details of establishments serving food and drink featured in this section may be found on the Travel Publishing website – www.travelpublishing.co.uk This website has a large database of establishments serving food and drink covering the whole of Britain and Ireland.

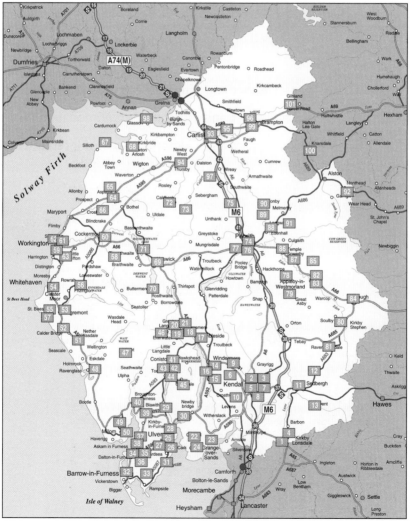

1	The Kings Arms, Kirkby Lonsdale
2	The Master's House Tea Room, Kendal
3	The Black Swan, Kendal
4	The Pheasant Inn, Casterton
5	The New Inn, Kendal
6	The Sun Inn, Crook
7	Prelude of Kendal, Kendal
8	The Garden House Hotel & Restaurant, Kendal
9	Wilf's Café, Staveley
10	The Wheatsheaf at Brigsteer, Brigsteer
11	The Bull Hotel, Sedburgh
12	The Cross Keys Temperance Inn, Cautley
13	Stone Close Tea Room & Guest House, Dent
14	The Two Eggcups Restaurant, Bowness-on-Windermere
15	The Nissi Restaurant, Bowness-on-Windermere
16	The Mariners Inn, Bowness-on-Windermere
17	Bizzy Lizzy's, Ambleside
18	Glen Rothay Hotel & Badger Bar, Rydal
19	The Wild Daffodil, Grasmere
20	Dale Lodge Hotel, Grasmere
21	Sara's Bistro, Grasmere
22	The Kings Arms, Cartmel
23	At Home, Grange-over-Sands
24	The Hope and Anchor, Flookburgh
25	Laurel's Bistro, Ulverston
26	Kings Café Wine Bar, Ulverston
27	Olde Ulverston Tea Rooms, Ulverston
28	The Armadale Country Restaurant & Hotel, Ulverston
29	The Red Lion Inn, Lowick Bridge
30	The Anglers Arms, Haverthwaite
31	The Farmers Arms, Baycliff
32	The Rams Head Hotel, Barrow-in-Furness
33	The Copper Dog, Leece
34	Chequers Hotel & Restaurant, Dalton-in-Furness
35	Clarence House Country Hotel and Restaurant, Skelgate
36	The Red Lion Inn, Dalton-in-Furness
37	The Askam Hotel, Askam-in-Furness
38	Furness Tavern, Askam-in-Furness
39	The Greyhound Inn, Grizebeck
40	The Bakehouse, Broughton-in-Furness
41	The Sun Hotel, Coniston
42	The Crown Hotel, Coniston
43	Spindles of Coniston, Coniston
44	Jumping Jenny Coffee House & Restaurant, Coniston
45	The Eagles Head, Satterthwaite
46	The Old Dungeon Ghyll Hotel, Great Langdale
47	Brook House Inn & Restaurant, Boot
48	Brown Cow Inn, Waberthwaite
49	Underwood Country Guest House, Millom
50	Cambridge House Hotel, Millom

51	Westlakes Hotel, Gosforth
52	White Mare, Beckermet
53	The Red Lion Hotel, Egremont
54	Cap'n Sennys, Whitehaven
55	Manor House Hotel & Coast-to-Coast Bar, St Bees
56	The Stork Hotel, Rowrah
57	Hartley's Beach Shop, St Bees
58	New House Farm, Lorton
59	Green Dragon Hotel, Workington
60	Hunters, Cockermouth
61	The Westlands Hotel, Workington
62	The Travellers Rest, Workington
63	The Galloping Horse, Workington
64	The Grapes Hotel, Aspatria
65	The Swan Inn and Restaurant, Westnewton
66	The Masons Arms, Gilcrux
67	The Skinburness Leisure Hotel, Skinburness
68	Joiners Arms Country Inn, Newton Arlosh
69	Ginger & Pickles Coffee Shop, Keswick
70	Grange Bridge Cottage, Grange-in-Borrowdale
71	The Old Sawmill Tearoom, Mirehouse
72	The Old Smithy Crafts, Gifts and Tearoom, Caldbeck
73	The Old Crown, Hesket Newmarket
74	Three Crowns Tea Shop, Penrith
75	The Globe Inn, Calthwaite
76	The Purple Sage Restaurant, Penrith
77	Kings Arms, Stainton
78	White Horse Inn, Kings Meaburn
79	Meaburn B&B and Restaurant, Maulds Meaburn
80	The Pennine Hotel, Kirkby Stephen
81	The Kings Head Hotel, Ravenstonedale
82	The Golden Ball, Appleby-in-Westmorland
83	The Bay Tree, Appleby-in-Westmorland
84	The Castle Hotel, Brough
85	The Stag Inn, Dufton
86	The Kings Arms Hotel, Temple Sowerby
87	Bridge End Inn, Kirkby Thore
88	Brief Encounter, Langwathby Station
89	The Highland Drove Inn, Great Salkeld
90	The Joiners Arms, Lazonby
91	The Fox Inn, Ousby
92	The Miners Arms, Nenthead
93	The Near Boot Inn, Tarraby
94	The Ship Inn, Thursby
95	Crosby Lodge Country House Hotel & Restaurant, Crosby-on-Eden
96	Farlam Hall Hotel, Brampton
97	The Crown Inn Restaurant, Southwaite
98	The Hope and Anchor Inn, Port Carlisle
99	The Capon Tree, Brampton
100	Kirkstyle Inn, Knarsdale
101	Samson Inn, Gilsland

1 THE KINGS ARMS

7 Market St, Kirkby Lonsdale,
Cumbria LA6 2AU
☎ 01524 271220
e-mail: bougourdj36@aol.com

The Kings Arms is a venerable inn whose history is linked with that of Kirkby Lonsdale itself. In 1558 the manor was sold to Thomas Carus, who built the manor hall that is today this fine inn. It has been tastefully refurbished over the years, but some original features – such as the fine fireplace – remain. Tenants David and Judith have well over 20 years' experience in the trade, and offer real ales and great food every day. Adjacent there are three cottages available for B&B or room-only accommodation.

2 THE MASTER'S HOUSE TEA ROOM

80b Highgate, Kendal, Cumbria LA9 4HE
☎ 01539 720723

Home-made scones and cakes, excellent range of sandwiches, hot and cold snacks and 15 teas together with coffees and cold drinks. Open Mon-Sat 10-5.

3 THE BLACK SWAN

8 Allhollows Lane, Kendal,
Cumbria LA9 4JH
☎ 01539 724278

The Black Swan dates back to the early 1700s. Three real ales from the Jennings Brewery are available, together with excellent home-made meals. Four good-sized guest rooms are available all year round.

4 THE PHEASANT INN

Casterton, Kirkby Lonsdale,
Cumbria LA6 2RX
☎ 01524 271230 Fax: 01524 274267
e-mail: pheasantinn@fsbdial.co.uk
⊕ www.pheasantinn.co.uk

Just a short drive or walk from Kirkby Lonsdale on the A683, **The Pheasant Inn** at Casterton dates to the 18th century, and is owned and run by the Dixon family, a local farming family. The Inn boasts a superb bar area, with three real ales – Theakstons Best, Cod Cask and a rotating guest ale. Quality

food is available daily at lunch (12-2) and dinner (6-9). The no-smoking restaurant seats 50. Booking is essential on Saturday evening and Sunday lunchtime. Guests choose from the menu or specials board from a varied menu of fine English dishes.

The Inn offers 10 quality en suite rooms, available all year round. Two of the rooms are on the ground floor; one of these is suitable for people with disabilities. An ideal place to stay and use as a base while visiting this lovely area, it is also a short drive to North Yorkshire and close to the Settle-Carlisle Railway. Children welcome.

5 THE NEW INN

**98 High Gate, Kendal,
Cumbria LA9 4HE
☎ 01539 722484 Fax: 01539 738088
e-mail: farrelldrwer@ktdinternet.com**

A former coaching inn dating back to the early 18th century, **The New Inn** stands on Kendal's main thoroughfare. Popular with locals and visitors alike, this convivial and attractive inn offers great food, drink and accommodation. Open all day, every day for ale, with one real ale and a good selection of keg bitters, lagers, wines, and spirits, food is served at

lunch and dinner. Guests choose from a wide range of tempting dishes such as filled Yorkshire puddings, home-made steak and ale pie and home-made chilli. Thursday night is Steak Night – booking advised. The four comfortable guest rooms are available all year round.

6 THE SUN INN

**Crook, Kendal, Cumbria LA8 8LA
☎ 01539 821351 Fax: 01539 821351**

Situated at Crook, on the B5284 between Kendal and Bowness-on-Windermere, **The Sun Inn** boasts two cosy rooms serving a wide range of traditional hand-drawn ales and home-cooked food. Run by Peter and Gill Sykes, this proper village inn has four real ales on tap –

Coniston Bluebird (brewed locally), Theakstons and two rotating guest ales, and an excellent bar menu, specials board and restaurant menu at lunch and dinner Monday to Friday, and all day at weekends. The inn enjoys a quiet setting away from the Lake District bustle while still being handy for all the sights and attractions of the region.

7 PRELUDE OF KENDAL

**Library Road, Kendal, Cumbria LA9 4QB
☎ 01539 732929**

A top-of-the-range licensed coffee house and restaurant, **Prelude of Kendal** is located just yards off the main street of the town. Experienced restaurateurs Janet and Melvyn Pares own and run this fine establishment as well as two other eateries in nearby Windermere. Beautifully furnished and decorated throughout, the restaurant is adorned with handsome photographs of the Lake District, blown up from old postcards. People come from miles around to

admire these images and to enjoy the excellent food and drink served. Open Monday to Saturday 8.30 a.m. to 5 p.m., guests choose from the menu and specials board from a range of tempting dishes including full breakfasts, morning and afternoon light bites such as toasted tea cakes, scones and home-made cakes, hot main courses such as home-made quiche, spinach and ricotta pancakes and home-made steak pie, a range of hot and cold sandwiches, baguettes and more. There's also a mouth-watering range of desserts. Children welcome. All major credit cards. Adjacent car park.

8 THE GARDEN HOUSE HOTEL & RESTAURANT

Fowl Ing Lane, Kendal, Cumbria LA9 6PH
☎ 01539 731131 Fax: 01539 740064
e-mail: gardenhousehotel@btinternet.com
🌐 www.gardenhousehotel.co.uk

The Garden House Hotel and Restaurant in Kendal is a charming and tasteful establishment run by Warwick and Shelley McKiever, who have many years' experience in the trade. Before this they ran luxury safari lodges in South Africa. They have undertaken a complete refurbishment. So far, the handsome bar and restaurant downstairs have been tastefully transformed to offer the perfect place to enjoy a relaxing drink or meal.

The bar area is very cosy and welcoming. The restaurant is open by prior arrangement at lunch, and Monday to Saturday evenings (from 6.30 to last orders at 8.30) for residents and non-residents. Booking essential for non-residents. Each of the 11 en suite bedrooms is also due to undergo individual renovation. Open all year round and set in its own grounds, the hotel boasts a good choice of bedrooms of different sizes – one on the ground floor. Even before their refurbishment they offer a high standard of comfort and quality. Guests can stay on a bed-and-breakfast or bed, breakfast and dinner basis. Children welcome.

9 WILF'S CAFÉ

Mill Yard, Back Lane, Staveley, Kendal, Cumbria LA8 9LR
☎ 01539 822329 Fax: 01539 822969
🌐 www.wilfs-cafe.co.uk

Situated a mile off the A591 between Kendal and Windermere, the village of Staveley is home to the marvellous **Wilf's Café**. Chef Martin Lovett and his dedicated team create an excellent range of everything from breakfasts ('meaty' and 'veggie') to delicious sandwiches, hot snacks like rarebit, jacket spuds and chilli, salads and a good selection of mouthwatering home-made cakes, shortbreads, tiffin, flapjacks and hot and cold puddings.

Guests are drawn from near and far to enjoy the many home-cooked and expertly prepared delights on offer. To drink, there's a good range of Fairtrade coffees, teas, hot chocolate and also cold drinks such as fresh juices and milk shakes. Spacious and welcoming, the café is attractive and comfortable, with modern furnishings and tasteful paintings on the walls, and summer seating overlooking the River Kent. Opened in 1997, this popular and convivial café also hosts a series of 'speciality evenings' and in the winter months slide and supper evenings with guest speakers. The café is also available for hire for private parties, functions and classes.

Brigsteer, Kendal, Cumbria LA8 8AN
☎ 01539 568254
e-mail: email@brigsteer.gb.com
⊕ www.brigsteer.gb.com

Great food expertly prepared is the *raison d'etre* of **The Wheatsheaf at Brigsteer**, a superb restaurant and inn hidden away in the tranquil and picturesque village of Brigsteer, just three miles from Kendal found either west off the A591 or north of the A590 via the village of Levens. It's also just a short drive from Junction 36 of the M6. Parts of

the premises date back to 1762, and began life as three cottages plus a 'shoe-ing' room for horses. It then became an alehouse and was licensed back in the early 1800s.

Tasteful and handsome throughout, this welcoming inn has attractive and comfortable furnishings and décor. Ale is served at lunchtime and evening, and includes regular Cumbrian Ales along with two rotating guest ales. The bar menu offers an excellent choice of soups, salads, sandwiches and tasty hot dishes and is served Monday to Saturday lunchtime.

The restaurant, which seats 50, serves lunch (12-2pm) and dinner (6pm-9pm) daily. The mouthwatering choices included on the truly impressive menu use locally-sourced produce whenever possible and there is an excellent selection of wines to accompany your meal. Booking is required at all times to avoid disappointment.

This fine inn also boasts four excellent double en suite guest bedrooms. All have superb facilities and the tariff includes a

hearty breakfast. The Wheatsheaf provides private off road parking and has outside seating for sunny days.

Being centrally located yet peaceful and relaxed, the village makes the perfect base from which to explore the many sights and attractions of the region. Children welcome. No smoking throughout.

139

11 THE BULL HOTEL

Main Street, Sedbergh, Cumbria LA10 5BL
☎ 01539 620264 Fax: 01539 620212
e-mail: info@bull-hotel.com
🌐 www.bull-hotel.com

The excellent **Bull Hotel** boasts real ales, hearty food and superb accommodation. Open all day, every day for ale, there are four in summer and two in winter, the regular being Black Sheep. Most of the dishes on the menu and specials board are home-made, and served every evening 6-9 and Weds-Sun lunchtime (12-2.30). Booking is advised for Friday and Saturday evening. Specialities include lamb and Lakeland steaks. Accommodation is available all year round with 15 comfortable and welcoming en suite guest bedrooms, rated 4 Diamonds by the ETC. Guests can stay on a bed-and-breakfast or bed, breakfast and dinner basis.

12 THE CROSS KEYS TEMPERANCE INN

Cautley, nr Sedbergh, Cumbria LA10 5NE
☎ 01539 620284
e-mail: clowes@freeuk.com
🌐 www.cautleyspout.co.uk

An alcohol-free zone – though guests are welcome to bring their own. Charming tea rooms, restaurant and two guest rooms.

Explore Britain and Ireland with *Hidden Places* guides - a fascinating series of national and local travel guides.

www.travelpublishing.co.uk

0118-981-7777

info@travelpublishing.co.uk

13 STONE CLOSE TEA ROOM & GUEST HOUSE

Main Street, Dent, Sedbergh, Cumbria LA10 5QL
☎ 01539 625231
e-mail: stoneclose@btinternet.com
🌐 www.dentdale.com

A lovely traditional tea room, serving light lunches, cakes, teas and coffees. Three excellent bed-and-breakfast rooms available.

14 THE TWO EGGCUPS RESTAURANT

60 Ash Street, Bowness-on-Windermere, Cumbria LA23 3EB
☎ 01539 445979
e-mail: jimsuegee@aol.com

A varied menu of home-made dishes made with local produce in a charming setting just two minutes' walk from the Lake. Open: Fri-Weds until 5 p.m.

15 THE NISSI RESTAURANT

Westmoreland House, Lake Road, Bowness-on-Windermere, Cumbria LA23 3DJ
☎ 01539 445055
e-mail: p.harris@btinternet.com

Paul Harris is an accomplished chef who offers all guests to **The Nissi Restaurant** the authentic flavours of Greece and the Mediterranean. The attractive and stylish interior is comfortable and welcoming, while the menu offers a varied selection of starters and main courses such as hummus, roasted field mushrooms, dolmades, taramasalata, pan-fried crevettes, smoked chicken breast Caesar salad, moussaka, kleftico, roasted aubergine, char-grilled fillet steak, fried salt cod and a range of souvlakia (kebabs), all expertly prepared and presented. Booking is recommended. Open: Tues-Sun 6-10.30.

16 THE MARINERS INN

Lake Road, Bowness-on-Windermere,
Cumbria LA23 3AP
☎ 01539 445678 Fax: 01539 444078
e-mail: steve@mariners-inn.co.uk
⊕ www.mariners-inn.co.uk

The Mariners Inn began life in the late 1700s as the home of a wealthy local merchant. Over the course of its life it has fulfilled many roles, including that of ironmongers, fish and chip shop and, of course, a licensed inn. With leaseholders Steve and Helen at the helm, it welcomes visitors all day, every day for drinks which include three real ales (four in summer), all from the local Jennings Brewery – Jennings Bitter and Jennings Cumberland Ale are the regulars – together with a good range of draught and bottled beers, lagers, stout, cider, wines, spirits and soft drinks.

The bar has recently been refurbished and is a happy mix of traditional and modern comforts, the walls adorned with nautical memorabilia. The Mariners is also an excellent choice for accommodation, with eight attractive and comfortable en suite guest bedrooms – six doubles and two family rooms. The tariff includes a hearty English breakfast.

17 BIZZY LIZZY'S

Old Bank Building, Lake Road, Ambleside,
Cumbria LA22 0AD
☎ 01539 434972

Bizzy Lizzy's is a welcoming coffee house and take-away open every day from 10 to 4.30. Tasty sandwiches, salads, cakes, toasties, panninis and more.

18 GLEN ROTHAY HOTEL & BADGER BAR

Rydal, Ambleside, Cumbria LA22 9LR
☎ 01539 434500
e-mail: JhPckrng9@aol.com
⊕ www.theglenrothay.com

Grade II listed 17th-century coaching inn. Excellent menu using Cumbrian produce. Eight en suite bedrooms available all year round.

19 THE WILD DAFFODIL

Stock Lane, Grasmere, Cumbria LA22 9SL
☎ 01539 436770 Fax: 01539 448773

There are two menus at **The Wild Daffodil**, one served between 9.30 and 6 and another for the evening meal (6-9 p.m.). Well-placed for all the attractions of Grasmere, this excellent café and restaurant is run by Carl and Sarah McAllister. Local produce goes into creating a range of dishes including everything from all-day breakfasts to superb sandwiches and snacks, meat, fish and vegetarian dishes to teacakes and home-made cakes. The carvery is available at both lunch and dinner. The restaurant stocks locally-brewed beers in bottles as well as locally-made liqueurs and also relishes, pickles and preserves, which are also for sale.

Grasmere, Cumbria LA22 9SW
☎ 01539 435300 Fax: 01539 435570
e-mail: enquiries@dalelodgehotel.co.uk
🌐 www.dalelodgehotel.co.uk

Taste and elegance are the hallmarks of **Dale Lodge Hotel**. Graciously appointed in every quarter, the Lodge is surrounded by stunning scenery and is set in the heart of Grasmere in three-and-a-half acres of its own beautiful, well-tended gardens. It's the perfect location for a relaxing break, a family holiday or for weddings and other celebrations.

This is a family-owned and –run establishment, owned by Brian and Gillian Roberts, whose son James is Head Chef while son Alexander manages the bar. Dating back to 1840, the hotel has undergone extensive and tasteful refurbishment. Tweedies Bar and Restaurant is open all day, every day, with meals served at lunch (12-3pm) and dinner (6-9 p.m.). Warm woods and flagstone floors add to the traditional and comfortable ambience. Outside there's a spacious and attractive beer garden. In Tweedies Bar there are five real ales on tap: Timothy Taylor Landlord is the mainstay, with four changing guest ales. Winner of a CAMRA award, the beers are well-kept and tasty.

The Lodge restaurant, in the main hotel building, serves fine cuisine 7 days a week that will please every palate. Head Chef James has worked alongside the likes of Raymond Blanc, and his experience shows in every dish. The wine cellar is distinctive, while the menu includes delicious and expertly prepared starters and main courses such as home-made country paté, warm Jersey salad, roasted rack of lamb, duck confit, fillet steak, monkfish and the pasta du jour. The daily dessert menu offers a selection of mouth-watering choices. Booking is advised at all times, but is essential for the traditional Sunday roast lunch (served 12-4pm).

Each of the 14 en suite guest bedrooms is individually styled, beautifully appointed and decorated to a high standard of comfort and quality. For guests with disabilities, the hotel offers excellent access to the hotel, restaurant and Tweedies, and there is a guest room on the ground floor with first-class facilities. Guests can stay on a room-only, B&B or Dinner and B&B basis off-season, while during the high season all rooms are offered on a Dinner and B&B basis. This superb hotel is open all year round. Off-road parking within the grounds. Late availability for B&B on request.

21 SARA'S BISTRO

Broadgate, Grasmere, Cumbria LA22 9TA
☎ 01539 435266 Fax: 01539 435266

Daytime and evening menus offer a range of tempting dishes using local produce, most of which are home-made. Open: Tues-Sun and Bank Hols 10.30-4 and 6-9.

22 THE KINGS ARMS

The Square, Cartmel, Cumbria LA11 6QB
☎ 01539 536220

Near Cartmel's famous racecourse, **The Kings Arms** is a stunning public house serving four to seven real ales and great food. Booking advised at weekends. Cosy and welcoming; outdoor seating along the riverbank.

23 AT HOME

Danum House, 2 Main Street, Grange-over-Sands, Cumbria LA11 6AB
☎ 01539 534400

Renowned for its food, which has made it one of the most popular eateries in the Lake District, **At Home** is a café and restaurant open Tues-Sat 10-4 and Fri-Sat from 6.30 (last orders 9 p.m.). Booking advised at all times. All dishes are home-made using locally-sourced ingredients and produce. The café menu includes soups, sandwiches (hot and cold), light bites, cakes and scones, while the evening menu boasts main courses such as roast lamb, sirloin steaks and salmon fillet. No smoking. Children welcome.

24 THE HOPE AND ANCHOR

11 Market Street, Flookburgh,
Cumbria LA11 7JU
☎ 01539 558733 Fax: 01539 559003
e-mail: hopeandanchor@colowebworld.co.uk

Run by Gill Gardner, ably assisted by her daughters Katie and Verity, **The Hope and Anchor** is a welcoming and friendly public house with great food, drink and accommodation. Gill has been in the licensing trade for over 25 years and is a superb cook. The interior of this fine pub is rich in warm woods and comfortable seating, while outside there's a well-tended beer garden.

Open all day, every day for ale, there are always two to three real ales available. Hartleys XB is

the regular here, together with changing guest ales. Food is served Tues-Fri 12-3 and 5-8.30, Sat-Sun 12-8.30. Guests choose from the menu or specials board from a range of hearty traditional dishes such as Westmorland steak meat pie, Cumberland sausage, home-made pork and apricot casserole, Flookburgh Fluke and roasted vegetable lasagne. The inn also boasts five comfortable and cosy en suite guest bedrooms on a room-only or bed-and-breakfast basis. Children welcome. Live entertainment second Saturday of each month from 8.30 p.m.

25 LAUREL'S BISTRO

13 Queen Street, Ulverston,
Cumbria LA12 7AF
☎ 01229 583961 Fax: 01229 583961

The Ferretti family have been restaurateurs since 1902, and this long tradition of quality and service shows in every part of **Laurel's Bistro**, a convivial and attractive place in the heart of Ulverston and named for famous son, Stan Laurel. The interior is splendid, with a wealth of ornaments and memorabilia depicting the great comedian's life and times. The lunch, early evening and evening menus boast tasty dishes from all over the world. Head chef Richard Hill and second chef Kell Armstrong expertly prepare and present more than 30 main courses.

26 KINGS CAFÉ WINE BAR

15-17 Queen Street, Ulverston,
Cumbria LA12 7AF
☎ 01229 588947 Fax: 01229 588949
e-mail: gary@3mail.com

Kings Café Wine Bar is a stylish and welcoming place. Open for coffee, lunch, afternoon tea and evening meals, the menus offer an impressive range of delicious fresh dishes.

27 OLDE ULVERSTON TEA ROOMS

2 Lower Brook Street, Ulverston,
Cumbria LA12 7EE
☎ 01229 580280 Fax: 01229 580280
🌐 www.oldeulverstontearooms.co.uk

Superb home-cooked food, ranging from soups and sandwiches to toasted snacks and scrumptious pastries. The specials board features savoury pies, roasts and hearty casseroles.

28 THE ARMADALE COUNTRY RESTAURANT & HOTEL

Arrad Foot, Ulverston, Cumbria LA12 7SL
☎ 01229 861257 Fax: 01229 861733
🌐 www.thearmadale.co.uk

Elegant and pretty as a picture, **The Armadale Country Restaurant and Hotel** is set in its own grounds and can be found just off the A590 between Ulverston and Greenodd. Excellent fresh local food is served Tues to Sun (weekend booking required) in the restaurant. The house began life as a quiet retreat for a local cotton mill owner, and boasts en suite rooms and a family suite, each of which has its own motel-style private entrance. Tastefully decorated and furnished, they make an excellent, great value base for touring the Lakes.

29 THE RED LION INN

Lowick Bridge, nr Ulverston,
Cumbria LA12 8EF
☎ 01229 885366

Three real ales, an excellent menu and two comfortable guest bedrooms mark out **The Red Lion Inn** as a cut above the rest. The attractive beer garden overlooks the Old Man of Coniston.

Looking for:

- *Places to Visit?*
- *Places to Stay?*
- *Places to Eat & Drink?*
- *Places to Shop?*

www.travelpublishing.co.uk

30 THE ANGLERS ARMS

Haverthwaite, Ulverston,
Cumbria LA12 8AJ
☎ 01539 531216 Fax: 01539 530695
e-mail: theanglersarms@aol.com

Situated in the heart of charming Haverthwaite, just a minute's walk from the Lakeside and Haverthwaite Private Railway and a couple of hundred yards off the A590, **The Anglers Arms** is an impressive establishment well known for its fine array of well-kept ales and excellent food. Tenants Michael and Linda Cairns have many years' experience in the trade and have been here since 2003, bringing their vast knowledge of hospitality and how to make all their guests feel welcome.

Open all day every day for ale, there are no fewer than 10 real ales available – two from the Moorhouses and Hawkshead Brewery along with eight rotating guest ales. Delicious food is served every day at lunch (12-2, until 2.30 on Sundays) and Monday to Saturday evenings (5.30-8.30, until 9 on Saturdays). Guests choose off the menu or daily specials board from a range of tempting favourites such as Cumberland sausage, steak and kidney pie, mixed grills, game, salads and more. Booking required at weekends.

31 THE FARMERS ARMS

Main Road, Baycliff, Ulverston,
Cumbria LA12 9RP
☎ 01229 869382 Mobile: 07713 621471
⊕ www.farmersarmsbaycliff.co.uk

The Farmers Arms in Baycliff is a superior village inn, traditional and welcoming. Found just off the coastal A5087 southeast of Ulverston, it's just a short walk from the sands at Morecambe Bay. Popular with walkers, bird-watchers and anyone in search of  a good pint or meal, the real ales here are Hartleys XB and a changing guest ale, while the menu offers a good range of hearty favourites expertly prepared. This fine inn also boasts two excellent letting rooms, available all year round.

32 THE RAMS HEAD HOTEL

110 Rawlinson Street, Barrow-in-Furness,
Cumbria LA14 2DG
☎ 01229 821728

A large and imposing late-Victorian inn on a corner site an easy walk from the town centre, **The Rams Head Hotel**'s location and reputation make it popular with visitors and locals alike, and the inn always has a friendly atmosphere. Open all day everyday, there's one changing guest ale together with a good range of  wines, spirits, lagers and soft drinks, and a selection of hot and cold snacks served throughout the day. There are also seven comfortable guest bedrooms, available all year round.

145

33 THE COPPER DOG

Leece, nr Ulverston, Cumbria LA12 0QP
☎ 01229 877088
e-mail: cchrischef@msn.com

Standing on the edge of the village of Leece, about 1½ miles off the A5087 and about 7 miles from Ulverston, **The Copper Dog** is a superb public house and restaurant. Spacious and comfortable, this fine establishment has a relaxed and friendly ambience. Owners Sheena and Chris Bryant (Chris is also the accomplished chef) have been here since November of 2004. Chris has over 22 years' experience in the trade, and he and Sheena have, in a short time, made The Copper Dog one of the premier places to dine in the area.

This Free House has three rotating guest ales

from all over the UK, together with a good selection of lagers and bottled beers from around the world, cider, stout, a wide range of wines to suit every palate and accompany your meal, spirits and soft drinks. The interior is a charming and welcoming mix of traditional and modern, with a large open fireplace, a wealth of warm woods and nearly floor-to-ceiling windows in the restaurant, making the most of the sunlight that fills the room on fine days.

Fresh coffee and cream teas are available, and the full menu and chef's specials are served at both lunchtime and evening. The choice is outstanding, with delicious dishes using the freshest locally-sourced produce and including Cumberland sausage, sirloin steaks, lamb chops, home-made beef lasagne, roast of the day and a good range of fish dishes. The tempting desserts are well worth leaving room for. Booking required Friday and Saturday evenings in the eye-catching restaurant, which seats 52 and is no-smoking throughout.

The bar area seats a further 36, with more room outside overlooking the surrounding, picturesque countryside. Children welcome. Large off-road car park. Opening hours: Mon-Fri 11.30-3 & 5.30-11 (restaurant open 12-2.30 & 6-9.30), Saturday 11.30-11 (restaurant 12-9.30), Sunday 12-10.30 (restaurant 12-9.30).

34 CHEQUERS HOTEL & RESTAURANT

10 Abbey Road, Dalton-in-Furness,
Cumbria LA15 8LF
☎ 01229 462124 Fax: 01229 464624
e-mail: chequers@chequers-hotel.co.uk
🌐 www.chequers-hotel.co.uk

Set adjacent to the Castle in Dalton-in-Furness, **Chequers Hotel and Restaurant** is a distinguished and distinctive place offering the highest standard of comfort and quality, Dating back to late-Victorian days, this privately owned hotel began life as a school, and is located on the edge of the Lake District, just a 20-minute drive from Lake Windermere. Now fully renovated, it offers the best in modern comforts while retaining its traditional charm.

Family-run by the Benn family since 1988, the hotel has a well-deserved reputation as one of the finest places to stay in the southern Lakes. The accommodation is nothing short of superb, with 25 en suite guest bedrooms that are tastefully appointed to provide every comfort and convenience. Eight rooms are on the ground floor; one is fully equipped to meet the needs of guests with disabilities. No expense has been spared in creating these guest rooms – each is individually decorated and furnished with taste and style.

In the bar, the friendly, helpful staff serve up a range of real ales, all from the Thwaites Brewery, together with a good selection of lagers, cider, stout, wines, spirits (including over 60 malt whiskies) and soft drinks. Renowned for the excellent food, served Wednesday to Saturday from 12 – 2 and 4 – 9.30, Sundays 11.30 – 9.30, booking is required at all times. The menus and specials board boast a variety of tempting

dishes, all using the freshest local ingredients in season.

Making an excellent touring base, this fine hotel is within easy reach of Barrow Dock Museum, Bowness, Coniston Water, Furness Abbey, Holker Hall, Swarthmoor Hall, Gleaston Water Mill and Piel Castle, among the many other sights and attractions of the region, and is particularly suited for walkers and bird-watchers, being near Walney Bird Observatory and Muncaster Castle (the latter the home of the World Owl Centre).

Skelgate, Dalton-in-Furness,
Cumbria LA15 8BQ
☎ 01229 462508 Fax: 01229 467177
e-mail: info@clarencehouse-hotel.co.uk
⊕ www.clarencehouse-hotel.co.uk

Elegance and first-class service are assured at the superb **Clarence House Country Hotel and Restaurant**. Set in two acres with grounds that include outstanding ornamental gardens and breathtaking views, this is truly Furness' jewel in the crown. Open all year round, from early morning breakfast (from 7 a.m.) right through to 9 p.m., this distinguished and distinctive hotel has merited the highest awards from bodies that include the RAC (2 Stars Dining) – and is the only hotel in Furness with an AA Rosette.

The interior is stunning – a happy marriage of traditional features and modern comforts. In the bar there's a wealth of burnished wood and a wonderful selection of real ales, wines, whiskies, lagers, ciders, stouts and soft drinks – something to please every palate. Every public space is decorated and furnished to the highest standard of taste, with elegant touches that add up to the best in luxury and comfort. This high standard continues in the beautifully decorated and furnished restaurant, where the menu

offers the freshest and finest ingredients expertly prepared and presented by the hotel's cadre of professional chefs. From light lunches to speciality five-course meals, all dishes are delicious and memorable. For afternoon tea there's a mouth-watering selection of cakes prepared by the hotel's dedicated Patisserie Chef.

The cellar provides a vast selection of excellent vintages. The ambience throughout this gracious hotel is always relaxed and welcoming. There are 17

luxurious and supremely comfortable guest bedrooms, five of which are situated on the ground floor. The hotel has always been renowned for its unique and individually-themed bedrooms, each with its own style and private facilities. As a touring base it is second to none, being within easy distance of Lake Windermere, the fells and the many scenic sights and attractions of the region. The Garden Lodge, a recently-converted traditional barn building, is now available for small conferences, weddings and celebrations.

36 THE RED LION INN

5 Market Street, Dalton-in-Furness,
Cumbria LA15 8AE
☎ 01229 467914
⊕ www.redliondalton.co.uk

Dating back to the early 17th century, **The Red Lion Inn** is a pristine and tasteful inn with traditional features and a friendly, welcoming ambience. Holts is the regular ale, together with three changing guest ales. Chef Danny Richards, who was trained by Raymond Blanc, and second chef Jamie create a menu of tempting dishes, complemented by an excellent selection of daily specials, using the freshest locally-produced ingredients. Booking is advised at all times, and is essential Fri-Sun. The inn also boasts seven superb guest bedrooms.

Open: Mon 6-11, Tues-Thurs 11-3 and 6-11, Fri-Sat 11-11, Sun 11-10.30.

37 THE ASKAM HOTEL

1-3 Victoria Street, Askam-in-Furness,
Cumbria LA16 7BX
☎ 01229 466161
e-mail: askamhotel@btconnect.com

Here in the village of Askam-in-Furness, just half a mile off the main A595, **The Askam Hotel** does double duty as a public house and hotel, with bed and breakfast accommodation available in three pleasant and comfortable guest bedrooms. Located just a few hundred yards from the beach, and close to South Lakes Animal Park, this fine inn's selection of ales includes Worthingtons Bitter and Cumberland Ale. Food is served Saturdays until 6 p.m. and Sunday lunchtime (from midday until 3 p.m.).

38 FURNESS TAVERN

140 Duke Street, Askam-in-Furness,
Cumbria LA16 7AE
☎ 01229 462692

The Furness Tavern in Askam is a traditional inn with a delightful beer garden. Open evenings Monday to Thursday, Fridays from 3 p.m. and weekends from midday, there are two changing guest ales complemented by a good range of wines, spirits, lagers, cider, stout and soft drinks. Food is served Sunday (12-3pm), with a selection of tasty home-

made snacks and bar meals. Booking advised for the Sunday lunch roast dinners. Three guest bedrooms available all year round, complete the excellent facilities offered by this traditional tavern.

39 THE GREYHOUND INN

Grizebeck, Kirkby-in-Furness,
Cumbria LA17 7XJ
☎ 01229 889224 Fax: 01229 889900
e-mail: thegreyhound@grizebeck.fsworld.co.uk

The Greyhound Inn has a well-earned reputation for quality and service. Rotating guest ales, excellent food and seven recently refurbished letting rooms.

40 THE BAKEHOUSE

Princes Street, Broughton-in-Furness,
Cumbria LA20 6HQ
☎ 01229 716284

Baking with 100% natural ingredients, locally sourced, organic and Fairtrade. Speciality breads, desserts and cakes. Shop, Café and Accommodation. Farmers Markets.

41 THE SUN HOTEL

Coniston, Cumbria LA21 8HQ
☎ 015394 41248 Fax: 015394 41219
e-mail: TheSun@hotelconiston.com
🌐 www.thesunconiston.com

The Sun Hotel is situated in the heart of Coniston. Built before 1600 on the old Walna Scar packhorse trail, the inn enjoys a Lakeland setting and traditional features including the stone walls, stone floor and exposed beamwork. Open all day, every day for ale, the hotel is well known for its various premium real ales. There are always five real ales – regulars Coniston Bluebird and

Hawkshead, together with three changing guest ales.

Meals are served daily at lunch and dinner, expertly prepared by the chef and his team, who bring great inventiveness and exotic influences to bear on creating an excellent menu and daily specials. The select wine list complements the menu perfectly. Outside, the hotel's attractive beer garden looks down to Coniston Water. There are nine en suite guest bedrooms and one room with private bath. The hotel also boasts a fine new conservatory, where guests can enjoy superb views in every direction.

42 THE CROWN HOTEL

Coniston, Cumbria LA21 8ED
☎ 01539 441243 Fax: 01539 441804
e-mail: info@crown-hotel-coniston.com
🌐 www.crown-hotel-coniston.com

The stylish and welcoming **Crown Hotel** has it all: great food, drink and accommodation. Situated in the heart of Coniston, this fine inn boasts three real ales from the Robinsons

Brewery range, together with a selection of lagers, spirits, cider, stout, wines and soft drinks. The good, varied menu and specials board offer a range of excellent dishes using the best local produce. The 12 guest bedrooms are tasteful and comfortable, and have been awarded a 4 Diamonds rating by the English Tourist Board.

43 SPINDLES OF CONISTON

Lake Road, Coniston, Cumbria LA21 8EW
☎ 01539 441256
🌐 www.spindlesofconiston.co.uk

Situated on the edge of the centre of town, **Spindles of Coniston** is a delightful tea rooms and restaurant, where locally-sourced produce is used to create the superb dishes. Owners Stewart and Lesley Barker have been here for three years and Stewart is the chef, with over 20 years' experience in catering. The evening menu boasts a good range of tasty

dishes such as Cumbrian pork tenderloin, sirloin steaks, Barbary duck and a choice of fish and seafood meals. Open seven days a week in the summer months and five days a week the rest of the year. Booking required Friday to Sunday.

44 JUMPING JENNY COFFEE HOUSE & RESTAURANT

Brantwood, Coniston, Cumbria LA21 8AD
☎ 015394 41715 Mobile: 07974 090310
Fax: 0709 200 4 112
⊕ www.jumpingjenny.com
e-mail: chris@addison.ms

Make a beeline for **Jumping Jenny Coffee House & Licensed Restaurant** while visiting the Lake District, and enjoy Chris & Gillie Addison's superb food, drink and hospitality. Situated in the grounds of famous Brantwood, home of artist John Ruskin in the 19th Century, this charming place takes its name from Ruskin's rowing boat and occupies the former stables. There is a large terrace overlooking Coniston Water.

Jumping Jenny is open from 11am **ALL YEAR**, every day, (except Mondays and Tuesdays between mid-November and mid-March) for splendid home cooking, such as Gillie's famous Tarte au Citron. The restaurant can be booked for evening private parties for between 12 and 50 guests, with the option of a cruise on the Lake as a special prelude to an evening meal. Wedding Evening Parties are a speciality. In 2006, Chris and Gillie will be opening another venture nearby, which will be a wedding venue with capacity for 100 guests, and a very special private guest house. See website for details.

45 THE EAGLES HEAD

Satterthwaite, nr Ulverston,
Cumbria LA12 8LN
☎ 01229 860237

A charming traditional inn, rustic and comfortable in equal measure, **The Eagles Head** began life as a farmhouse back in the 1500s. It is set in the heart of Grizedale Forest, west of Lake Windermere. Over the years the pub has been modernised and refurbished, but remains cosy, warm and welcoming. Head chef Paul Brady creates a range of tempting dishes using meats delivered fresh from local suppliers and other

locally-sourced produce. All meals are cooked to order. The range of real ales includes local brews. Booking advised evenings and is essential at weekends.

Looking for:

- *Places to Visit?*
- *Places to Stay?*
- *Places to Eat & Drink?*
- *Places to Shop?*

COUNTRY LIVING RURAL GUIDES

HIDDEN INNS

HIDDEN PLACES

COUNTRY Pubs & Inns

off the motorway 3rd edition

46 THE OLD DUNGEON GHYLL HOTEL

Great Langdale, Ambleside,
Cumbria LA22 9JY
☎ 01539 437272 Fax: 01539 437272
e-mail: neil.odg@lineone.net
🌐 www.odg.co.uk

In a magnificent setting at the head of the Great Langdale Valley, **The Old Dungeon Ghyll Hotel** has been dispensing hospitality to fellwalkers, climbers and tourists for over 300 years. Since 1984 this fine old inn has been run by Neil Walmsley, a keen fell-runner, and his wife Jane. They have continued to improve and develop its amenities, and the 14 guest bedrooms, some with four-

posters, some with en suite shower facilities, offer warmth and comfort in abundance, and keen walkers will be pleased that the hotel has the essential amenity of a drying room.

The first port of call for many visitors is the Hikers Bar, where a selection of real ales is on hand to quench outdoor thirsts. Both Neil and Jane enjoy cooking, and the accent is very much on home-made food, from bar meals to evening meals served in the comfort of the dining room (open to non-residents with advance booking). The hotel takes its name from one of the most dramatic of the Lake District waterfalls, which tumbles 60 feet down the fellside.

47 BROOK HOUSE INN & RESTAURANT

Boot, Eskdale, Cumbria CA19 1TG
☎ 01946 723288 Fax: 01946 723160
e-mail: stay@brookhouseinn.co.uk
🌐 www.brookhouseinn.co.uk

With six real ales in peak season, great food (booking required at weekends) and seven comfortable en suite guest bedrooms, **Brook House Inn & Restaurant** is well worth seeking out. Located in the unspoilt Eskdale Valley in the heart of the Lake District, it makes an excellent base from which to explore the Western valleys and fells and the many other natural and man-made sights and attractions of the region.

Built in the 1870s, the inn enjoys glorious views in all directions. Owner Gareth Thornley and his family provide excellent hospitality. Gareth is also a superb chef who numbers many home-cooked dishes from around the world among his many specialities. Among the accolades won by this fine inn and restaurant are ratings of 4 Diamonds by the ETC and RAC, the RAC Dining Award, and recommendations in the *Good Beer Guide* and *Good Pub Guide* for 2004.

Waberthwaite, Cumbria LA19 5YJ
☎ 01229 717243 Fax: 01229 717295
e-mail: keith-Freda@browncowinn.com
🌐 www.browncowinn.com

The **Brown Cow Inn** is a delightful hostelry conveniently located on the A595 about three miles south of Ravenglass. Enjoying a well-deserved reputation for its excellent food, available from breakfast at 10 a.m. through lunch, afternoon tea and dinner served until 8.30 p.m. Resident owners Keith and Freda Hitchen keep customers happy with their friendly service and excellent hospitality. The cooking is simply splendid, with a menu of local

delicacies including Waberthwaite ham and Cumberland gammon or sausage, together with fish dishes, Indian meals, vegetarian specials and a good choice of children's meals. The portions are hearty and always delicious. There's a take-away service available and, on Sundays, a choice of two tempting roasts with all the trimmings.

This fine inn also boasts a good range of real ales, lagers, cider, stout, wines, spirits and soft drinks. And for those wishing to prolong their stay in this beautiful part of the world, The Brown Cow also offers a comfortable and charming self-catering flat which sleeps four.

49 UNDERWOOD COUNTRY GUEST HOUSE

The Hill, Millom, Cumbria LA18 5EZ
☎ 01229 771116 Fax: 01229 719900
e-mail: enquiries@underwoodhouse.co.uk
🌐 www.underwoodhouse.co.uk

Set in eight acres of beautiful countryside, with superb views in every direction, **Underwood Country Guest House** is the last word in comfort, elegance and relaxation. Dating back to the mid-1860s, this distinguished oasis of peace and tranquillity nestles on the edge of woodland between the scenic Whicham Valley and Duddon Estuary, and speaks of quality in every department. The interior décor and furnishings are simply splendid, and each guest room is individually and stylishly decorated. Given a 5-diamond rating by the AA, this beautifully restored former vicarage offers five double and two twin en suite guest bedrooms, all tastefully furnished. There are two elegant lounges in which to relax, an attractive and

welcoming dining room, conference facilities and much more. Found off the A5093 a short drive from the junction with the A595, the guest house also boasts an excellent restaurant, open seven evenings a week between 7 and 8 p.m. The menu changes to make the best use of the freshest local produce in season; a small sample would include main courses such as rack of lamb with redcurrant gravy, pan-friend port tenderloin in an apple and Calvados sauce, and linguine with roasted pine nuts, basil and watercress. The starters and desserts are equally sumptuous and satisfying.

Owners Andrew and Wendy Miller have been here since 1999; both are accomplished chefs with international culinary experience who create a superior range of tempting dishes. The wine list has been put together carefully to complement the fine food. Open all year round, the many excellent amenities and facilities at this superb guest house include the magnificent 12-metre indoor swimming pool, croquet lawn, tennis court and ample off-road parking. Away from the hustle and bustle yet within easy reach of Lake Windermere, Coniston Water and Wast Water, it is the perfect base for exploring the region.

154

50 CAMBRIDGE HOUSE HOTEL

1 Cambridge Street, Millom,
Cumbria LA18 5BD
☎ 01229 774982
e-mail: info@cambridge-house-hotel.co.uk
🌐 www.cambridge-house-hotel.co.uk

The new owners John and Joy Fernley offer a warm and friendly welcome at the **Cambridge House Hotel**. Recently refurbished to offer the best of traditional touches and ensuring guest's comfort and convenience.

The premises has a licenced bar and meals are served every evening, and a traditional Sunday lunch is served 12-3 p.m. (meals are available to non-residents) Meals are freshly prepared catering for specific diets, vegetarians or special occasion requests. All rooms are en suites and the price includes a full English breakfast. There are 4 twin rooms and 2 doubles. Ideally situated for a touring base, just two miles from the beach at Haverigg and within easy reach of the Western Lakes.

51 WESTLAKES HOTEL

Gosforth, Cumbria CA20 1HP
☎ 01946 725221 Fax: 01946 725099
e-mail: stay@westlakeshotel.com
🌐 www.westlakeshotel.com

Westlakes Hotel is set in a beautiful and historic country house dating back to 1827. Built for a wealthy fruit merchant of the era and originally named Haverigg Hall, the hotel stands in three acres of eye-catching gardens. It's the perfect place to relax, unwind and recharge your batteries in luxurious comfort. Open all year round, there are nine tasteful, elegant and comfortable en suite guest

bedrooms, in a mixture of sizes, each individually furnished and decorated.

This superior hotel also boasts a gracious and elegant restaurant open to residents and non-residents. Open from 7 p.m. Monday to Saturday, the menu features a range of tempting dishes such as chicken mignons, minted lamb Henry, red snapper fillet, Cajun chicken salad and mushroom stroganoff, all making use of the freshest locally-sourced ingredients. The mouth-watering desserts are well worth leaving room for! Booking essential for non-residents.

Beckermet, Cumbria CA21 2XS
☎ 01946 841246 Fax: 01946 841100
e-mail: phil@whitemare.co.uk
🌐 www.whitemare.co.uk

Philip Ward is the friendly, energetic licensee at the **White Mare**, an outstanding country inn and hotel set in the quiet and picturesque West Cumbrian village of Beckermet, just a mile off the A595. An ideal base for exploring the hidden places of the

Westlakes and lake District, it also attracts an appreciative local clientele. With its smart white-painted frontage and small-paned windows, the White Mare, which dates back to the early 1800s, is a place of considerable charm and character, and open fires in the main lounge make it a warm, inviting spot for a drink.

Open both at lunchtime and in the evenings, the public bar has been nicknamed the

Sports Bar and boasts a wealth of sporting memorabilia on display, while raised above the lounge is a delightful restaurant. There are always at least six real ales on tap, an ever-changing selection from local and far-flung breweries. A dedicated team in the kitchen cater well for their customers, providing a good choice of bar and restaurant menus, including daily specials and a wide selection of vegetarian meals.

Weddings can also be catered for as the White Mare has two approved venues for Civil Ceremonies and superbly appointed marquees that can seat up to 150 guest during the day and 250 for the evening function. Their wedding portfolio is available on request.

For overnight guests the White Mare has six double and two twin en suite guest bedrooms. Four of the

rooms have convertible sofas, making them particularly suitable for families, and all the rooms are no-smoking. Details of tarriffs can be found on their website or by telephoning the hotel. The White Mare has an excellent car park and a beer garden. Local groups and singers perform in the restaurant once a month, and other social events include a quiz on Wednesdays and a knock-out dominoes competition every Friday. The Lakes are within an easy drive, the sea even closer, and among the attractions in the vicinity are Egremont Castle and the Florence Mine Heritage Centre.

53 THE RED LION HOTEL

2 Market Place, Egremont,
Cumbria CA22 IAE
☎ 01946 824050
e-mail: redlionhotel@btopenworld.com

One of the biggest plaster red lions you will ever see adorns the frontage at **The Red Lion Hotel**, which is easy to spot on Egremont's main street. This excellent hotel began life in the early 1700s as a coaching inn, and became an important stopping-place along what was then the main Whitehaven-to-Barrow road. Its early prominence was but a distant memory when John Walker came here in 1998; since then he has invested a great deal of time and effort in a major refurbishment programme that has seen the hotel restored to its rightful style and elegance.

The 11 guest bedrooms offer a choice of accommodation to suit all guests, running from simple and homely with shared facilities to top-of-the-range rooms with en suite facilities. The tariff varies accordingly. In the bar, guests and locals can enjoy a full range of beers, including real ales, together with a good complement of lagers, cider, stout, wines, spirits and soft drinks. John has also widened the scope of their pub by serving hearty home-prepared food every lunchtime and evening, and in the process has made the pub one of the town's most popular meeting places.

Entertainment on offer includes regular karaoke session and discos, and to the rear of the pub there is a spacious function room available for private parties. Egremont, lying among the low hills of the Ehen Valley, is a little town with a lot of history, and is well worth taking the time to explore. It's famous for its castle, its annual medieval festival and, most of all, for the Crab Fayre Day in September, when the entertainments include the World Gurning Championships. Thanks to John's continuing programme of tasteful renovation, his hard work and dedication, the Red Lion has become an excellent base from which to enjoy everything Egremont and the surrounding area has to offer.

54 CAP'N SENNYS

2 Senhouse Street, Whitehaven,
Cumbria CA28 7ES
☎ 01946 62222
e-mail: andy2sennys@aol.com

Family-owned-and-run since 2001, **Cap'n Sennys** is a friendly, welcoming place that takes its name (as does Senhouse Street) from one Captain Richard Senhouse, who was instrumental in the development of both Whitehaven and Maryport. He bought the land in 1685 and, with a grant from the Lowther Estate, built the Mansion (Tangier House) and Warehouse in 1688. In 1692 he

built the first distillery in Whitehaven, and it is this building which today forms the major part of the inn, tastefully renovated over the years so that the interior is spacious and comfortable, with handsome oak beams and a wealth of original features.

Open Tuesday to Sunday, til late (1 a.m.) Thurs, Fri and Sat, the pub has a good selection of liquid refreshment. A DJ spins the discs Thurs-Sat, and owner Andrew Conoley does the cooking, serving up a range of tasty dishes at weekends between 12 and 3 p.m.

55 MANOR HOUSE HOTEL & COAST-TO-COAST BAR

Main Street, St Bees, Cumbria CA27 0DE
☎ 01946 822425 Fax: 01946 824949

Real ales, great food at lunch and dinner and eight en suite guest bedrooms in spacious, pristine and distinctive hotel and bar.

Explore Britain and Ireland with *Hidden Places* guides - a fascinating series of national and local travel guides.

www.travelpublishing.co.uk

0118-981-7777

info@travelpublishing.co.uk

56 THE STORK HOTEL

Rowrah Road, Rowrah, Cumbria CA26 3XJ
☎ 01946 861213
e-mail: joan@storkhotel.co.uk

Completely refurbished from top to bottom while retaining all its origin charm, **The Stork Hotel** at Rowrah is a friendly inn with accommodation. The two regular real ales here are Jennings Bitter and Jennings Cumberland Ale along with a changing guest ale. Owners Joan and Paul Keswell are ably assisted by their daughters Jayne and Joanne. Joanne is the chef, and her home-made dishes are justly popular. Guests choose from the menu or specials board for a range of freshly prepared dishes using the best in local produce. Booking advised for Sunday lunch.

Upstairs, there are six cosy and comfortable en suite guest bedrooms, available all year round.

St Bees Foreshore, St Bees,
Cumbria CA27 0ES
☎ 01946 820175 Fax: 01946 820456
⊕ www.hartleys-ice-cream.co.uk

Occupying an enviably beautiful location overlooking the foreshore at St Bees, **Hartley's Beach Shop & Tea Rooms** has justly become one of the most popular places in the region to enjoy a drink and snack. It's a particularly welcome amenity for anyone starting (or especially finishing!) a spell of exercise along the Coast-to-Coast walk, which runs across the Pennines to Robin Hood's Bay in North Yorkshire.

The long-established owners of this excellent premises are the Richardson family. Open every day between mid-March and New Year's day from 9 a.m. to 5 p.m. (high season 8 a.m. to 7 p.m.), the shop has recently undergone refurbishment to make it even more attractive and welcoming.

There are no-smoking seats for 48 inside, and outdoor tables when the weather is fine. Home-made cakes, toasted tea cakes and scones are among the specialities here, along with the famous ice-creams – in 1981 the family took over an ice-cream business founded 50 years previously, boasting a range that includes more than 30 flavours, with a selection of sorbets as well, made on the premises at the family's ice-cream shop in Church Street, Egremont (open March to early January 11 a.m. to 5 p.m., 7 p.m. in the busy summer months).

On the savoury side the choice comprises soup, beans on toast and made-to-order sandwiches with a variety of generous, tasty fillings – tuna savoury, corned beef and onion, chicken mayonnaise and ham with cheese and pineapple are just a few of the options. Coffee is the favourite beverage, coming in several varieties and two sizes.

The Beach Shop, on the right-hand side of the long, low, modern building, is stocked with a wide range of foods, drinks, gifts and everything that walkers or campers might need.

St Bees is a place of many attractions including the priory church, the school, a nature reserve and wonderful walks along the coastal footpath – and for the past 20 years and more, no visit to St Bees has been complete without sampling the goodies on offer at Hartley's.

58 NEW HOUSE FARM

Lorton, Cockermouth,
Cumbria CA13 9UU
☎ 01900 85404 Fax: 01900 85478
e-mail: hazel@newhouse-farm.co.uk
🌐 www.newhouse-farm.co.uk

Enjoying a truly outstanding setting amid 17 acres of lovely gardens and pastureland, **New House Farm** is a magnificent 17th-century farmhouse surrounded by superb Lortondale countryside. Owner Hazel Thompson has been offering comfortable and relaxing accommodation here since 1990. The five bedrooms take their names from local mountains; each is individually furnished and decorated to provide the very best in quality and comfort. All have en suite facilities and offer wonderful views. One room is on the ground floor.

Guests also can make use of the two elegant and gracious lounges, while the hearty and delicious breakfast is served in the separate dining room. Children over 6 are welcome; special arrangements can be made for younger children. Awarded 5 Diamonds by the AA, this no-smoking establishment is a truly special guest house and makes the perfect base from which to explore one of the loveliest parts of the county. Bookings are taken on a bed and breakfast or dinner, bed and breakfast basis.

Open all year round, New House Farm stands by the B5289 in Lorton Vale, south of Cockermouth. Other places of beauty and interest nearby include Keswick, Bassenthwaite Lake,

Derwent Water, the spectacular Whinlatter Pass and Forest Park. The Lortons, High and Low, are peaceful, enchanting places, and behind the former's village hall stands the yew tree made famous by poet William Wordsworth. Right next door is the charming Barn, a handsome building dating back to the 1880s and now tastefully converted into a tea room, seating 40 and serving mouth-watering food from 11 to 5 every day from March to October. As well as serving excellent traditional teas, it also has appetising home-cooked hot and cold snacks throughout the day.

59 GREEN DRAGON HOTEL

Portland Square, Workington,
Cumbria CA14 4BJ
☎ 01900 603803

Taste and quality are the bywords at the gracious **Green Dragon Hotel** in Workington. Standing in one of the oldest parts of town, in Portland Square with its distinctive cobbled streets, The Green Dragon began life in the mid-1700s as a coaching inn. Having undergone a careful and tasteful refurbishment, this fine hotel can offer the very best in food, drink, accommodation and hospitality to all its guests. A happy blend of modern and traditional, it's a friendly, welcoming place to enjoy a tasty drink or meal, or enjoy first-class comfort in one of the guest bedrooms.

New owners Stephen and Angela Bell are ably assisted by their sons Stephen, Andrew and Paul. Andrew is the chef, creating a delicious range of excellent dishes and daily specials using the freshest locally-sourced ingredients, with plenty of choice to appeal to every appetite. Open every session for ale, there are two changing guest ales to choose from, together with a good selection of wines, spirits, soft drinks, lagers and more. The newly refurbished restaurant is open evenings from 5.30 p.m. and seats more than 40 diners. Open all year round, the hotel boasts 12 lovely guest bedrooms.

Ten rooms are en suite, the other two have private bath. All are located on the first or second floor. Guests stay on a bed-and-breakfast basis, and the hotel is ideally sited for anyone wanting a base from which to explore Workington, the River Derwent and the many sights and attractions of the region. The Bells also own and run the nearby 'Well' public house in Washington Street, offering a similarly good choice of quality food and drink. The hidden courtyard at this pub is just one of its distinctive features.

60 HUNTERS

43a Main Street, Cockermouth, Cumbria CA13 9JS
☎ 01900 826560
e-mail: hunters1@fsmail.net

Cheerful and pristine inside and out, **Hunters** is a very welcoming and convivial inn with lots of style and class. Polished wood floors, modern furnishings and tasteful décor and layout add to the pleasant and relaxing ambience. Owned and run by Chris and Ghislain Smithson, it's open all day, every day, there are two real ales – Jennings Bitter and Jennings Cumberland Ale – together with a good selection of keg bitters, lagers, cider, stout, wines, spirits and soft drinks. The menu boasts a majority of home-made dishes, with the steak-and-ale pie just one of Ghislain's many specialities.

HIDDEN PLACES GUIDES

Explore Britain and Ireland with *Hidden Places* guides - a fascinating series of national and local travel guides.

Packed with easy to read information on hundreds of places of interest as well as places to stay, eat and drink.

Available from both high street and internet booksellers

For more information on the full range of *Hidden Places* guides and other titles published by Travel Publishing visit our website on

www.travelpublishing.co.uk or ask for our leaflet by phoning **0118-981-7777** or emailing **info@travelpublishing.co.uk**

61 THE WESTLANDS HOTEL

Branthwaite Road, Workington, Cumbria CA14 4TD
☎ 01900 604544 Fax: 01900 68830
e-mail: davidwestlands@hotmail.co.uk
⊕ www.westlandshotel.com

Set in six-and-a-half acres of grounds on the outskirts of Workington, **The Westlands Hotel** is a superb establishment owned and personally run by Iona and David Sale. The Sales are a friendly and welcoming couple who have many years' experience in offering the finest standard of comfort and hospitality. They

have been here at Westlands for a year and are restoring the eminence and prestige enjoyed by the hotel in the 1970s and 80s, when visits from royalty, prime ministers and other dignitaries was a common occurrence.

Open all year round, this spacious and elegant hotel has 70 superbly appointed en suite guest bedrooms, a number of which are on the ground floor. The hotel bar is open throughout the day and serves four regular real ales alongside guest ales and the full complement of lagers, spirits, wines and soft drinks. Tasty traditional English meals are served at lunch and dinner – booking required for Sunday lunch. The owners are also re-opening the Westlands Theatre, adjacent to the hotel, as a venue for entertainments of all kinds.

62 THE TRAVELLERS REST

63 High Street/Whitehaven Road,
Workington, Cumbria CA14 4EU
☎ 01900 602064 Fax: 01900 602064

The Travellers Rest enjoys a growing reputation for its excellent menu and welcoming ambience. Tim Lewis-Dalby is a well-known chef in the region; he and his wife Dawn became tenants here in early 2004. Together they have made it one of the premier destinations in the area.

Open all day, every day, there's something to quench every thirst and also excellent food

at lunch and dinner. Guests choose from the menu or specials board from an across-the-board range of delicious dishes using the best of local produce. Booking required for Saturday evening and Sunday lunch. There's also a children's menu. Tim and Dawn have brought their experience of running the Old Town House Restaurant in Portland Street, Workington, which has earned them 2 Rosettes and boasts over 100 main courses from which to choose, to bear on this newer venture, and it shows in the quality and service on hand.

63 THE GALLOPING HORSE

High Harrington, Workington,
Cumbria CA14 4NQ
☎ 01946 830083
e-mail: craigdlowery@aol.com

High Harrington is just a short drive from Workington on the A597. Here can be found **The Galloping Horse**, a large and impressive pub with great food, drink and hospitality. There's been a pub on this site for hundreds of years, this is the latest incarnation, built in 1946. Open every session weekdays and all day at weekends, the real ale here is Jennings Bitter, complemented

by a good selection of lagers, cider, stout, wines, spirits and soft drinks. Excellent food is served daily at lunch and dinner. The meals are justly popular, so it's first come, first served here. Many of the dishes are home-made using local produce.

64 THE GRAPES HOTEL

Market Square, Aspatria,
Cumbria CA7 3HB
☎ 01697 322550

Free House with adjacent café, serving hot and cold dishes Tues-Sat 9 a.m.-4 p.m. Five spacious and comfortable guest bedrooms.

65 THE SWAN INN AND RESTAURANT

Westnewton, Aspatria, Wigton,
Cumbria CA7 3PQ
☎ 01687 320627
e-mail: info@theswaninnwestnewton.co.uk
🌐 www.theswaninnwestnewton.co.uk

Justly renowned inn with real ales and an impressive menu of fresh local produce expertly prepared. Open Thurs-Mon for lunch and dinner; booking advised.

Gilcrux, Wigton, Cumbria CA7 2QX
☎ 01697 320765
e-mail: thepubgilcrux@btconnect.com

The Masons Arms is a truly outstanding inn with accommodation set in the tranquil village of Gilcrux. Once a busy little coal-mining village, Gilcrux stands on a hillside overlooking the Ellen Valley commanding superb views across the Solway Firth to Scotland. When the coal industry was in its heyday the village supported no fewer than seven licensed premises; today The Masons Arms is the only original one left.

The original oak beams and open fireplace contribute to the inn's warm and welcoming traditional ambience. It's a welcome enforced by owners Esther and Paul Bowness, a friendly local couple who took over as tenants in 2000 and became the owners in 2001. They have established a fine reputation not just for their hospitality but also for the quality of their ales, excellent range of wines

and great food. The inn is open every lunchtime and evening , serving a range of hearty and tasty dishes expertly prepared. Warm crusty baguettes, jacket potatoes, salads, omelettes and cheese bakes make for tasty quick snacks, while the choices from the grill include 16-oz steaks, Cumberland sausages, gammon and an exotic selection including wild boar, ostrich and kangaroo! Home-made pies (chicken, leek and Stilton, venison and red wine pie, steak and ale) and main courses such as chicken Stroganoff, salmon fillet and peppered pork complete this fine inn's superb choice of delicious dishes. For Sunday lunch, traditional roasts are added to the regular evening menu.

This family-friendly inn has a spacious beer garden and a games room; there's occasional live entertainment on Bank holidays, and all are welcome for the quiz every other Monday evening. In a former barn next to the main inn, tastefully converted, comfortable and cosy, are three top-of-the-range en suite guest bedrooms, stylish and homely with every amenity guests could want.

67 THE SKINBURNESS LEISURE HOTEL

Skinburness, Silloth-on-Solway,
Cumbria CA7 4QY
☎ 01697 332332 Fax: 01697 332549
e-mail: events.skinburness@ntlworld.com
🌐 www.skinburnessleisurehotel.co.uk

Dating back to 1745 and a hotel since 1809,
The Skinburness Leisure Hotel occupies a
stunning location at the edge of the Solway
Firth. Open all year round, there are 26 guest
bedrooms including three executive rooms
and a ground-floor room adapted for guests
with disabilities. All rooms are en suite and
the hotel boasts a 3 Star rating from the AA and RAC and is also an AA Pet Friendly Hotel. The
hotel's name is a hint of the many leisure facilities on hand, which include an indoor plunge pool,
sauna, sunbed and fitness suite.

Outside in the lovely gardens, guests can enjoy use of
the bowling greens and croquet pitch. The restaurant is
open to residents and non-residents alike, and is open
daily for lunch (12-3), afternoon tea and dinner (5-9). The
menu offers a varied choice of dishes to suit all palates.
Booking required for Saturday evening and Sunday lunch.
The hotel bar is open all day, every day for a range of
thirst-quenchers including draught keg bitters, lagers,
wines and soft drinks.

68 JOINERS ARMS COUNTRY INN

Newton Arlosh, Wigton,
Cumbria CA7 5ET
☎ 01697 351470

A truly outstanding place, the **Joiners Arms
Country Inn** is a picture-postcard
establishment set in a lovely village and with
an interior that is tasteful and traditional, in
keeping with
the history of
the inn but
affording every
comfort. Open
every session,

there are three real ales from the Jennings Brewery together with a
good range of lagers, cider, stout, wines, spirits and soft drinks.
Delicious food is served every lunchtime (12-2) and evening (6-
9). Guests choose off the menu and specials board from a range of
dishes using the best and freshest local produce to create home-
made specialities including Cumberland sausage, steak pie, rack of
lamb, lasagne, chicken curry, Scottish salmon and more. Owners
Allan and Dorothy Burton have been here for two years; it's their
first venture into this type of business but Dorothy has 34 years'
experience in the catering and licensing trade, and offers all her
guests the highest standard of service and hospitality.

165

69 GINGER & PICKLES COFFEE SHOP

7 Lake Road, Keswick, Cumbria CA12 5BS
☎ 01768 780006

Delicious food and drink for morning coffee, lunches and afternoon tea – the outstanding **Ginger & Pickles Coffee Shop** has it all. Charming and welcoming, it is owned and run by Judith and Norman, both of whom are accomplished cooks. Most of the dishes and cakes –
from the menu and daily specials board – are home-cooked using the best and freshest local produce. Open seven days a week, summer 9.30-7.00 and winter 10-5.30. Children welcome. No smoking.

70 GRANGE BRIDGE COTTAGE TEASHOP

Grange-in-Borrowdale, Keswick, Cumbria CA12 5UQ
☎ 01768 777201
e-mail: info@grange-teashop.co.uk
🌐 www.grange-teashop.co.uk

In a superb location and boasting excellent home cooking and baking, this superb teashop is justly popular.

71 THE OLD SAWMILL TEAROOM

Mirehouse, Keswick, Cumbria CA12 4QE
☎ 01768 774317
🌐 www.theoldsawmill.co.uk

Within the Mirehouse Estate at Bassenthwaite Lake, charming and welcoming tearoom. Mouthwatering home-made dishes using the best local produce.

72 THE OLD SMITHY CRAFTS, GIFTS AND TEAROOM

Caldbeck, Wigton, Cumbria CA7 8EL
☎ 01697 478246 Fax: 01697 361186
e-mail: richard@rawsonpottery.fsnet.co.uk
🌐 www.caldbeckvillage.co.uk *or*
www.rawsonpottery.co.uk

Open all year round seven days a week from 9.30-6, **The Old Smithy Crafts, Gifts and Tearoom** is a business run by Kathryn and Richard Rawson based on the Quaker ethos. The tearoom is the perfect place to enjoy a relaxing cup of tea or coffee. Superb home-made cakes, light meals or snacks are served all day and freshly prepared to order. As far as possible all ingredients are from supplies which are Fairtrade and ethically sourced and organic where available. In the fine weather you can enjoy your food outside on the grassy area by the beck. Shop visitors can browse among the wide range of locally-produced crafts including ceramics

by Rawson Pottery, Eddie Stobart merchandise, sweets, confectionery and speciality foods such as pickles, sauces, honey, jams and Kendal mint cake. The shop also hosts regular events such as guided walks, pottery painting workshops, crafts demonstrations and more. Everyone is welcome including walkers, cyclists, dog owners and the disabled. They will endeavour to provide access to all comers. Every Thursday, Kathryn and Richard have two stalls on Keswick Market where they display a selection of the many crafts and speciality foods available at The Old Smithy.

73 THE OLD CROWN ❢

Hesket Newmarket, Cumbria CA7 8JG
☎ 01697 478288
e-mail: louhogg@onetel.com
⊕ www.theoldcrownpub.co.uk

Co-operative pub owned by 125 locals and
supporters, traditional
and characterful with a
wide range of real ales
from the famed
brewery at the rear of
the pub.

74 THREE CROWNS TEA SHOP ❢

Three Crowns Yard, Bluebell Lane, Penrith,
Cumbria CA11 7PH
☎ 01768 899789

Delicious light bites, sandwiches and home-
made cakes, scones
and more. Open
every day in
summer, Mon-Sat at
other times, 9-5
(8.30-5 on
Saturdays).

75 THE GLOBE INN ❢

Calthwaite, Penrith, Cumbria CA11 9QT
☎ 01768 885238
e-mail: calthwaiteglobe@aol.com
⊕ www.theglobeinn-calthwaite.co.uk

Set in the picturesque village of Calthwaite,
west off the A6 or a short drive off J41 of
the M6, **The Globe Inn** is an outstanding
traditional coaching inn dating back to 1690.
The interior is welcoming and attractive,
while outside
there's a beer
garden and
children's
play area.
Open all day
every day for
ale, there is

one real ale available from the local Cumbrian
Hesket Newmarket Brewery. A range of
tempting dishes are served Tues-Sun and
Bank Holidays between midday and 9 p.m.
The speciality is the excellent steak-and-ale
pie. This wonderful inn also boasts two guest
bedrooms.

76 THE PURPLE SAGE RESTAURANT ❢

8 St Andrew's Church Yard, Penrith,
Cumbria CA11 9QT
☎ 01768 895555
e-mail: strandbud@aol.com
⊕ www.purplesage.info

Located in a
charming
17th-century
house near
the splendid
Church of St

Andrew, **The Purple Sage Restaurant** is one of the region's
most popular eateries, and justly so. Owners Martin and Jan
Strand are highly praised by locals and visitors alike, and
warmly recommended by many of the local guest houses and
Bed & Breakfast establishments.

Martin is an experienced and very talented chef
and his menus make mouthwatering reading. Results on
the plate fully live up to expectations, whether it's a
simple daytime snack or a three- or four-course evening
meal. Open Tues-Thurs 6.30-8.45, Fri-Sat 10-2.30 and
6.30-8.45 (closed Sun and Mon except for privately-
booked parties), the impressive evening menu includes
pan-fried Sea Bass fillets, Barbary duck breast with star-
anise and black cherry sauce, roast butternut squash,
vegetable and feta cheese crumble, and a chef's daily
recommendation such as rump of Lakeland lamb with
pesto crust. Themed food nights are a regular feature at
this first-class establishment, and are held on the last
Friday of the month. Booking essential at weekends.

77 KINGS ARMS

**The Green, Stainton, Penrith,
Cumbria CA11 0EP
☎ 01768 862778**

The impressive **Kings Arms** was built as an inn and dates back to 1721. Open every session and all day on Saturdays, the inn boasts two regular ales – Worthington and Black Sheep – along with an occasional guest ale. Tasty food is served at lunch and dinner, guests choosing from the menu or specials board from a varied range of home-made

dishes including an excellent steak-and-kidney pie. The interior is spacious and traditional, while outside there's a small garden to the rear and patio seating to the front. Leaseholders Richard Jakeman and his son Adam have many years' experience in providing excellent food, drink and service to all their guests.

78 WHITE HORSE INN

**Kings Meaburn, Penrith,
Cumbria CA10 3BU
☎ 01931 714256
e-mail: whitehorse-inn@yahoo.co.uk
⊕ www.pubsineden.co.uk**

Dating back to the early 1700s, the **White Horse Inn** began life as a string of cottages. With a lovely traditional interior and ambience, the inn boasts real ales and excellent food. Dinner is served Mon-Sun evening (excluding Wed);

lunch is available on Thursdays and weekends. The experienced chef creates a varied menu of locally-sourced dishes including specialities such as steaks, chops, roasts and a very good vegetarian selection. Booking required Fri-Sun. In late July the inn hosts a beer festival with over 40 ales to sample, craft stalls and live jazz bands – please ring or visit their website for full details.

79 MEABURN B&B AND RESTAURANT

**Meaburn Hill Farmhouse, Maulds Meaburn,
Penrith, Cumbria CA10 3HN
☎ 01931 715168
e-mail: meaburnhillfarm@pentalk.org
⊕ www.cumbria-bed-breakfast.co.uk**

Meaburn B&B and Restaurant is an outstanding place. Owners Annie and Brian have a great deal of experience, and it shows: Annie was voted Landlady of the Year for the UK and Ireland by the AA in 2004. Open six nights a week, the restaurant's impressive menu boasts such delights as roast duck with damson sauce, Annie's game pie

and Michel Roux's 7-hour lamb. Ideal as a base while touring the Eden Valley, there are three comfortable and attractive en suite guest bedrooms and also a charming self-catering cottage. 4 Diamonds AA.

80 THE PENNINE HOTEL

**Market Square, Kirkby Stephen,
Cumbria CA17 4QT
☎ 01768 371382 Fax: 01768 372686**

Friendly inn open all day, every day. Real ales, real cider, home-made dishes at lunch and dinner and six comfortable guest bedrooms.

Looking for:
- *Places to Visit?*
- *Places to Stay?*
- *Places to Eat & Drink?*
- *Places to Shop?*

www.travelpublishing.co.uk

Ravenstonedale, Cumbria CA17 4NH
☎ 01539 623284
e-mail: enquiries@kings-head.net
🌐 www.kings-head.net

A traditional village inn in the best sense of the word, **The Kings Head Hotel** offers great food, drink and accommodation. Set in Ravenstonedale in an area of outstanding natural beauty in the foothills of the Eden Valley, this fine hotel has recently been completely refurbished and is now a happy mix of ancient and modern.

One of the oldest buildings in the village, the hotel began life in 1627 as three cottages, later served as the village courthouse, and was later converted to create this picture-postcard establishment owned and run by Gary and Susan Kirby. They are friendly and welcoming hosts, ably assisted by their capable, efficient staff. Other regulars include Spot the dog and three amiable resident ghosts! There are four charming and convivial public rooms, perfect for enjoying the ales and other liquid refreshment on offer, including a very good wine list. In the no-smoking restaurant, the best of traditional English home-cooking is served every lunchtime and evening.

Member of the Good Beer Guide for 2004/2005/2006, and of the Cumbria Good Beer Guide 2005/06, this fine hotel has much to recommend it. Outside, the attractive beer garden runs alongside the beck. There are three charming and comfortable en suite guest bedrooms. Handy for exploring the Eden Valley, the many sights and attractions of the region include the village itself with its ancient parish church, school and remains of a Gilbertine abbey dating back to the 13th century, horse-riding and fishing (fly and coarse), nearby Howgill fells and beautiful countryside boasting a profusion of bird life and wildflowers. Sedbergh is just 20 minutes away, while the centres of Penrith and Kendal are only 45 minutes away. Closer to home, tennis and golf are available.

82 THE GOLDEN BALL

4 High Wiend, Appleby-in-Westmorland,
Cumbria CA16 6RD
☎ 01768 351493

Superb pub dating back to the early 1600s with handsome traditional décor and friendly ambience. Real ales, great food and four guest bedrooms. Rear courtyard garden is a sun trap. Children and dogs welcome.

83 THE BAY TREE

1 Bridge Street, Appleby-in-Westmorland,
Cumbria CA16 6QH
☎ 01768 353700 Fax: 01768 353700
e-mail: info@theybaytree.biz
⊕ www.thebaytree.biz

Ground-floor showroom with crafts and gifts; upstairs there's an excellent coffee shop overlooking the river. Open Fri-Sat and Mon-Weds 10-4.30; Thurs 10-2.

84 THE CASTLE HOTEL

Main Street, Brough, Cumbria CA17 4AX
☎ 01768 341252 Fax: 01768 341775
⊕ www.castlehotelbrough.co.uk

Feature murals on the restaurant walls are just one highlight at this fine hotel with 14 tasteful rooms. Real ales and great food.

Looking for:

- *Places to Visit?*
- *Places to Stay?*
- *Places to Eat & Drink?*
- *Places to Shop?*

www.travelpublishing.co.uk

HIDDEN PLACES GUIDES

Explore Britain and Ireland with *Hidden Places* guides - a fascinating series of national and local travel guides.

Packed with easy to read information on hundreds of places of interest as well as places to stay, eat and drink.

Available from both high street and internet booksellers

For more information on the full range of *Hidden Places* guides and other titles published by Travel Publishing visit our website on

www.travelpublishing.co.uk
or ask for our leaflet by phoning **0118-981-7777** or emailing **info@travelpublishing.co.uk**

85 THE STAG INN

Dufton, Appleby-in-Westmorland,
Cumbria CA16 6DB
☎ 01768 351608

Outstanding country inn with 3-4 real ales including one from local Tirril Brewery and a varied selection of dishes. Cosy cottage adjacent.

86 THE KINGS ARMS HOTEL

Temple Sowerby, Penrith,
Cumbria CA10 1SB
☎ 01768 361211
⊕ www.kingsarmshoteltemplesowerby.com

Real ales, bar and restaurant menus, ten guest bedrooms in a spacious and handsome traditional pub/hotel with a relaxed and welcoming atmosphere.

87 BRIDGE END INN

**Main Street, Kirkby Thore, Penrith,
Cumbria CA10 1UZ
☎ 01768 362180 Fax: 01768 363772**

Adjacent to the main A66 in Kirkby Thore, **Bridge End Inn** is a distinctive and impressive establishment serving up great food, drink and hospitality. There is one changing guest ale available together with a good selection of lagers, cider, stout, wines, spirits and soft drinks – something to slake every thirst. Afternoon teas are also available.

The décor is traditional throughout, with traditional features such as the open fireplace and large casement windows letting in plenty of light on fine days.

Food is served every day from midday until 8.30 p.m. (and until 10 p.m. during the summer months). Guests choose off the menu or specials board from a good and varied range of dishes, most of them home-made. Owner Paul Coward is also the chef, and he's a past master at creating delicious snacks and meals. The inn is well placed for exploring the many sights and attractions of the region. Please ring for details.

88 BRIEF ENCOUNTER

**Langwathby Station, Penrith,
Cumbria CA10 1NB
☎ 01768 881902 Fax: 01228 631501
e-mail: geeedgar@aol.com
🌐 www.briefencounterlangwathby.co.uk**

Langwathby Station on the famous Settle-Carlisle line is home to **Brief Encounter** café and restaurant, housed in the beautifully restored station building on the north platform which retains all the elegance of a bygone era.

Open for morning coffee, light lunches, afternoon tea and Sunday lunch, as

well as evening dinner parties by prior arrangement, this charming establishment is open seven days a week March to October, 9-5, and Tues-Sun in November and December, 10-4. Owners Gordon and Elsie Edgar personally run this popular place.

171

89 THE HIGHLAND DROVE INN

**Great Salkeld, Penrith,
Cumbria CA11 9NA
☎ 01768 898349 Fax: 01768 898708
e-mail: highlanddroveinn@btinternet.com
⊕ www.highland-drove.co.uk**

Father-and-son team Donald and Paul Newton have been welcoming visitors to **The Highland Drove Inn** since 1998. The inn has been providing hospitality for over 200 years, and the Newtons continue this tradition in great style. There are three real ales – John Smiths Cask,

Theakstons Black Bull and a changing guest ale – while in the superb Kyloes Restaurant the dishes range from fish, charcuterie and meze plates to Peking duck, snapper with a risotto cake and Moroccan-style chicken. Five comfortable and attractive guest bedrooms are available.

90 THE JOINERS ARMS

**Townfoot, Lazonby, Penrith,
Cumbria CA10 1BL
☎ 01768 898728**

Dating back to the 1700s, **The Joiners Arms** began life as a cottage, later becoming an alehouse. Owners Terry and Marlene, who bought the inn in 2004, have completely refurbished the inn to the highest standard of comfort and quality. Theakstons Best and a brew from the Cumbrian Hesket Newmarket Brewery are the regular ales here, and tasty food is

served at lunch Weds-Sun and every evening 6-9. Marlene does the cooking, using only the freshest local produce to create a range of excellent dishes. The inn also offers one letting room with bath, available all year round.

91 THE FOX INN

**Ousby, Penrith, Cumbria CA10 1QA
☎ 01768 881374**

Situated in the picturesque village of Ousby, found some two-and-a-half miles off the A686 after the turn-off between Langwathby and Melmerby, **The Fox Inn** dates back to 1790. Owned and run by Sid and Katy Hughes, this Free House serves two real ales, one from the local Tirril brewery and a changing guest ale. Excellent food is served every evening from 6 until

9 p.m. and at Sunday lunchtime (12-2). Guests choose from the menu or specials board from a range of tempting traditional home-made dishes making use of the freshest local produce. To the rear of the inn there's a privately-owned static caravan park set in two acres with room for up to 39 caravans. To the front, across the road, there's a caravan and camping park with toilet block. The owners also run the Country Coffee Shop in Prince's Road, Penrith, and an outside catering service.

92 THE MINERS ARMS

Nenthead, Alston, Cumbria CA9 3PF
☎ 01434 381427
e-mail: minersarms@cybermoor.org.uk
🌐 www.nenthead.com

The Miners Arms dates to the mid-18th century and is a popular stop along the Coast-to-Coast cycle route and the Pennine Way. Open all day, every day from May to September, and every session the rest of the year, there are good ales (Black Sheep plus a changing guest ale) and quality food served at lunch and dinner. Alison is a superb cook, having published her own recipe book, and among the

home-made dishes to enjoy is her famous Alston Pie. This fine establishment also boasts a cosy and comfortable guest bedroom and, adjacent to the inn, a luxurious bunkhouse sleeping 12 and available all year round.

93 THE NEAR BOOT INN

Whiteclosegate, Tarraby, Carlisle, Cumbria CA3 0JA
☎ 01228 540100
e-mail: rob877y@aol.com

Four to six real ales and excellent food served at lunch and dinner Tues-Sun and Bank Hol Mondays. Booking advised at weekends.

94 THE SHIP INN

Church Lane, Thursby, Carlisle, Cumbria CA5 6PE
☎ 01228 710600

Family-run early 19th-century pub open every session and all day at weekends for great food, real ale and warm hospitality. Booking advised for evening meal.

VISIT THE TRAVEL PUBLISHING WEBSITE

Looking for:

- *Places to Visit?*
- *Places to Stay?*
- *Places to Eat & Drink?*
- *Places to Shop?*

Then why not visit the Travel Publishing website...

- Informative pages on places to visit, stay, eat, drink and shop throughout the British Isles.

- Detailed information on Travel Publishing's wide range of national and regional travel guides.

www.travelpublishing.co.uk

95 CROSBY LODGE COUNTRY HOUSE HOTEL & RESTAURANT

High Crosby, Crosby-on-Eden, Carlisle,
Cumbria CA6 4QZ
☎ 01228 573618 Fax: 01228 573428
e-mail: enquiries@crosbylodge.co.uk
🌐 www.crosbylodge.co.uk

Situated close the Hadrian's Wall, the newly refurbished **Crosby Lodge Country House Hotel & Restaurant** is a beautiful and tranquil retreat offering excellent food and accommodation. Gracious and elegant in every quarter, the lodge is decorated and furnished in the finest Georgian style, and this romantic mansion just five minutes from the M6 and near the many sights and attractions of Carlisle and the surrounding region is perfect as a base while exploring the Lake District, the Scottish borders and of course, Hadrian's Wall itself.

Chef Roger Herring has been here nearly 30 years, presiding over the renowned restaurant. His experience and shows in the varied range of expertly prepared dishes served at lunch and dinner, and the lodge can also host weddings (holding a civil licence) and other celebrations as well as business entertaining or conferences. The best of the freshest locally-sourced ingredients are used to create memorable dishes. In the grounds, the walled garden has been restored and there's also an attractive gazebo. Each of the 11 en suite guest bedrooms has been individually designed and furnished with taste and style.

96 FARLAM HALL HOTEL

Brampton, Cumbria CA8 2NG
☎ 01697 746234 Fax: 01697 746683
e-mail: farmlamhall@dial.pipex.com
🌐 www.farmlamhall.co.uk

One of the finest country house hotels in the country, **Farlam Hall** is a gracious and elegant establishment. Lavishly furnished with antiques, it is a real retreat, perfect for unwinding. Parts of the premises date to the 17th century, with Victorian additions. It is set in 12 acres of outstanding grounds, with landscaped gardens, an ornamental lake and stream.

Many leading guides nominate Farlam Hall as the most highly rated country house hotel in the region. Family run by the Quinion and Stevenson families, there are 12 beautiful and supremely comfortable en suite guest bedrooms. Two are on the ground floor, and one has a glorious four-poster bed. Most visitors plump for the dinner, bed and breakfast option, so that they can take advantage not just of the hearty and delicious breakfasts but

also the superb freshly-made dishes served at the evening meal. Non-residents can also dine here, but booking is essential at this superb and distinguished place.

97 THE CROWN INN RESTAURANT ‖

Broadfield, Southwaite, Carlisle,
Cumbria CA4 0PT
☎ 016974 73467
e-mail: crowninnrestaurant@i12.com
⊕ www.crowninnrestaurant.co.uk

Just a stone's throw from the M6 motorway
and two miles from Southwaite, **The Crown
Inn Restaurant** is an excellent Free House
with a superb menu of tempting dishes.
Owners Nick and Marie Pinnell have been
here since
2003. Nick
has been a
chef for 10
years –
experience
that shows
in the
delicious

meals he creates at lunch and dinner. The
selection of starters and main courses take
their inspiration from world cuisine, and
make use of only the freshest locally-sourced
ingredients. Closed Monday and Wednesday
lunchtime and all day Tuesday.

98 THE HOPE AND ANCHOR INN ‖

Port Carlisle, Cumbria CA7 5BU
☎ 01697 351460

Pristine inn with two real ales, excellent food
– lamb Henry, fish &
chips and more – and
attractive
accommodation, in
stunning location
overlooking the
Solway Firth.

99 THE CAPON TREE ‖

27 Front Street, Brampton,
Cumbria CA8 1NG
☎ 01697 73649

The freshest locally-
sourced produce is used
in the delicious dishes –
rolls, sandwiches, soups,
salads, scones, cakes and
more – served 9.15-4.30
Mon-Sat.

100 KIRKSTYLE INN ‖

Knarsdale, Brampton,
Northumbria CA8 7PB
☎ 01434 381559
e-mail: davidanddebbie@kirkstyle.com
⊕ www.kirkstyle.com

The **Kirkstyle Inn** is situated just off the
A689 between Alston and Brampton with
picturesque countryside in every direction.
Owners David and Debbie Lister are
welcoming hosts who offer all their guests
great food and ales. The two real ales are
Yates, a local Cumbrian brew, and a changing
guest ale. Debbie is a superb cook and the
majority of dishes are home-made using
locally-sourced produce. Food is served
12.30-2.30 and 6.30-8.30 p.m. (closed
Tuesday lunch in summer, Tues-Thurs
lunchtime
Oct-May).
Booking
required for
Sunday
lunch and
Wednesday
evenings.

101 SAMSON INN ‖

Gilsland, Brampton, Carlisle,
Cumbria CA8 7DR
☎ 01697 747220

Beautiful early 18th-
century Free House open
all day, every day for ales,
great food (noon-9 p.m.)
and comfortable
accommodation. Booking
required at weekends.

Accommodation in Cumbria

The accommodation featured in this section includes hotels, inns, guest houses, bed & breakfasts and self catered establishments. Each establishment has an entry number which is used to identify its location on the map below and its name and short address in the list below the map. The entry number can also be used to find more information and contact details for the accommodation in the ensuing pages. In addition full details of all this accommodation may be found on the Travel Publishing website - www.travelpublishing.co.uk. This website has a comprehensive database of accommodation covering the whole of Britain and Ireland.

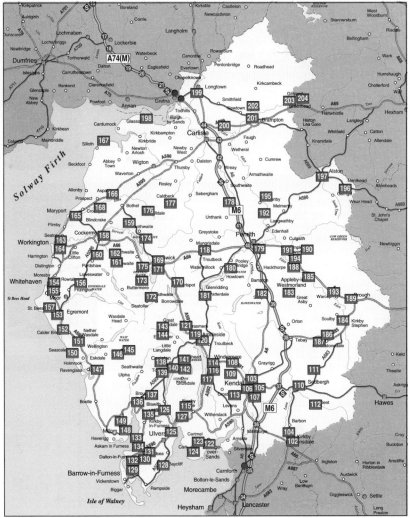

ACCOMMODATION

102	The Kings Arms, Kirkby Lonsdale	153	The Red Lion Hotel, Egremont
103	Sundial Guest House, Kendal	154	Cap'n Sennys, Whitehaven
104	The Pheasant Inn, Casterton	155	Glenfield Guest House, Whitehaven
105	The New Inn, Kendal	156	The Stork Hotel, Rowrah
106	The Black Swan, Kendal	157	Manor House Hotel & Coast-to-Coast Bar, St Bees
107	The Garden House Hotel & Restaurant, Kendal	158	Rook Guest House, Cockermouth
108	Brunt Knoll Farm Holiday Cottages, Staveley	159	Irton House Farm, Isel
109	Mitchelland House, Crook	160	The Howe, Mosser
110	The Bull Hotel, Sedbergh	161	New House Farm, Lorton
111	The Cross Keys Temperance Inn, Cautley	162	The Old Vicarage, Lorton
112	Stone Close Tea Room & Guest House, Dent	163	The Westlands Hotel, Workington
113	The Wheatsheaf at Brigsteer, Brigsteer	164	Green Dragon Hotel, Workington
114	May Cottage, Bowness-on-Windermere	165	Riverside B&B, Maryport
115	Trundle Brow Cottage, Brow Edge	166	The Grapes Hotel, Aspatria
116	Packway House, Bowness-on-Windermere	167	The Skinburness Leisure Hotel, Skinburness
117	The Mariners Inn, Bowness-on-Windermere	168	The Masons Arms, Gilcrux
118	Greenah Crag, Troutbeck	169	Brookfield Guest House, Keswick
119	Glen Rothay Hotel & Badger Bar, Rydal	170	Stybeck Farm, Thirlmere
120	Cottages on the Green, Ambleside	171	Grassmoor Guest House, Keswick
121	Dale Lodge Hotel, Grasmere	172	Hazel Bank Country House, Borrowdale
122	Blackrock Holiday Flats, Grange-over-Sands	173	Littletown Farm, Newlands
123	Prior's Yeat, Cartmel	174	Ravenstone Lodge, Bassenthwaite
124	The Hope and Anchor, Flookburgh	175	Braithwaite Farm, Braithwaite
125	The Armadale Country Restaurant & Hotel, Ulverston	176	Ponderosa Guest House, Uldale
126	The Red Lion Inn, Lowick Bridge	177	Swaledale Watch, Caldbeck
127	Crook Farm, Haverthwaite	178	The Globe Inn, Calthwaite
128	The Farmers Arms, Baycliff	179	Hornby Hall, Brougham
129	The Rams Head Hotel, Barrow-in-Furness	180	Park Foot Caravan and Camping Park, Pooley Bridge
130	Chequers Hotel & Restaurant, Dalton-in-Furness	181	Old Water View, Patterdale
131	Clarence House Country Hotel and Restaurant, Skelgate	182	The Hermitage, Shap
132	The Red Lion Inn, Dalton-in-Furness	183	Meaburn B&B and Restaurant, Maulds Meaburn
133	The Askam Hotel, Askam-in-Furness	184	The Pennine Hotel, Kirkby Stephen
134	Furness Tavern, Askam-in-Furness	185	The Golden Ball, Appleby-in-Westmorland
135	The Greyhound Inn, Grizebeck	186	The Kings Head Hotel, Ravenstonedale
136	The Bakehouse, Broughton-in-Furness	187	Stouphill Gate, Ravenstonedale
137	Ring House Cottages, Woodland	188	Tarka House, Bolton
138	The Crown Hotel, Coniston	189	The Castle Hotel, Brough
139	The Sun Hotel, Coniston	190	Milburn Grange, Knock
140	The Coppermines and Lakes Cottages, Coniston	191	The Kings Arms Hotel, Temple Sowerby
141	Esthwaite Old Hall, Hawkshead	192	The Highland Drove Inn, Great Salkeld
142	Borwick Fold, Outgate	193	Haybergill Centre, Warcop
143	The Old Dungeon Ghyll Hotel, Great Langdale	194	Bridge End Inn, Kirkby Thore
144	Millbeck Farm and Side House Farm & Cottage, Great Langdale	195	Howscales, Kirkoswald
145	Stanley Ghyll House, Boot	196	The Miners Arms, Nenthead
146	Brook House Inn & Restaurant, Boot	197	Lowbyer Manor Country House, Alston
147	Brown Cow Inn, Waberthwaite	198	The Hope and Anchor Inn, Port Carlisle
148	Cambridge House Hotel, Millom	199	Home From Home, Longtown
149	Underwood Country Guest House, Millom	200	Crosby Lodge Country House Hotel & Restaurant, Crosby-on-Eden
150	Westcliff Hotel, Seascale	201	Farlam Hall Hotel, Brampton
151	Westlakes Hotel, Gosforth	202	Walton High Rigg Farm, Walton
152	White Mare, Beckermet	203	Samson Inn, Gilsland
		204	Holmhead Guest House, Greenhead

177

102 THE KINGS ARMS

7 Market, Kirkby Lonsdale,
Cumbria LA6 2AU
☎ 01524 271220
e-mail: bougourdj36@aol.com

The Kings Arms is a venerable inn whose
history is linked with that of Kirkby Lonsdale
itself. In 1558 the manor was sold to Thomas
Carus, who built
the manor hall that
is today this fine
inn. It has been
tastefully
refurbished over
the years, but some
original features –
such as the fine
fireplace – remain.
Tenants David and
Judith have well
over 20 years'
experience in the
trade, and offer
real ales and great
food every day. Adjacent there are three
cottages available for B&B or room-only
accommodation.

103 SUNDIAL GUEST HOUSE

51 Milnthorpe Road, Kendal,
Cumbria LA9 5QG
☎ 01539 724468
e-mail:
info@sundialguesthousekendal.co.uk
🌐 www.sundialguesthousekendal.co.uk

Situated on the main approach road into
Kendal after leaving the M6 (Junction 36),
Sundial Guest House is a top-of-the-range
establishment built in 1877 and owned and
run by local couple Sue and Andrew McLeod.
This impressive property offers six superb
guest bedrooms on
three floors, including
one ground-floor
room. Making an
excellent touring base,
with plenty of off-
road parking for
guests, you can stay on
a B&B or room-only
basis. Packed lunches
available by
arrangement. Children
welcome. No smoking.

104 THE PHEASANT INN

Casterton, Kirkby Lonsdale,
Cumbria LA6 2RX
☎ 01524 271230 Fax: 01524 274267
e-mail: pheasantinn@fsbdial.co.uk
🌐 www.pheasantinn.co.uk

Just a short drive or walk from Kirkby
Lonsdale on the A683, **The Pheasant Inn** at
Casterton dates to the 18th century, and is
owned and run by the Dixon family, a local
farming family. The Inn boasts a superb bar
area, with three real ales – Theakstons Best,
Cod Cask and a rotating guest ale. Quality

food is available daily at lunch (12-2) and dinner (6-9).
The no-smoking restaurant seats 50. Booking is
essential on Saturday evening and Sunday lunchtime.
Guests choose from the menu or specials board from a
varied menu of fine English dishes.

The Inn offers 10 quality en suite rooms, available
all year round. Two of the rooms are on the ground
floor; one of these is suitable for people with
disabilities. An ideal place to stay and use as a base
while visiting this lovely area, it is also a short drive to
North Yorkshire and close to the Settle-Carlisle
Railway. Children welcome.

105 THE NEW INN

98 High Gate, Kendal,
Cumbria LA9 4HE
☎ 01539 722484 Fax: 01539 738088
e-mail: farrelldrwer@ktdinternet.com

A former coaching inn dating back to the early 18th century, **The New Inn** stands on Kendal's main thoroughfare. Popular with locals and visitors alike, this convivial and attractive inn offers great food, drink and accommodation. Open all day, every day for ale, with one real ale and a good selection of keg bitters, lagers, wines, and spirits, food is served at

lunch and dinner. Guests choose from a wide range of tempting dishes such as filled Yorkshire puddings, home-made steak and ale pie and home-made chilli. Thursday night is Steak Night – booking advised. The four comfortable guest rooms are available all year round.

106 THE BLACK SWAN

8 Allhollows Lane, Kendal,
Cumbria LA9 4JH
☎ 01539 724278

The Black Swan dates back to the early 1700s. Three real ales from the Jennings Brewery are available, together with excellent home-made meals. Four good-sized guest rooms are available all year round.

Explore Britain and Ireland with *Hidden Places* guides - a fascinating series of national and local travel guides.

www.travelpublishing.co.uk

0118-981-7777

info@travelpublishing.co.uk

107 THE GARDEN HOUSE HOTEL & RESTAURANT

Fowl Ing Lane, Kendal, Cumbria LA9 6PH
☎ 01539 731131 Fax: 01539 740064
e-mail: gardenhousehotel@btinternet.com
🌐 www.gardenhousehotel.co.uk

The Garden House Hotel and Restaurant in Kendal is a charming and tasteful establishment run by Warwick and Shelley McKiever, who have many years' experience in the trade. Before this they ran luxury safari lodges in South Africa. They have undertaken a complete refurbishment. So far, the handsome bar and restaurant downstairs have

been tastefully transformed to offer the perfect place to enjoy a relaxing drink or meal.

The bar area is very cosy and welcoming. The restaurant is open by prior arrangement at lunch, and Monday to Saturday evenings (from 6.30 to last orders at 8.30) for residents and non-residents. Booking essential for

non-residents. Each of the 11 en suite bedrooms is also due to undergo individual renovation. Open all year round and set in its own grounds, the hotel boasts a good choice of bedrooms of different sizes – one on the ground floor. Even before their refurbishment they offer a high standard of comfort and quality. Guests can stay on a bed-and-breakfast or bed, breakfast and dinner basis. Children welcome.

108 BRUNT KNOTT FARM HOLIDAY COTTAGES

Staveley, Kendal, Cumbria LA8 9QX
☎ 01539 821030 Fax: 01539 822680
e-mail: margaret@bruntknott.demon.co.uk
🌐 www.bruntknott.demon.co.uk

Surrounded by hundreds of miles of scenic countryside, **Brunt Knott Farm Holiday Cottages** comprise four beautiful self-catering cottages sleeping between two and five guests. Rated 3 Stars by the English Tourist Board, these former farm buildings have been tastefully refurbished, and each traditional

stonebuilt cottage commands wonderful views of Lakeland fells. Weekly bookings in season, while between November and Easter shorter breaks are available: three nights over the weekend and four nights mid-week. The facilities include a separate laundry room.

109 MITCHELLAND HOUSE

Crook, nr Kendal, Cumbria LA8 8LL
☎ 015394 48589
e-mail: marie.mitchelland@talk21.com

Set in seven acres of beautiful countryside with scenic views in all directions, **Mitchelland House** is a listed building dating back in parts to 1681. There are three spacious and attractive guest bedrooms.

Charming and full of character, the many extras available here include stabling and paddocks,

and free use of mountain bikes, maps and information. Packed lunches and flask-filling provided on arrangement. 4 Diamonds ETC. Reached via the A591 (off J36 of the M6) towards Windermere, then the B5284 (signposted Hawkshead and Ferry), turning left after 4 miles and taking the country road to reach the second house on the right.

110 THE BULL HOTEL

Main Street, Sedbergh, Cumbria LA10 5BL
☎ 01539 620264 Fax: 01539 620212
e-mail: info@bull-hotel.com
🌐 www.bull-hotel.com

The excellent **Bull Hotel** boasts real ales, hearty food and superb accommodation. Open all day, every day for ale, there are four in summer and two in winter, the regular being Black Sheep. Most of the dishes on the menu and specials board are home-made, and served every evening 6-9 and Weds-Sun lunchtime (12-2.30). Booking is advised for Friday and Saturday evening. Specialities include lamb and Lakeland steaks. Accommodation is available all year round with 15 comfortable and welcoming en suite guest bedrooms, rated 4 Diamonds by the ETC. Guests can stay on a bed-and-breakfast or bed, breakfast and dinner basis.

111 THE CROSS KEYS TEMPERANCE INN

Cautley, nr Sedbergh, Cumbria LA10 5NE
☎ 01539 620284
e-mail: clowes@freeuk.com
🌐 www.cautleyspout.co.uk

An alcohol-free zone – though guests are welcome to bring their own. Charming tea rooms, restaurant and two guest rooms.

112 STONE CLOSE TEA ROOM & GUEST HOUSE

Main Street, Dent, Sedbergh, Cumbria LA10 5QL
☎ 01539 625231
e-mail: stoneclose@btinternet.com
🌐 www.dentdale.com

A lovely traditional tea room, serving light lunches, cakes, teas and coffees. Three excellent bed-and-breakfast rooms available.

113 THE WHEATSHEAF AT BRIGSTEER

Brigsteer, Kendal, Cumbria LA8 8AN
☎ 01539 568254
e-mail: email@brigsteer.gb.com
🌐 www.brigsteer.gb.com

Great food expertly prepared is the *raison d'etre* of **The Wheatsheaf at Brigsteer**, a superb restaurant and inn hidden away in the tranquil and picturesque village of Brigsteer, just three miles from Kendal found either west off the A591 or north of the A590 via the village of Levens. It's also just a short drive from Junction 36 of the M6. Parts of

the premises date back to 1762, and began life as three cottages plus a 'shoe-ing' room for horses. It then became an alehouse and was licensed back in the early 1800s.

Tasteful and handsome throughout, this welcoming inn has attractive and comfortable furnishings and décor. Ale is served at lunchtime and evening, and includes regular Cumbrian Ales along with two rotating guest ales. The bar menu offers an excellent choice of soups, salads, sandwiches and tasty hot dishes and is served Monday to Saturday lunchtime.

The restaurant, which seats 50, serves lunch (12-2pm) and dinner (6pm-9pm) daily. The mouthwatering choices included on the truly impressive menu use locally-sourced produce whenever possible and there is an excellent selection of wines to accompany your meal. Booking is required at all times to avoid disappointment.

This fine inn also boasts four excellent double en suite guest bedrooms. All have superb facilities and the tariff includes a

hearty breakfast. The Wheatsheaf provides private off road parking and has outside seating for sunny days.

Being centrally located yet peaceful and relaxed, the village makes the perfect base from which to explore the many sights and attractions of the region. Children welcome. No smoking throughout.

114 MAY COTTAGE

Kendal Road, Bowness-on-Windermere,
Cumbria LA23 3EW
☎ 01539 446478 Mobile: 07793 056322
e-mail: kc@may-cottage.com

Lake? Restaurants? Shops?
- All close! Parking; Clean,
light, comfortable, en-suite
rooms; Hearty breakfasts;
Leisure Facilities. (You'll
know you've made the
right decision).

115 TRUNDLE BROW COTTAGE

Brow Edge, Newby Bridge,
Cumbria LA12 8QT
☎ 01539 531941
e-mail: dandsdean@tinyworld.co.uk
🌐 www.trundlebrow.co.uk

Outstanding property
dating back over 300
years, two attractive and
comfortable guest
bedrooms amid
spectacular countryside.

116 PACKWAY HOUSE

Stuart & Mary Robinson
Crook Road, Bowness-on-Windermere,
Cumbria LA23 3NE
☎ 01539 443532

In a scenic location just a short walk from the
centre of Bowness, **Packway House** is the
ideal place to relax and unwind. Set in two
acres of stunning grounds which include a
stream, woodland where wildlife roam free,
there are 5 spacious and attractive apartments
available all year round. Children welcome.
Each apartment takes its names from a nearby
fell, and command open views. Sleeping
between two and six people, there's an
apartment to suit every taste and budget here.

117 THE MARINERS INN

Lake Road, Bowness-on-Windermere,
Cumbria LA23 3AP
☎ 01539 445678 Fax: 01539 444078
e-mail: steve@mariners-inn.co.uk
🌐 www.mariners-inn.co.uk

The Mariners Inn began life in the late 1700s as
the home of a wealthy local merchant. Over the
course of its life it has fulfilled many roles,
including that of ironmongers, fish and chip shop
and, of course, a licensed inn. With leaseholders
Steve and Helen at the helm, it welcomes visitors
all day, every day for drinks which include three real ales (four in summer), all from the local
Jennings Brewery – Jennings Bitter and Jennings
Cumberland Ale are the regulars – together with a good
range of draught and bottled beers, lagers, stout, cider,
wines, spirits and soft drinks.

The bar
has recently
been
refurbished
and is a
happy mix
of traditional
and modern
comforts, the
walls adorned with nautical memorabilia. The Mariners
is also an excellent choice for accommodation, with
eight attractive and comfortable en suite guest
bedrooms – six doubles and two family rooms. The
tariff includes a hearty English breakfast.

118 GREENAH CRAG

Troutbeck, Penrith, Cumbria CA11 0SQ
☎ 01768 483233
e-mail: stay@greenahcrag.co.uk
🌐 www.greenahcrag.co.uk

B&B in beautiful old farmhouse plus self-catering cottage amid superb countryside. B&B available Feb-Nov.

119 GLEN ROTHAY HOTEL & BADGER BAR

Rydal, Ambleside, Cumbria LA22 9LR
☎ 01539 434500
e-mail: JhPckrng9@aol.com
🌐 www.theglenrothay.com

Grade II listed 17th-century coaching inn. Excellent menu using Cumbrian produce. Eight en suite bedrooms available all year round.

120 COTTAGES ON THE GREEN

The Haven, The Green, Ambleside, Cumbria LA22 9AU
☎ 015394 32441
e-mail:
twosparrows@havengreen.fsbusiness.co.uk
🌐 www.havengreen.fsbusiness.co.uk

Located in a tranquil part of Ambleside, close to the town centre yet in a secluded position in the original old part of town, **Cottages on the Green** offer three self-catering cottages part of a late 19th-century terrace. Rocklea, Sunnydene and Wilwyn cottages sleep four and are fully equipped to make your stay comfortable and enjoyable, with full kitchen facilities, lounge and dining area. All cottages share a lovely garden looking onto Loughrigg Fell. Available all year round.

HIDDEN PLACES GUIDES

Explore Britain and Ireland with *Hidden Places* guides - a fascinating series of national and local travel guides.

Packed with easy to read information on hundreds of places of interest as well as places to stay, eat and drink.

Available from both high street and internet booksellers

For more information on the full range of *Hidden Places* guides and other titles published by Travel Publishing visit our website on

www.travelpublishing.co.uk
or ask for our leaflet by phoning **0118-981-7777** or emailing **info@travelpublishing.co.uk**

THE HIDDEN PLACES OF
DORSET, HAMPSHIRE AND ISLE OF WIGHT

THE HIDDEN PLACES OF
THE LAKE DISTRICT AND CUMBRIA

THE HIDDEN PLACES OF
NORTHUMBERLAND AND DURHAM

EXPLORE

121 DALE LODGE HOTEL

Grasmere, Cumbria LA22 9SW
☎ 01539 435300 Fax: 01539 435570
e-mail: enquiries@dalelodgehotel.co.uk
🌐 www.dalelodgehotel.co.uk

Taste and elegance are the hallmarks of **Dale Lodge Hotel**. Graciously appointed in every quarter, the Lodge is surrounded by stunning scenery and is set in the heart of Grasmere in three-and-a-half acres of its own beautiful, well-tended gardens. It's the perfect location for a relaxing break, a family holiday or for weddings and other celebrations.

This is a family-owned and –run establishment, owned by Brian and Gillian Roberts, whose son James is Head Chef while son Alexander manages the bar. Dating back to 1840, the hotel has undergone extensive and tasteful refurbishment. Tweedies Bar and Restaurant is open all day, every day, with meals served at lunch (12-3pm) and dinner (6-9 p.m.). Warm woods and flagstone floors add to the traditional and comfortable ambience. Outside there's a spacious and attractive beer garden. In Tweedies Bar there are five real ales on tap: Timothy Taylor Landlord is the mainstay, with four changing guest ales. Winner of a CAMRA award, the beers are well-kept and tasty.

The Lodge restaurant, in the main hotel building, serves fine cuisine 7 days a week that will please every palate. Head Chef James has worked alongside the likes of Raymond Blanc, and his experience shows in every dish. The wine cellar is distinctive, while the menu includes delicious and expertly prepared starters and main courses such as home-made country paté, warm Jersey salad, roasted rack of lamb, duck confit, fillet steak, monkfish and the pasta du jour. The daily dessert menu offers a selection of mouth-watering choices. Booking is advised at all times, but is essential for the traditional Sunday roast lunch (served 12-4pm).

Each of the 14 en suite guest bedrooms is individually styled, beautifully appointed and decorated to a high standard of comfort and quality. For guests with disabilities, the hotel offers excellent access to the hotel, restaurant and Tweedies, and there is a guest room on the ground floor with first-class facilities. Guests can stay on a room-only, B&B or Dinner and B&B basis off-season, while during the high season all rooms are offered on a Dinner and B&B basis. This superb hotel is open all year round. Off-road parking within the grounds. Late availability for B&B on request.

122 BLACKROCK HOLIDAY FLATS

Morecambe Bank, Grange-over-Sands,
Cumbria LA11 6DX
☎ 01539 534107 Daytime: 01539 532836

In the heart of Grange-over-Sands, facing
Morecambe Bay and just a few minutes' walk
from the shops, gardens and promenade,
Blackrock Holiday Flats are three self-
catering accommodation units. From the
balcony of Dolphin Cottage there are superb
views over the Bay, and

Black Rock
flat No 1
also has
excellent
views. Just
a few steps
outside
Black Rock
flat No 2,

which is on the ground floor, brings you
alongside the Bay. All three are cosy and
comfortable, have private parking and sleep
two. They are available all year round, for
weekly booking in season and shorter breaks
(3 nights or more) out of season.

123 PRIOR'S YEAT

Aynsome Road, Cartmel, Grange-over-
Sands, Cumbria LA11 6PR
☎ 01539 535178
e-mail: priorsyeat@hotmail.com
⊕ www.priorsyeat.co.uk

Three en suite rooms rated 4 Diamonds by
the ETC in charming
Edwardian home. Fantastic
breakfasts - kedgeree,
scrambled egg with smoked
salmon or vegetarian choice.

124 THE HOPE AND ANCHOR

11 Market Street, Flookburgh,
Cumbria LA11 7JU
☎ 01539 558733 Fax: 01539 559003
e-mail: hopeandanchor@colowebworld.co.uk

Run by Gill Gardner, ably assisted by her
daughters Katie and Verity, **The Hope and
Anchor** is a welcoming and friendly public
house with great food, drink and
accommodation. Gill has been in the licensing
trade for over 25 years and is a superb cook.
The interior of this fine pub is rich in warm
woods and comfortable seating, while outside
there's a well-tended beer garden.

Open all day, every day for ale, there are always two to three real ales available. Hartleys XB is

the regular here, together with changing guest ales. Food is
served Tues-Fri 12-3 and 5-8.30, Sat-Sun 12-8.30. Guests
choose from the menu or specials board from a range of
hearty traditional dishes such as Westmorland steak meat
pie, Cumberland sausage, home-made pork and apricot
casserole, Flookburgh Fluke and roasted vegetable lasagne.
The inn also boasts five comfortable and cosy en suite
guest bedrooms on a room-only or bed-and-breakfast
basis. Children welcome. Live entertainment second
Saturday of each month from 8.30 p.m.

125 THE ARMADALE COUNTRY RESTAURANT & HOTEL

Arrad Foot, Ulverston, Cumbria LA12 7SL
☎ 01229 861257 Fax: 01229 861733
🌐 www.thearmadale.co.uk

Elegant and pretty as a picture, **The Armadale Country Restaurant and Hotel** is set in its own grounds and can be found just off the A590 between Ulverston and Greenodd. Excellent fresh local food is served Tues to Sun (weekend booking required)

in the restaurant. The house began life as a quiet retreat for a local cotton mill owner, and boasts en suite rooms and a family suite, each of which has its own motel-style private entrance. Tastefully decorated and furnished, they make an excellent, great value base for touring the Lakes.

128 THE FARMERS ARMS

Main Road, Baycliff, Ulverston, Cumbria LA12 9RP
☎ 01229 869382 Mobile: 07713 621471
🌐 www.farmersarmsbaycliff.co.uk

The Farmers Arms in Baycliff is a superior village inn, traditional and welcoming. Found just off the coastal A5087 southeast of Ulverston, it's just a short walk from the sands at Morecambe Bay. Popular with walkers, bird-watchers and anyone in search of

a good pint or meal, the real ales here are Hartleys XB and a changing guest ale, while the menu offers a good range of hearty favourites expertly prepared. This fine inn also boasts two excellent letting rooms, available all year round.

126 THE RED LION INN

Lowick Bridge, nr Ulverston, Cumbria LA12 8EF
☎ 01229 885366

Three real ales, an excellent menu and two comfortable guest bedrooms mark out **The Red Lion Inn** as a cut above the rest. The attractive beer garden overlooks the Old Man of Coniston.

127 CROOK FARM

Bouth, Haverthwaite, Ulverston, Cumbria LA12 8JL
☎ 01229 861481 Fax: 01539 861768

Set in 126 acres of scenic countryside, **Crook Farm** is a traditional farmhouse offering superb accommodation in two en suite bedrooms. There is also a luxury static caravan on site.

129 THE RAMS HEAD HOTEL

110 Rawlinson Street, Barrow-in-Furness, Cumbria LA14 2DG
☎ 01229 821728

A large and imposing late-Victorian inn on a corner site an easy walk from the town centre, **The Rams Head Hotel**'s location and reputation make it popular with visitors and locals alike, and the inn always has a friendly atmosphere. Open all day everyday, there's one changing guest ale together with a good range of wines, spirits, lagers and soft

drinks, and a selection of hot and cold snacks served throughout the day. There are also seven comfortable guest bedrooms, available all year round.

130 CHEQUERS HOTEL & RESTAURANT

10 Abbey Road, Dalton-in-Furness,
Cumbria LA15 8LF
☎ 01229 462124 Fax: 01229 464624
e-mail: chequers@chequers-hotel.co.uk
🌐 www.chequers-hotel.co.uk

Set adjacent to the Castle in Dalton-in-Furness, **Chequers Hotel and Restaurant** is a distinguished and distinctive place offering the highest standard of comfort and quality, Dating back to late-Victorian days, this privately owned hotel began life as a school, and is located on the edge of the Lake District, just a 20-minute drive from Lake Windermere. Now fully renovated, it offers the best in modern comforts while retaining its traditional charm.

Family-run by the Benn family since 1988, the hotel has a well-deserved reputation as one of the finest places to stay in the southern Lakes. The accommodation is nothing short of superb, with 25 en suite guest bedrooms that are tastefully appointed to provide every comfort and convenience. Eight rooms are on the ground floor; one is fully equipped to meet the needs of guests with disabilities. No expense has been spared in creating these guest rooms – each is individually decorated and furnished with taste and style.

In the bar, the friendly, helpful staff serve up a range of real ales, all from the Thwaites Brewery, together with a good selection of lagers, cider, stout, wines, spirits (including over 60 malt whiskies) and soft drinks. Renowned for the excellent food, served Wednesday to Saturday from 12 – 2 and 4 – 9.30, Sundays 11.30 – 9.30, booking is required at all times. The menus and specials board boast a variety of tempting

dishes, all using the freshest local ingredients in season.

Making an excellent touring base, this fine hotel is within easy reach of Barrow Dock Museum, Bowness, Coniston Water, Furness Abbey, Holker Hall, Swarthmoor Hall, Gleaston Water Mill and Piel Castle, among the many other sights and attractions of the region, and is particularly suited for walkers and bird-watchers, being near Walney Bird Observatory and Muncaster Castle (the latter the home of the World Owl Centre).

131 CLARENCE HOUSE COUNTRY HOTEL AND RESTAURANT

Skelgate, Dalton-in-Furness,
Cumbria LA15 8BQ
☎ 01229 462508 Fax: 01229 467177
e-mail: info@clarencehouse-hotel.co.uk
🌐 www.clarencehouse-hotel.co.uk

Elegance and first-class service are assured at the superb **Clarence House Country Hotel and Restaurant**. Set in two acres with grounds that include outstanding ornamental gardens and breathtaking views, this is truly Furness' jewel in the crown. Open all year round, from early

morning breakfast (from 7 a.m.) right through to 9 p.m., this distinguished and distinctive hotel has merited the highest awards from bodies that include the RAC (2 Stars Dining) – and is the only hotel in Furness with an AA Rosette.

The interior is stunning – a happy marriage of traditional features and modern comforts. In the bar there's a wealth of burnished wood and a wonderful selection of real ales, wines, whiskies, lagers, ciders, stouts and soft drinks – something to please every palate. Every public space is decorated and furnished to the highest standard of taste, with elegant touches that add up to the best in luxury and comfort. This high standard continues in the beautifully decorated and furnished restaurant, where the menu

offers the freshest and finest ingredients expertly prepared and presented by the hotel's cadre of professional chefs. From light lunches to speciality five-course meals, all dishes are delicious and memorable. For afternoon tea there's a mouth-watering selection of cakes prepared by the hotel's dedicated Patisserie Chef.

The cellar provides a vast selection of excellent vintages. The ambience throughout this gracious hotel is always relaxed and welcoming. There are 17

luxurious and supremely comfortable guest bedrooms, five of which are situated on the ground floor. The hotel has always been renowned for its unique and individually-themed bedrooms, each with its own style and private facilities. As a touring base it is second to none, being within easy distance of Lake Windermere, the fells and the many scenic sights and attractions of the region. The Garden Lodge, a recently-converted traditional barn building, is now available for small conferences, weddings and celebrations.

132 THE RED LION INN

5 Market Street, Dalton-in-Furness,
Cumbria LA15 8AE
☎ 01229 467914
🌐 www.redliondalton.co.uk

Dating back to the early 17th century, **The Red Lion Inn** is a pristine and tasteful inn with traditional features and a friendly, welcoming ambience. Holts is the regular ale, together with three changing guest ales. Chef Danny Richards, who was trained by Raymond Blanc, and second chef Jamie create a menu of tempting dishes, complemented by an excellent selection of daily specials, using the freshest locally-produced ingredients. Booking is advised at all times, and is essential Fri-Sun. The inn also boasts seven superb guest bedrooms.

Open: Mon 6-11, Tues-Thurs 11-3 and 6-11, Fri-Sat 11-11, Sun 11-10.30.

133 THE ASKAM HOTEL

1–3 Victoria Street, Askam-in-Furness,
Cumbria LA16 7BX
☎ 01229 466161
e-mail: askamhotel@btconnect.com

Here in the village of Askam-in-Furness, just half a mile off the main A595, **The Askam Hotel** does double duty as a public house and hotel, with bed and breakfast accommodation available in three pleasant and comfortable guest bedrooms. Located just a few hundred yards from the beach, and close to

South Lakes Animal Park, this fine inn's selection of ales includes Worthingtons Bitter and Cumberland Ale. Food is served Saturdays until 6 p.m. and Sunday lunchtime (from midday until 3 p.m.).

134 FURNESS TAVERN

140 Duke Street, Askam-in-Furness,
Cumbria LA16 7AE
☎ 01229 462692

The Furness Tavern in Askam is a traditional inn with a delightful beer garden. Open evenings Monday to Thursday, Fridays from 3 p.m. and weekends from midday, there are two changing guest ales complemented by a good range of wines, spirits, lagers, cider, stout and soft drinks. Food is served Sunday (12-3pm), with a selection of tasty home-

made snacks and bar meals. Booking advised for the Sunday lunch roast dinners. Three guest bedrooms available all year round, complete the excellent facilities offered by this traditional tavern.

135 THE GREYHOUND INN

Grizebeck, Kirkby-in-Furness,
Cumbria LA17 7XJ
☎ 01229 889224 Fax: 01229 889900
e-mail: thegreyhound@grizebeck.fsworld.co.uk

The Greyhound Inn has a well-earned reputation for quality and service. Rotating guest ales, excellent food and seven recently refurbished letting rooms.

136 THE BAKEHOUSE

Princes Street, Broughton-in-Furness,
Cumbria LA20 6HQ
☎ 01229 716284

Baking with 100% natural ingredients, locally sourced, organic and Fairtrade. Speciality breads, desserts and cakes. Shop, Café and Accommodation. Farmers Markets.

137 RING HOUSE COTTAGES

Woodland, Broughton-in-Furness,
Cumbria LA20 6DG
☎ 01229 716578 Fax: 01229 716850
e-mail: info@ringhouse.co.uk
www.ringhouse.co.uk

Ring House Cottages are situated in the secluded Woodland Valley in the Lake District National Park between Coniston and Broughton-in-Furness. Five delightful Farmhouse Cottages set amongst woods, meadowlands and fells. Ring House offers easy access to all Lakeland activities. Weekly bookings run from Friday or Monday and short breaks are available all

through the year. All the Cottages are central heated and double glazed and some have log fires. There is ample parking and.the Cottages are fully equiped. Bedding and towels are provided and beds are made up before you arrive. Electricity and other extras are provided in the fully inclusive prices.

138 THE CROWN HOTEL

Coniston, Cumbria LA21 8ED
☎ 01539 441243 Fax: 01539 441804
e-mail: info@crown-hotel-coniston.com
www.crown-hotel-coniston.com

The stylish and welcoming **Crown Hotel** has it all: great food, drink and accommodation. Situated in the heart of Coniston, this fine inn boasts three real ales from the Robinsons

Brewery range, together with a selection of lagers, spirits, cider, stout, wines and soft drinks. The good, varied menu and specials board offer a range of excellent dishes using the best local produce. The 12 guest bedrooms are tasteful and comfortable, and have been awarded a 4 Diamonds rating by the English Tourist Board.

139 THE SUN HOTEL

Coniston, Cumbria LA21 8HQ
☎ 015394 41248 Fax: 015394 41219
e-mail: TheSun@hotelconiston.com
www.thesunconiston.com

The Sun Hotel is situated in the heart of Coniston. Built before 1600 on the old Walna Scar packhorse trail, the inn enjoys a Lakeland setting and traditional features including the stone walls, stone floor and exposed beamwork. Open all day, every day for ale, the hotel is well known for its various premium real ales. There are always five real ales – regulars Coniston Bluebird and

Hawkshead, together with three changing guest ales.

Meals are served daily at lunch and dinner, expertly prepared by the chef and his team, who bring great inventiveness and exotic influences to bear on creating an excellent menu and daily specials. The select wine list complements the menu perfectly. Outside, the hotel's attractive beer garden looks down to Coniston Water. There are nine en suite guest bedrooms and one room with private bath. The hotel also boasts a fine new conservatory, where guests can enjoy superb views in every direction.

140 THE COPPERMINES AND LAKES COTTAGES

The Estate Office, The Bridge, Coniston,
Cumbria LA21 8HJ
☎ 01539 441765   Fax: 01539 441944
🌐 www.coppermines.co.uk

The Coppermines and Lakes Cottages
offer an outstanding selection of over 60
cottages throughout the region. Each cottage
is brimming with character and quality.
Coniston, Sawtrey, Hawkshead, Duddon,
Ambleside, Windermere and Grasmere – all

these locations boast
a range of charming
accommodation.
Some cottages are cosy nooks for two, others can offer superior
accommodation for up to 30 people in interlinking cottages, the perfect
place to celebrate birthdays, weddings and other special occasions. Many
are over 100 years old; all retain their traditional charm and original
features while being sympathetically restored and refurbished to offer the
highest standard of comfort and modern-day conveniences.

Stunning scenery is a hallmark of the region, of course, and these
cottages offer the opportunity to enjoy the rest and relaxation that comes
of spending time in this surpassingly lovely part of the world. Apart from
the sights and attractions there is great walking and activities such as
watersports, climbing, mountain biking and horse-riding available.

141 ESTHWAITE OLD HALL

Hawkshead, Ambleside,
Cumbria LA22 0QF
☎ 01539 436007

Standing in its own grounds and surrounded
by breathtaking scenery, **Esthwaite Old Hall**
is an outstanding place to enjoy peace,
relaxation and superb accommodation. Dating
back in parts to 1541, the building was once
part of the local estate and has recently been
completely
and
sensitively
refurbished.
Opened to
the public in
October
2004, the
Hall is

beautifully furnished and decorated
throughout. There are three en suite guest
bedrooms here, where taste and elegance are
the bywords. Situated just a mile and a half
out of Hawkshead on the Newby Bridge
Road, it is within easy reach of the many
sights and attractions of the region.

142 BORWICK FOLD COTTAGES

Hawkshead, Ambleside,
Cumbria LA22 0PU
☎ 015394 36742
e-mail: borwickfoldcottages@firenet.uk.net
🌐 www.borwickfold.com

Very special barn conversion. Idyllic setting.
Panoramic mountain/valley views. Character/
comfort. Books.
Beautifully
furnished/
excellently
equipped. Walking/
cycling facilities.

Explore Britain and Ireland with
Hidden Places guides - a fascinating
series of national and local travel
guides.

www.travelpublishing.co.uk

0118-981-7777

info@travelpublishing.co.uk

191

143 THE OLD DUNGEON GHYLL HOTEL

Great Langdale, Ambleside,
Cumbria LA22 9JY
☎ 01539 437272 Fax: 01539 437272
e-mail: neil.odg@lineone.net
🌐 www.odg.co.uk

In a magnificent setting at the head of the
Great Langdale Valley, **The Old Dungeon
Ghyll Hotel** has been dispensing hospitality
to fellwalkers, climbers and tourists for over
300 years. Since 1984 this fine old inn has
been run by Neil Walmsley, a keen fell-
runner, and his wife Jane. They have
continued to improve and develop its amenities, and the 14 guest bedrooms, some with four-

posters, some with en suite shower facilities, offer warmth
and comfort in abundance, and keen walkers will be pleased
that the hotel has the essential amenity of a drying room.

The first port of call for many visitors is the Hikers Bar,
where a selection of real ales is on hand to quench outdoor
thirsts. Both Neil and Jane enjoy cooking, and the accent is
very much on home-made food, from bar meals to evening
meals served in the comfort of the dining room (open to
non-residents with advance booking). The hotel takes its
name from one of the most dramatic of the Lake District
waterfalls, which tumbles 60 feet down the fellside.

144 MILLBECK FARM AND SIDE HOUSE FARM & COTTAGE

Millbeck Farm, Great Langdale, Ambleside,
Cumbria LA22 9JU
☎ 01539 437364 Fax: 01539 437570
e-mail: millbeckfarm@btinternet.com
🌐 www.millbeckfarm.co.uk

Enjoying truly spectacular views in great
walking country near the head of the
stunning Langdale Valley, the 17th-century
**Millbeck Farm and Side House Farm &
Cottage** provide the setting for a relaxing
and memorable break. Bed and breakfast
accommodation is available at Millbeck Farm,
in three warm and spotless bedrooms. Self-
catering accommodation is on hand at Side
House Farm, which sleeps six, or the cottage,
which sleeps three. Owners Sue and Eric
Taylforth are also noted suppliers of
Herdwick
lamb and
Angus beef,
fresh from
the Fells,
which is also
sold here.

145 STANLEY GHYLL HOUSE

Boot, Eskdale, Cumbria CA19 1TF
☎ 01946 723327
e-mail: stanley.ghyll@virgin.net
⊕ www..stanleyghyll-eskdale.co.uk

Set in the Eskdale Valley just east off the A595 between Eskdale Green and Boot, **Stanley Ghyll House** boasts outstanding panoramic views in every direction, extensive gardens to the rear and, to the front, stands across the road from the Ravenglass-to-Eskdale Railway, known locally as 'The Ratty'. Since April 2003 this superb premises has been family-run by Gary and Suzanne Howard, ably assisted by Gary's mum, Sally.

Extensively renovated and refurbished throughout, it offers a high standard of comfort and quality. Dating back to the mid-1800s, it is open all year round for accommodation, with 12 en suite guest bedrooms, all of which are spacious and very comfortable. Log fires in the reception and dining areas add to the traditional feel and warm ambience of this excellent place. Situated in the heart of the Lake District National Park, there are fine walks from the doorstep. Children welcome. No smoking.

146 BROOK HOUSE INN & RESTAURANT

Boot, Eskdale, Cumbria CA19 1TG
☎ 01946 723288 Fax: 01946 723160
e-mail: stay@brookhouseinn.co.uk
⊕ www.brookhouseinn.co.uk

With six real ales in peak season, great food (booking required at weekends) and seven comfortable en suite guest bedrooms, **Brook House Inn & Restaurant** is well worth seeking out. Located in the unspoilt Eskdale Valley in the heart of the Lake District, it makes an excellent base from which to explore the Western valleys and fells and the many other natural and man-made sights and attractions of the region.

Built in the 1870s, the inn enjoys glorious views in all directions. Owner Gareth Thornley and his family provide excellent hospitality. Gareth is also a superb chef who numbers many home-cooked dishes from around the world among his many specialities. Among the accolades won by this fine inn and restaurant are ratings of 4 Diamonds by the ETC and RAC, the RAC Dining Award, and recommendations in the *Good Beer Guide* and *Good Pub Guide* for 2004.

147 BROWN COW INN

Waberthwaite, Cumbria LA19 5YJ
☎ 01229 717243 Fax: 01229 717295
e-mail: keith-Freda@browncowinn.com
⊕ www.browncowinn.com

The **Brown Cow Inn** is a delightful hostelry conveniently located on the A595 about three miles south of Ravenglass. Enjoying a well-deserved reputation for its excellent food, available from breakfast at 10 a.m. through lunch, afternoon tea and dinner served until 8.30 p.m. Resident owners Keith and Freda Hitchen keep customers happy with their friendly service and excellent hospitality. The cooking is simply splendid, with a menu of local

delicacies including Waberthwaite ham and Cumberland gammon or sausage, together with fish dishes, Indian meals, vegetarian specials and a good choice of children's meals. The portions are hearty and always delicious. There's a take-away service available and, on Sundays, a choice of two tempting roasts with all the trimmings.

This fine inn also boasts a good range of real ales, lagers, cider, stout, wines, spirits and soft drinks. And for those wishing to prolong their stay in this beautiful part of the world, The Brown Cow also offers a comfortable and charming self-catering flat which sleeps four.

148 CAMBRIDGE HOUSE HOTEL

1 Cambridge Street, Millom,
Cumbria LA18 5BD
☎ 01229 774982
e-mail: info@cambridge-house-hotel.co.uk
⊕ www.cambridge-house-hotel.co.uk

The new owners John and Joy Fernley offer a warm and friendly welcome at the **Cambridge House Hotel**. Recently refurbished to offer the best of traditional touches and ensuring guest's comfort and convenience.

The premises has a licenced bar and meals are served every evening, and a traditional Sunday lunch is served 12-3 p.m. (meals are available to non-residents) Meals are freshly prepared catering for specific diets, vegetarians or special occasion requests. All rooms are en suites and the price includes a full English breakfast. There are 4 twin rooms and 2 doubles. Ideally situated for a touring base, just two miles from the beach at Haverigg and within easy reach of the Western Lakes.

149 UNDERWOOD COUNTRY GUEST HOUSE

The Hill, Millom, Cumbria LA18 5EZ
☎ 01229 771116 Fax: 01229 719900
e-mail: enquiries@underwoodhouse.co.uk
⊕ www.underwoodhouse.co.uk

Set in eight acres of beautiful countryside, with superb views in every direction, **Underwood Country Guest House** is the last word in comfort, elegance and relaxation. Dating back to the mid-1860s, this distinguished oasis of peace and tranquillity nestles on the edge of woodland between the scenic Whicham Valley and Duddon Estuary, and speaks of quality in every department. The interior décor and furnishings are simply splendid, and each guest room is individually and stylishly decorated.

Given a 5-diamond rating by the AA, this beautifully restored former vicarage offers five double and two twin en suite guest bedrooms, all tastefully furnished. There are two elegant lounges in

which to relax, an attractive and welcoming dining room, conference facilities and much more. Found off the A5093 a short drive from the junction with the A595, the guest house also boasts an excellent restaurant, open seven evenings a week between 7 and 8 p.m. The menu changes to make the best use of the freshest local produce in season; a small sample would include main courses such as rack of lamb with redcurrant gravy, pan-friend port tenderloin in an apple and Calvados sauce, and linguine with roasted pine nuts, basil and watercress. The starters and desserts are equally sumptuous and satisfying.

Owners Andrew and Wendy Miller have been here since 1999; both are accomplished chefs with international culinary experience who create a superior range of tempting dishes. The wine list has been put together carefully to complement the fine food. Open all year round, the many excellent amenities and facilities at this superb guest house include the magnificent 12-metre indoor swimming pool, croquet lawn, tennis court and ample off-road parking. Away from the hustle and bustle yet within easy reach of Lake Windermere, Coniston Water and Wast Water, it is the perfect base for exploring the region.

150 WESTCLIFF HOTEL

Drigg Road, Seascale, Cumbria CA20 1NS
☎ 01946 728298 Fax: 01946 728298
🌐 www.westcliffhotelcumbria.com

Just a couple of miles off the A595 in Seascale, **The Westcliff Hotel** sits opposite the sea with private gardens leading down to the sands. Dating back to the late 19th century and built as the private residence of a wealthy local brewer, the hotel has been recently refurbished to provide guests with every comfort. Stylish, tasteful

and very comfortable, it's open all year round and has nine en suite guest bedrooms, most with simply outstanding views. The tariff includes a wonderful breakfast; evening meals by arrangement. Children welcome. No smoking.

HIDDEN PLACES GUIDES

Explore Britain and Ireland with *Hidden Places* guides - a fascinating series of national and local travel guides.

Packed with easy to read information on hundreds of places of interest as well as places to stay, eat and drink.

Available from both high street and internet booksellers

For more information on the full range of *Hidden Places* guides and other titles published by Travel Publishing visit our website on

www.travelpublishing.co.uk or ask for our leaflet by phoning **0118-981-7777** or emailing **info@travelpublishing.co.uk**

151 WESTLAKES HOTEL

Gosforth, Cumbria CA20 1HP
☎ 01946 725221 Fax: 01946 725099
e-mail: stay@westlakeshotel.com
🌐 www.westlakeshotel.com

Westlakes Hotel is set in a beautiful and historic country house dating back to 1827. Built for a wealthy fruit merchant of the era and originally named Haverigg Hall, the hotel stands in three acres of eye-catching gardens. It's the perfect place to relax, unwind and recharge your batteries in luxurious comfort. Open all year round, there are nine tasteful, elegant and comfortable en suite guest

bedrooms, in a mixture of sizes, each individually furnished and decorated.

This superior hotel also boasts a gracious and elegant restaurant open to residents and non-residents. Open from 7 p.m. Monday to Saturday, the menu features a range of tempting dishes such as chicken mignons, minted lamb Henry, red snapper fillet, Cajun chicken salad and mushroom stroganoff, all making use of the freshest locally-sourced ingredients. The mouth-watering desserts are well worth leaving room for! Booking essential for non-residents.

152 WHITE MARE

Beckermet, Cumbria CA21 2XS
☎ 01946 841246 Fax: 01946 841100
e-mail: phil@whitemare.co.uk
🌐 www.whitemare.co.uk

Philip Ward is the friendly, energetic licensee at the **White Mare**, an outstanding country inn and hotel set in the quiet and picturesque West Cumbrian village of Beckermet, just a mile off the A595. An ideal base for exploring the hidden places of the

Westlakes and lake District, it also attracts an appreciative local clientele. With its smart white-painted frontage and small-paned windows, the White Mare, which dates back to the early 1800s, is a place of considerable charm and character, and open fires in the main lounge make it a warm, inviting spot for a drink.

Open both at lunchtime and in the evenings, the public bar has been nicknamed the

Sports Bar and boasts a wealth of sporting memorabilia on display, while raised above the lounge is a delightful restaurant. There are always at least six real ales on tap, an ever-changing selection from local and far-flung breweries. A dedicated team in the kitchen cater well for their customers, providing a good choice of bar and restaurant menus, including daily specials and a wide selection of vegetarian meals.

Weddings can also be catered for as the White Mare has two approved venues for Civil Ceremonies and superbly appointed marquees that can seat up to 150 guest during the day and 250 for the evening function. Their wedding portfolio is available on request.

For overnight guests the White Mare has six double and two twin en suite guest bedrooms. Four of the

rooms have convertible sofas, making them particularly suitable for families, and all the rooms are no-smoking. Details of tarriffs can be found on their website or by telephoning the hotel. The White Mare has an excellent car park and a beer garden. Local groups and singers perform in the restaurant once a month, and other social events include a quiz on Wednesdays and a knock-out dominoes competition every Friday. The Lakes are within an easy drive, the sea even closer, and among the attractions in the vicinity are Egremont Castle and the Florence Mine Heritage Centre.

197

153 THE RED LION HOTEL

2 Market Place, Egremont,
Cumbria CA22 1AE
☎ 01946 824050
e-mail: redlionhotel@btopenworld.com

One of the biggest plaster red lions you will ever see adorns the frontage at **The Red Lion Hotel**, which is easy to spot on Egremont's main street. This excellent hotel began life in the early 1700s as a coaching inn, and became an important stopping-place along what was then the main Whitehaven-to-Barrow road. Its early prominence was but a distant memory when John Walker came here in 1998; since then he has invested a great deal of time and effort in a major refurbishment programme that has seen the hotel restored to its rightful style and elegance.

The 11 guest bedrooms offer a choice of accommodation to suit all guests, running from simple and homely with shared facilities to top-of-the-range rooms with en suite facilities. The tariff varies accordingly. In the bar, guests and locals can enjoy a full range of beers, including real ales, together with a good complement of lagers, cider, stout, wines, spirits and soft drinks. John has also widened the scope of their pub by serving hearty home-prepared food every lunchtime and evening, and in the process has made the pub one of the town's most popular meeting places.

Entertainment on offer includes regular karaoke session and discos, and to the rear of the pub there is a spacious function room available for private parties. Egremont, lying among the low hills of the Ehen Valley, is a little town with a lot of history, and is well worth taking the time to explore. It's famous for its castle, its annual medieval festival and, most of all, for the Crab Fayre Day in September, when the entertainments include the World Gurning Championships. Thanks to John's continuing programme of tasteful renovation, his hard work and dedication, the Red Lion has become an excellent base from which to enjoy everything Egremont and the surrounding area has to offer.

154 CAP'N SENNYS

2 Senhouse Street, Whitehaven,
Cumbria CA28 7ES
☎ 01946 62222
e-mail: andy2sennys@aol.com

Family-owned-and-run since 2001, **Cap'n Sennys** is a friendly, welcoming place that takes its name (as does Senhouse Street) from one Captain Richard Senhouse, who was instrumental in the development of both Whitehaven and Maryport. He bought the land in 1685 and, with a grant from the Lowther Estate, built the Mansion (Tangier House) and Warehouse in 1688. In 1692 he

built the first distillery in Whitehaven, and it is this building which today forms the major part of the inn, tastefully renovated over the years so that the interior is spacious and comfortable, with handsome oak beams and a wealth of original features.

Open Tuesday to Sunday, til late (1 a.m.) Thurs, Fri and Sat, the pub has a good selection of liquid refreshment. A DJ spins the discs Thurs-Sat, and owner Andrew Conoley does the cooking, serving up a range of tasty dishes at weekends between 12 and 3 p.m.

155 GLENFIELD GUEST HOUSE

Corkickle, Whitehaven,
Cumbria CA28 7TS
☎ 01946 691911 Fax: 01946 694060

Rated 4 Diamonds RAC and winner of the RAC Warm Welcome Award in May 2005, **Glenfield Guest House** is an elegant late-Victorian townhouse open all year round with six stylish and tasteful en suite guest bedrooms. Just a five-minute walk from the Georgian town of Whitehaven, and ten minutes from the historic harbour and marina, it's also convenient for the start of the Coast-to-Coast walk and cycle routes.
Owners Margaret and
Andrew Davies are
the most welcoming
of hosts, and their
guests can look
forward to home-
from-home comforts
and the guarantee of a
relaxing break.
Evening meals are
served in the attractive
dining room.

156 THE STORK HOTEL

Rowrah Road, Rowrah, Cumbria CA26 3XJ
☎ 01946 861213
e-mail: joan@storkhotel.co.uk

Completely refurbished from top to bottom while retaining all its origin charm, **The Stork Hotel** at Rowrah is a friendly inn with accommodation. The two regular real ales here are Jennings Bitter and Jennings Cumberland Ale along with a changing guest ale. Owners Joan and Paul Keswell are ably assisted by their daughters Jayne and Joanne. Joanne is the chef, and her home-made dishes are justly popular. Guests choose from the menu or specials board for a range of freshly prepared dishes using the best in local produce. Booking advised for Sunday lunch.
Upstairs,
there are six
cosy and
comfortable
en suite
guest
bedrooms,
available all
year round.

157 MANOR HOUSE HOTEL & COAST-TO-COAST BAR

Main Street, St Bees, Cumbria CA27 0DE
☎ 01946 822425 Fax: 01946 824949

Real ales, great food at lunch and dinner and eight en suite guest bedrooms in spacious, pristine and distinctive hotel and bar.

158 ROOK GUEST HOUSE

9 Castlegate, Cockermouth, Cumbria CA13 9EU
☎ 01900 828496
⊕ www.therookguesthouse.gbr.cc/

Cosy and welcoming accommodation in early 18th-century home close to Cockermouth Castle. Three stylish and comfortable rooms, 1 ensuite, 1 with shower.

159 IRTON HOUSE FARM

Isel, Cockermouth, Cumbria CA13 9ST
☎ 01768 776380
e-mail: almond@farmersweekly.net
⊕ www.irtonhousefarm.com

Set in 240 acres of pasture and woodland, **Irton House Farm** enjoys one of the finest views to be found in the northern Lakes. Ideal for a tranquil and relaxing holiday, the farm boasts five immaculate, spacious and superbly decorated and furnished self-catering apartments sleeping

between two and six people. Specifically designed to provide easy access for all guests, this luxury accommodation offers a very high standard of comfort and quality. Located off the A66/A591, it makes a perfect base from which to explore Derwent Water, Thirlmere, Ullswater, Carlisle and more, and golf and fishing are available nearby.

160 THE HOWE

Mosser, Cockermouth, Cumbria CA13 0RA
☎ 01900 823660
e-mail: millie@mosserhowe.freeserve.co.uk
⊕ www.mosserhowe.co.uk

Superb accommodation in three handsome and comfortable traditional stonebuilt cottages sleeping between two and six people.

161 NEW HOUSE FARM

Lorton, Cockermouth,
Cumbria CA13 9UU
☎ 01900 85404 Fax: 01900 85478
e-mail: hazel@newhouse-farm.co.uk
🌐 www.newhouse-farm.co.uk

Enjoying a truly outstanding setting amid 17 acres of lovely gardens and pastureland, **New House Farm** is a magnificent 17th-century farmhouse surrounded by superb Lortondale countryside. Owner Hazel Thompson has been offering comfortable and relaxing accommodation here since 1990. The five bedrooms take their names from local mountains; each is individually furnished and decorated to provide the very best in quality and comfort. All have en suite facilities and offer wonderful views. One room is on the ground floor.

Guests also can make use of the two elegant and gracious lounges, while the hearty and delicious breakfast is served in the separate dining room. Children over 6 are welcome; special arrangements can be made for younger children. Awarded 5 Diamonds by the AA, this no-smoking establishment is a truly special guest house and makes the perfect base from which to explore one of the loveliest parts of the county. Bookings are taken on a bed and breakfast or dinner, bed and breakfast basis.

Open all year round, New House Farm stands by the B5289 in Lorton Vale, south of Cockermouth. Other places of beauty and interest nearby include Keswick, Bassenthwaite Lake,

Derwent Water, the spectacular Whinlatter Pass and Forest Park. The Lortons, High and Low, are peaceful, enchanting places, and behind the former's village hall stands the yew tree made famous by poet William Wordsworth. Right next door is the charming Barn, a handsome building dating back to the 1880s and now tastefully converted into a tea room, seating 40 and serving mouth-watering food from 11 to 5 every day from March to October. As well as serving excellent traditional teas, it also has appetising home-cooked hot and cold snacks throughout the day.

162 THE OLD VICARAGE

Church Lane, Lorton, Cumbria CA13 9UN
☎ 01900 85656
e-mail: enquiries@oldvicarage.co.uk
🌐 www.oldvicarage.co.uk

Close to the Whinlatter Pass, **The Old Vicarage** is a gracious and traditional country house offering excellent accommodation in a beautiful setting amid masses of countryside. Set in over an acre of wooded grounds, the vicarage was built in the 1890s and is a quiet and restful place to recharge your batteries while enjoying high-quality comfort.

There are five guest bedrooms in the main house and two in an adjacent annex which was once the stables and coach house. All rooms are en suite. The guests' sitting room has a real fire on cold days, and provides books, games and local newspapers for guests. Graded 4 Diamonds Red by the AA, this handsome and welcoming place boasts stunning views, log fires and real charm, and is a marvellous base from which to explore the many sights and attractions of the region. Evening dinner available by arrangement.

163 THE WESTLANDS HOTEL

Branthwaite Road, Workington,
Cumbria CA14 4TD
☎ 01900 604544 Fax: 01900 68830
e-mail: davidwestlands@hotmail.co.uk
🌐 www.westlandshotel.com

Set in six-and-a-half acres of grounds on the outskirts of Workington, **The Westlands Hotel** is a superb establishment owned and personally run by Iona and David Sale. The Sales are a friendly and welcoming couple who have many years' experience in offering the finest standard of comfort and hospitality. They have been here at Westlands for a year and are restoring the eminence and prestige enjoyed by the hotel in the 1970s and 80s, when visits from royalty, prime ministers and other dignitaries was a common occurrence.

Open all year round, this spacious and elegant hotel has 70 superbly appointed en suite guest bedrooms, a number of which are on the ground floor. The hotel bar is open throughout the day and serves four regular real ales alongside guest ales and the full complement of lagers, spirits, wines and soft drinks. Tasty traditional English meals are served at lunch and dinner – booking required for Sunday lunch. The owners are also re-opening the Westlands Theatre, adjacent to the hotel, as a venue for entertainments of all kinds.

164 GREEN DRAGON HOTEL

Portland Square, Workington,
Cumbria CA14 4BJ
☎ 01900 603803

Taste and quality are the bywords at the gracious **Green Dragon Hotel** in Workington. Standing in one of the oldest parts of town, in Portland Square with its distinctive cobbled streets, The Green Dragon began life in the mid-1700s as a coaching inn. Having undergone a careful and tasteful refurbishment, this fine hotel can offer the very best in food, drink, accommodation and hospitality to all its guests. A happy blend of modern and traditional, it's a friendly, welcoming place to enjoy a tasty drink or meal, or enjoy first-class comfort in one of the guest bedrooms.

New owners Stephen and Angela Bell are ably assisted by their sons Stephen, Andrew and Paul. Andrew is the chef, creating a delicious range of excellent dishes and daily specials using the freshest locally-sourced ingredients, with plenty of choice to appeal to every appetite. Open every session for ale, there are two changing guest ales to choose from, together with a good selection of wines, spirits, soft drinks, lagers and more. The newly refurbished restaurant is open evenings from 5.30 p.m. and seats more than 40 diners. Open all year round, the hotel boasts 12 lovely guest bedrooms.

Ten rooms are en suite, the other two have private bath. All are located on the first or second floor. Guests stay on a bed-and-breakfast basis, and the hotel is ideally sited for anyone wanting a base from which to explore Workington, the River Derwent and the many sights and attractions of the region. The Bells also own and run the nearby 'Well' public house in Washington Street, offering a similarly good choice of quality food and drink. The hidden courtyard at this pub is just one of its distinctive features.

165 RIVERSIDE B&B

10 Selby Terrace, Maryport,
Cumbria CA15 6NF
☎ 01900 813595

A wonderful Victorian townhouse just a short
walk from the centre of Maryport, the
Riverside offers excellent bed-and-breakfast
accommodation all year round. With four
spacious and comfortable bedrooms,
excellently furnished
and decorated, with
antiques and original
feature fireplaces, it
makes an ideal base for
exploring this part of
Cumbria and beyond.
The tariff includes a
tasty and hearty
breakfast, served
between 7 and 9 a.m.
Salmon & Sea Trout
fishing is available. You
will receive a warm and
friendly welcome from
owners Dale and Linda
Renac.

166 THE GRAPES HOTEL

Market Square, Aspatria,
Cumbria CA7 3HB
☎ 01697 322550

Free House with
adjacent café, serving
hot and cold dishes
Tues-Sat 9 a.m.-4 p.m.
Five spacious and
comfortable guest
bedrooms.

Looking for:
- *Places to Visit?*
- *Places to Stay?*
- *Places to Eat & Drink?*
- *Places to Shop?*

www.travelpublishing.co.uk

167 THE SKINBURNESS LEISURE HOTEL

Skinburness, Silloth-on-Solway,
Cumbria CA7 4QY
☎ 01697 332332 Fax: 01697 332549
e-mail: events.skinburness@ntlworld.com
🌐 www.skinburnessleisurehotel.co.uk

Dating back to 1745 and a hotel since 1809,
The Skinburness Leisure Hotel occupies a
stunning location at the edge of the Solway
Firth. Open all year round, there are 26 guest
bedrooms including three executive rooms
and a ground-floor room adapted for guests
with disabilities. All rooms are en suite and
the hotel boasts a 3 Star rating from the AA and RAC and is also an AA Pet Friendly Hotel. The
hotel's name is a hint of the many leisure facilities on hand, which include an indoor plunge pool,
sauna, sunbed and fitness suite.

Outside in the lovely gardens, guests can enjoy use of
the bowling greens and croquet pitch. The restaurant is
open to residents and non-residents alike, and is open
daily for lunch (12-3), afternoon tea and dinner (5-9). The
menu offers a varied choice of dishes to suit all palates.
Booking required for Saturday evening and Sunday lunch.
The hotel bar is open all day, every day for a range of
thirst-quenchers including draught keg bitters, lagers,
wines and soft drinks.

168 THE MASONS ARMS

Gilcrux, Wigton, Cumbria CA7 2QX
☎ 01697 320765
e-mail: thepubgilcrux@btconnect.com

The Masons Arms is a truly outstanding inn with accommodation set in the tranquil village of Gilcrux. Once a busy little coal-mining village, Gilcrux stands on a hillside overlooking the Ellen Valley commanding superb views across the Solway Firth to Scotland. When the coal industry was in its heyday the village supported no fewer than seven licensed premises; today The Masons Arms is the only original one left.

The original oak beams and open fireplace contribute to the inn's warm and welcoming traditional ambience. It's a welcome enforced by owners Esther and Paul Bowness, a friendly local couple who took over as tenants in 2000 and became the owners in 2001. They have established a fine reputation not just for their hospitality but also for the quality of their ales, excellent range of wines

and great food. The inn is open every lunchtime and evening, serving a range of hearty and tasty dishes expertly prepared. Warm crusty baguettes, jacket potatoes, salads, omelettes and cheese bakes make for tasty quick snacks, while the choices from the grill include 16-oz steaks, Cumberland sausages, gammon and an exotic selection including wild boar, ostrich and kangaroo! Home-made pies (chicken, leek and Stilton, venison and red wine pie, steak and ale) and main courses such as chicken Stroganoff, salmon fillet and peppered pork complete this fine inn's superb choice of delicious dishes. For Sunday lunch, traditional roasts are added to the regular evening menu.

This family-friendly inn has a spacious beer garden and a games room; there's occasional live entertainment on Bank holidays, and all are welcome for the quiz every other Monday evening. In a former barn next to the main inn, tastefully converted, comfortable and cosy, are three top-of-the-range en suite guest bedrooms, stylish and homely with every amenity guests could want.

169 BROOKFIELD GUEST HOUSE

Penrith Road, Keswick, Cumbria CA12 4LJ
☎ 01768 772867 Fax: 01768 772867
e-mail: brookfieldgh@supanet.com
🌐 www.brookfield-keswick.co.uk

Family-run guest house, dating back to 1896, with four en suite guest bedrooms decorated in period style.
Scenic walk to Keswick town centre.

170 STYBECK FARM

Thirlmere, Keswick, Cumbria CA12 4TN
☎ 01768 773232 Fax: 01768 773232
e-mail: stybeckfarm@farming.co.uk
🌐 www.stayfarmnorth.co.uk
or http://members.farmline.com/stybeckfarm

Excellent accommodation at traditional farmhouse, Barn-Gill House, Cumblands Farm near Ravenglass. Fishing and camping barn also available.

172 HAZEL BANK COUNTRY HOUSE

Rosthwaite, Borrowdale, Keswick, Cumbria CA12 5XB
☎ 01768 777248 Fax: 01768 777373
e-mail: enquiries@hazelbankhotel.co.uk
🌐 www.hazelbankhotel.co.uk

Set in four acres of lovely grounds, **Hazel Bank Country House** is an impressive place dating back to 1840 with eight outstanding guest bedrooms, each individually decorated and furnished to a high standard of taste and comfort. All are spacious; some boast four-poster

beds; two are on the ground floor. Guests stay on a dinner, bed and breakfast basis. In the handsome dining room, dinner is served from 7 p.m. onwards and is also available to non-residents (booking essential). To the rear of the hotel there's also a superb self-catering cottage. 5 Red Diamonds AA, Little Gem RAC, Gold Award ETC, Red Rosette for fine food AA, Best in Cumbria CTB..

171 GRASSMOOR GUEST HOUSE

10 Blencathra Street, Keswick, Cumbria CA12 4HP
☎ 01768 774008
e-mail: info@grassmoor-keswick.co.uk
🌐 www.grassmoor-keswick.co.uk

Situated in the heart of Keswick and dating back to 1815, **Grassmoor Guest House** is a friendly, family-run establishment offering first-class accommodation. Popular and with many repeat visitors thanks to its quality and hospitality – and filling, delicious breakfasts! – there are four comfortable and welcoming en suite guest bedrooms.
Each room offers eye-catching views and is fitted out with every amenity including TV and DVD, fresh milk in the fridges and zip-and-link beds. Open all year round, children are welcome. Rated 4 Diamonds by the ETC.

173 LITTLETOWN FARM

Newlands, Keswick, Cumbria CA12 5TU
☎ 01768 778353 Fax: 01768 778437
e-mail: littletown@btopenworld.com
🌐 www.littletownfarm.co.uk

Littletown Farm is a marvellous working farm in a quite outstanding scenic location where guests can enjoy comfort and relaxation in the fully modernised farmhouse that retains all its traditional character and charm. There are eight lovely guest bedrooms, all of which command wonderful views over the Newlands Valley, and the farm makes an excellent base

from which to explore the Lakelands. Walking, climbing, biking and sailing are all available nearby, whilst Buttermere and Crummock Water offer more stunning scenery and the centres at Keswick and Cockermouth are also within easy reach.

174 RAVENSTONE LODGE

Bassenthwaite, Keswick,
Cumbria CA12 4QG
☎ 01768 776629 Fax: 01768 776629
e-mail: ravenstone.lodge@talk21.com
🌐 www.ravenstonelodge.co.uk

Looking for the perfect rural getaway? Look no further. **Ravenstone Lodge** is a truly outstanding country guest house standing in six acres of pastureland and woodland, looking down towards Bassenthwaite Lake and up towards Skiddaw, and nestling at the foot of Ullock Pike, just four miles

north of Keswick on the A591. Family run by Roger and Jacqueline Charlton and their daughter Fiona, who have lived here since 1989, this excellent stonebuilt lodge was built in 1861 as a stable and groom's cottage for the Dower House, opposite. With its own private terrace, walled garden and ample off-road parking space, it's truly a welcoming retreat.

There are ten stylish and elegant en suite guest bedrooms, including a romantic four-poster bedroom and a spacious family room in what was once the old hay loft. Guests can stay on a

bed-and-breakfast or dinner, bed-and-breakfast basis. Dinner is taken at 7.30 p.m. either in the Stable Dining Room or the relaxing Conservatory. The lodge retains its Victorian character and boasts many features from bygone days, such as in the stable dining room, which has its original stalls and fittings. Roger is a self-taught chef who creates a menu that changes daily to make the most of the freshest local produce, and features such tempting dishes as roast duckling and poached Scottish salmon, along with mouthwatering puddings such as sticky toffee pudding or apricot Bavarois.

Outside, guests are welcome to wander the grounds, where wildflowers bloom in abundance and all the joys of nature are at hand. There are marvellous views towards the lake and the beautiful northwestern fells. Within easy access are many fine walks including the Allerdale Ramble. The Lodge is also happily placed for exploring Keswick, Cockermouth and the many sights and attractions of the region. Graded 4 Diamond with Silver Award by Visit Britain and 4 Diamond with Dining Award by the RAC.

207

175 BRAITHWAITE FARM

Braithwaite, Keswick, Cumbria CA12 5RY
☎ 01768 778411
e-mail: jenny@braithwaitefarm.co.uk
🌐 www.braithwaitefarm.co.uk

Set in magnificent scenic countryside, **Braithwaite Farm** offers superb bed-and-breakfast accommodation in two comfortable en suite guest bedrooms. Situated to the rear of the village cricket ground, it's a tranquil place where guests can relax and unwind. Both guest rooms are handsomely furnished and decorated,

and the breakfast sets you up for a day's sightseeing. Packed lunches are available by arrangement. Open all year round. Children welcome. No smoking. Owners Jenny and Steven Clark also have a charming self-catering cottage next to the village pub, which sleeps six.

176 PONDEROSA GUEST HOUSE

Uldale, Wigton, Cumbria CA7 1HA
☎ 01687 371805
🌐 www.ponderosakeswick.co.uk

Bed-and-breakfast accommodation in handsome and spacious home set in its own grounds in scenic village. Self-catering in adjacent cottage.

Explore Britain and Ireland with *Hidden Places* guides - a fascinating series of national and local travel guides.

www.travelpublishing.co.uk

0118-981-7777

info@travelpublishing.co.uk

177 SWALEDALE WATCH

Whelpo, Caldbeck, Wigton, Cumbria CA7 8HQ
☎ 01697 478409 Fax: 01697 478409
e-mail: nan.savage@talk21.com
🌐 www.swaledale-watch.co.uk

Set within the Lake District National Park and surrounded by glorious unspoilt countryside, **Swaledale Watch** is a working sheep farm where Nan and Arnold Savage have been welcoming bed-and-breakfast guests since the early 1980s. Guests are free to wander round the 300-acre farm – lambing

time is a great favourite with guests, and the owners also keep and breed miniature ponies.

Nan and Arnold will happily guide you to any of the delightful walks nearby, one of which leads to the village of Caldbeck, one mile away, via The Howk, a limestone gorge with a beautiful waterfall. Should you be unlucky with the weather, settle down in one of the lounges to

enjoy the selection of books, board games and jigsaw puzzles. Guests are accommodated either in the main house or in the nearby annex, a beautifully converted cowshed. There are five tasteful and comfortable rooms (including double, twin and family rooms), four en suite and one with private bath. The tariff includes a hearty breakfast, and Nan and Arnold can recommend several good local dining establishments. Children welcome. No smoking. 4 Diamonds ETC.

178 THE GLOBE INN

Calthwaite, Penrith, Cumbria CA11 9QT
☎ 01768 885238
e-mail: calthwaiteglobe@aol.com
🌐 www.theglobeinn-calthwaite.co.uk

Set in the picturesque village of Calthwaite,
west off the A6 or a short drive off J41 of
the M6, **The Globe Inn** is an outstanding
traditional coaching inn dating back to 1690.
The interior is welcoming and attractive,
while outside
there's a beer
garden and
children's
play area.
Open all day
every day for
ale, there is
one real ale available from the local Cumbrian
Hesket Newmarket Brewery. A range of
tempting dishes are served Tues-Sun and
Bank Holidays between midday and 9 p.m.
The speciality is the excellent steak-and-ale
pie. This wonderful inn also boasts two guest
bedrooms.

179 HORNBY HALL

Brougham, Penrith, Cumbria CA10 2AR
☎ 01768 891114 Fax: 01768 891114
e-mail: enquire@hornbyhall.co.uk
🌐 www.hornbyhall.co.uk

The finest country house accommodation is
on hand at the gracious **Hornby Hall**, set in
a working farm in a peaceful rural setting a
mile from the A66 and just three miles
southeast of
Penrith. This
Grade II
listed
building
dates back to
1550 and has
many
interesting
features and antique furnishings. There are
seven en suite guest bedrooms, a dining room
in the original 16th-century hall, and guests'
sitting room with log fire. All rooms overlook
the lovely garden. Booking can be arranged
for fishing and shooting parties or for those
who wish to entertain their own guests in a
private house ambience.

180 PARK FOOT CARAVAN AND CAMPING PARK

Howtown Road, Pooley Bridge, Penrith,
Cumbria CA10 2NA
☎ 01768 486309 Fax: 01768 486041
e-mail: holidays@parkfootullswater.co.uk
🌐 www.parkfootullswater.co.uk

Set adjacent to Lake Ullswater within 100
acres of countryside, **Park Foot Caravan
and Camping Park** offers self-catering
accommodation and camping/caravan berths
from Easter to the end of October. The
amenities and facilities on site include shop,
laundry room, playgrounds, tennis court, lake
access, boating, pony-trekking, cycle hire,
disco and live entertainment. Penrith is within
5 miles and
attractions such as
the Rheged
Discovery Centre,
Aira Force
Waterfall and the
Lowther Bird of
Prey Centre are
all within easy
reach.

181 OLD WATER VIEW

Patterdale, Penrith, Cumbria CA11 0NW
☎ 017684 82175 Fax: 017684 82860
e-mail: ask@oldwaterview.co.uk
🌐 www.oldwaterview.co.uk

Old Water View is a beautiful property with
lovely gardens and views, offering quality bed
and breakfast accommodation in four
charming and supremely comfortable guest
bedrooms. This Victorian country house is
built of
Lakeland stone
and has been
lovingly
restored. Each
room is
decorated and
furnished with
style and taste, and the house boasts many
original features. Located just a short walk
from Lake Ullswater, this fine establishment
also boasts a handsome guests' lounge with
wide-screen tv, video and CD player, maps,
books and board games. There's a hearty
breakfast, and packed lunches are available by
arrangement.

182 THE HERMITAGE

Shap, Penrith, Cumbria CA10 3LX
☎ 01931 716671
e-mail:
jeanjackson_hermitage@btopenworld.com
🌐 www.shapcumbria.co.uk

Dating back in parts to the mid-15th century and set in three-quarters of an acre of well-tended and attractive gardens, **The Hermitage** is an outstanding place to enjoy bed-and-breakfast accommodation. Here in the historic village of Shap, owner Jean Jackson, assisted by her son Joshua, has lived here and run this superb establishment for over 38 years.

Open all year round, there are four top-quality guest bedrooms, three twins and a double. All

have excellent facilities and are furnished and decorated to the highest standard of quality and comfort. Three are en suite; the fourth shares the house facilities. Features such as the large open stonebuilt fireplace and beautiful stained-glass window depicting Richard the Lionheart, purchased more than 40 years ago from nearby Lowther Castle, add to the warm and welcoming traditional ambience. The tariff includes a superb breakfast. Home-cooked evening meals are available by prior arrangement. Peaceful and relaxing yet within easy distance of the many sights and attractions of the region, it makes a perfect touring base.

183 MEABURN B&B AND RESTAURANT

Meaburn Hill Farmhouse, Maulds Meaburn,
Penrith, Cumbria CA10 3HN
☎ 01931 715168
e-mail: meaburnhillfarm@pentalk.org
🌐 www.cumbria-bed-breakfast.co.uk

Meaburn B&B and Restaurant is an outstanding place. Owners Annie and Brian have a great deal of experience, and it shows: Annie was voted Landlady of the Year for the UK and Ireland by the AA in 2004. Open six nights a week, the restaurant's impressive menu boasts such delights as roast duck with damson sauce, Annie's game pie

and Michel Roux's 7-hour lamb. Ideal as a base while touring the Eden Valley, there are three comfortable and attractive en suite guest bedrooms and also a charming self-catering cottage. 4 Diamonds AA.

184 THE PENNINE HOTEL

Market Square, Kirkby Stephen,
Cumbria CA17 4QT
☎ 01768 371382 Fax: 01768 372686

Friendly inn open all day, every day. Real ales, real cider, home-made dishes at lunch and dinner and six comfortable guest bedrooms.

185 THE GOLDEN BALL

4 High Wiend, Appleby-in-Westmorland,
Cumbria CA16 6RD
☎ 01768 351493

Superb pub dating back to the early 1600s with handsome traditional décor and friendly ambience. Real ales, great food and four guest bedrooms. Rear courtyard garden is a sun trap. Children and dogs welcome.

186 THE KINGS HEAD HOTEL

Ravenstonedale, Cumbria CA17 4NH
☎ 01539 623284
e-mail: enquiries@kings-head.net
🌐 www.kings-head.net

A traditional village inn in the best sense of the word, **The Kings Head Hotel** offers great food, drink and accommodation. Set in Ravenstonedale in an area of outstanding natural beauty in the foothills of the Eden Valley, this fine hotel has recently been completely refurbished and is now a happy mix of ancient and modern.

One of the oldest buildings in the village, the hotel began life in 1627 as three cottages, later served as the village courthouse, and was later converted to create this picture-postcard establishment owned and run by Gary and Susan Kirby. They are friendly and welcoming hosts, ably assisted by their capable, efficient staff. Other regulars include Spot the dog and three amiable resident ghosts! There are four charming and convivial public rooms, perfect for enjoying the ales and other liquid refreshment on offer, including a very good wine list. In the no-smoking restaurant, the best of traditional English home-cooking is served every lunchtime and evening.

Member of the Good Beer Guide for 2004/2005/2006, and of the Cumbria Good Beer Guide 2005/06, this fine hotel has much to recommend it. Outside, the attractive beer garden runs alongside the beck. There are three charming and comfortable en suite guest bedrooms. Handy for exploring the Eden Valley, the many sights and attractions of the region include the village itself with its ancient parish church, school and remains of a Gilbertine abbey dating back to the 13th century, horse-riding and fishing (fly and coarse), nearby Howgill fells and beautiful countryside boasting a profusion of bird life and wildflowers. Sedbergh is just 20 minutes away, while the centres of Penrith and Kendal are only 45 minutes away. Closer to home, tennis and golf are available.

187 STOUPHILL GATE

Ravenstonedale, Kirkby Stephen,
Cumbria CA17 4NN
☎ 01539 623653
e-mail: martin@wainhouse.f9.co.uk
🌐 www.accommodationkirkbystephen.co.uk

All guests at **Stouphill Gate** are assured a
warm and friendly welcome. This traditional
Cumbrian farmstead takes its name from its
proximity to the brow of Stoup Hill, and

enjoys
spectacular
views. The
holiday
cottage is full
of character
and charm
with
flexibility to

sleep up to four or six..The bed-and-breakfast
accommodation is adjacent with two double
rooms one of which is suitable for a family or
for guests with disabilities. The guest book is
filled with rave reviews – 'the perfect
getaway', 'a beautiful cottage in a beautiful
setting' – and a memorable stay is assured.

190 MILBURN GRANGE

Knock, Appleby-in-Westmorland,
Cumbria CA16 6DR
☎ 01768 361867 Fax: 01768 362337
e-mail: holidays@milburngrange.co.uk
🌐 www.milburngrange.co.uk

Outstanding self-catering
holiday cottages sleeping
between two and seven.
Set in three acres of
mature gardens with
glorious views.

191 THE KINGS ARMS HOTEL

Temple Sowerby, Penrith,
Cumbria CA10 1SB
☎ 01768 361211
🌐 www.kingsarmshoteltemplesowerby.com

Real ales, bar and restaurant menus, ten guest
bedrooms in a
spacious and
handsome traditional
pub/hotel with a
relaxed and welcoming
atmosphere.

188 TARKA HOUSE

Bolton, Appleby-in-Westmorland,
Cumbria CA16 6AW
☎ 01768 361422 Fax: 01768 361422
e-mail: neilson@tarka-house.fsnet.co.uk
🌐 www.tarka-house.com

Three outstanding en
suite guest bedrooms,
cosy and attractive with
excellent facilities in its
own grounds in a lovely
village setting.

189 THE CASTLE HOTEL

Main Street, Brough, Cumbria CA17 4AX
☎ 01768 341252 Fax: 01768 341775
🌐 www.castlehotelbrough.co.uk

Feature murals
on the restaurant
walls are just one
highlight at this
fine hotel with
14 tasteful
rooms. Real ales
and great food.

192 THE HIGHLAND DROVE INN

Great Salkeld, Penrith,
Cumbria CA11 9NA
☎ 01768 898349 Fax: 01768 898708
e-mail: highlanddroveinn@btinternet.com
🌐 www.highland-drove.co.uk

Father-and-son team Donald and Paul
Newton have been welcoming visitors to **The
Highland Drove Inn** since 1998. The inn
has been providing hospitality for over 200
years, and the
Newtons
continue this
tradition in
great style.
There are
three real ales
– John
Smiths Cask,

Theakstons Black Bull and a changing guest
ale – while in the superb Kyloes Restaurant
the dishes range from fish, charcuterie and
meze plates to Peking duck, snapper with a
risotto cake and Moroccan-style chicken. Five
comfortable and attractive guest bedrooms
are available.

193 HAYBERGILL CENTRE

Warcop, Appleby-in-Westmorland,
Cumbria CA16 6NP
☎ 01768 341970 Fax: 01768 341970
e-mail: enquiries@haybergill.co.uk
🌐 www.haybergill.co.uk

Created by owners Mick and Maggie Hickey, the unique **Haybergill Centre** opened in July of 1999. Standing within three acres of grounds and woodlands, it's a peerless establishment offering a venue with full disabled access for groups, training courses, retreats and holidays, some organised by the owners and some by the attending groups themselves. Taking up to a maximum of 30 people the Centre provides quite outstanding facilities, including those for people with disabilities.

The village of Warcop is just five miles southeast of Appleby-in-Westmorland on the B6259. It's a large village with a famous 16th-century bridge across the river, in the upper Eden Valley and within easy reach of the Lakes and the Yorkshire Dales. The grounds of the Centre offer the opportunity to take tranquil walks along the waymarked paths, and see a wealth of wildlife – pheasants, red squirrels, woodpeckers and more – in its natural setting. The

interior is modern and stylish, with a wealth of pale woods, supremely comfortable furnishings and a handsome verandah where guests can sit and relax while enjoying the tranquil surroundings. Both catered and self-catering accommodation are available.

The owners provide guests with exclusive use of this environmentally friendly timber building that blends in beautifully with its surroundings. For any groups, large or small, the Centre offers an alternative to more formal conference/meeting places, residential courses, short breaks and holidays. The Eden Valley provides a vast range of attractions such as walks, cycle routes, market towns and unspoilt villages, the Otter Trust Reserve, Smardale Nature Reserve, Orton Scar, Sunbiggin Tarn and the Ostrich Farm.

The Centre can easily arrange guided walks, cycle rides, bird-watching, riding, nature rambles, fishing and golf. The excellent facilities and amenities include seven en suite bedrooms, three dormer rooms, a spacious lounge/training room, dining room and sauna facility. Central heating and wood burning stove. Warm and comfortable all year round.

194 BRIDGE END INN

Main Street, Kirkby Thore, Penrith,
Cumbria CA10 1UZ
☎ 01768 362180 Fax: 01768 363772

Adjacent to the main A66 in Kirkby Thore, **Bridge End Inn** is a distinctive and impressive establishment serving up great food, drink and hospitality. There is one changing guest ale available together with a good selection of lagers, cider, stout, wines, spirits and soft drinks – something to slake every thirst. Afternoon teas are also available.

The décor is traditional throughout, with traditional features such as the open fireplace and large casement windows letting in plenty of light on fine days.

Food is served every day from midday until 8.30 p.m. (and until 10 p.m. during the summer months). Guests choose off the menu or specials board from a good and varied range of dishes, most of them home-made. Owner Paul Coward is also the chef, and he's a past master at creating delicious snacks and meals. The inn is well placed for exploring the many sights and attractions of the region. Please ring for details.

195 HOWSCALES

Kirkoswald, Penrith, Cumbria CA10 1JG
☎ 01768 898666 Fax: 01768 898710
e-mail: liz@howscales.co.uk
www.howscales.co.uk

Five charming cottages provide superb accommodation, set in beautiful award winning gardens, surrounded by spectacular countryside.
4 Stars ETC.

196 THE MINERS ARMS

Nenthead, Alston, Cumbria CA9 3PF
☎ 01434 381427
e-mail: minersarms@cybermoor.org.uk
🌐 www.nenthead.com

The Miners Arms dates to the mid-18th century and is a popular stop along the Coast-to-Coast cycle route and the Pennine Way. Open all day, every day from May to September, and every session the rest of the year, there are good ales (Black Sheep plus a changing guest ale) and quality food served at lunch and dinner. Alison is a superb cook, having published her own recipe book, and among the

home-made dishes to enjoy is her famous Alston Pie. This fine establishment also boasts a cosy and comfortable guest bedroom and, adjacent to the inn, a luxurious bunkhouse sleeping 12 and available all year round.

Looking for:
- *Places to Visit?*
- *Places to Stay?*
- *Places to Eat & Drink?*
- *Places to Shop?*

www.travelpublishing.co.uk

197 LOWBYER MANOR COUNTRY HOUSE

Hexham Road, Alston, Cumbria CA9 3JX
☎ 01434 381230 Fax: 01434 381425
e-mail: stay@lowbyer.com
🌐 www.lowbyer.com

Built in 1778, **Lowbyer Manor Country House** was then part of the Lowbyer estate, owned by the Radcliffe family, Earls of Derwentwater. Related by marriage to the Stuart kings, the lands were impounded by their successors William and Mary. Replacing the original farmhouse with something more suitably grand, the next owner, mining overseer Mr Paull, implemented many changes and additions. In Georgian times the Manor was a private girls' school for a time. Today, this stunning country house has been tastefully refurbished to provide guests with every comfort.

There are nine en suite guest bedrooms – rated 4 Diamonds by the RAC and AA and winner of an RAC Warm Welcome Award – each furnished and decorated with style and to offer guests a taste of luxurious country house living. The surrounding grounds comprise three-quarters of an acre of well-tended gardens. Guests take breakfast in the handsome and comfortable breakfast room, and there's a licensed bar for residents. No smoking.

198 THE HOPE AND ANCHOR INN

Port Carlisle, Cumbria CA7 5BU
☎ 01697 351460

Pristine inn with two real ales, excellent food – lamb Henry, fish & chips and more – and attractive accommodation, in stunning location overlooking the Solway Firth.

199 HOME FROM HOME

6 English Street, Longtown, Cumbria CA6 5SD
☎ 01228 792474

Living up to its name, this cosy, comfortable place boasts five excellent en suite bedrooms, one of which is located on the ground floor.

HIDDEN PLACES GUIDES

Explore Britain and Ireland with *Hidden Places* guides - a fascinating series of national and local travel guides.

Packed with easy to read information on hundreds of places of interest as well as places to stay, eat and drink.

Available from both high street and internet booksellers

For more information on the full range of *Hidden Places* guides and other titles published by Travel Publishing visit our website on

www.travelpublishing.co.uk
or ask for our leaflet by phoning
0118-981-7777 or emailing
info@travelpublishing.co.uk

200 CROSBY LODGE COUNTRY HOUSE HOTEL & RESTAURANT

High Crosby, Crosby-on-Eden, Carlisle,
Cumbria CA6 4QZ
☎ 01228 573618 Fax: 01228 573428
e-mail: enquiries@crosbylodge.co.uk
🌐 www.crosbylodge.co.uk

Situated close the Hadrian's Wall, the newly refurbished

Crosby Lodge Country House Hotel & Restaurant is a beautiful and tranquil retreat offering excellent food and accommodation. Gracious and elegant in every quarter, the lodge is decorated and furnished in the finest Georgian style, and this romantic mansion just five minutes from the M6 and near the many sights and attractions of Carlisle and the surrounding region is perfect as a base while exploring the Lake District, the Scottish borders and of course, Hadrian's Wall itself.

Chef Roger Herring has been here nearly 30 years, presiding over the renowned restaurant. His experience and shows in the varied range of expertly prepared dishes served at lunch and dinner, and the lodge can also host weddings (holding a civil licence) and other celebrations as well as business entertaining or conferences. The best of the freshest locally-sourced ingredients are used to create memorable dishes. In the grounds, the walled garden has been restored and there's also an attractive gazebo. Each of the 11 en suite guest bedrooms has been individually designed and furnished with taste and style.

201 FARLAM HALL HOTEL

Brampton, Cumbria CA8 2NG
☎ 01697 746234 Fax: 01697 746683
e-mail: farmlamhall@dial.pipex.com
🌐 www.farmlamhall.co.uk

One of the finest country house hotels in the country, **Farlam Hall** is a gracious and elegant establishment. Lavishly furnished with antiques, it is a real retreat, perfect for unwinding. Parts

of the premises date to the 17th century, with Victorian additions. It is set in 12 acres of outstanding grounds, with landscaped gardens, an ornamental lake and stream.

Many leading guides nominate Farlam Hall as the most highly rated country house hotel in the region. Family run by the Quinion and Stevenson families, there are 12 beautiful and supremely comfortable en suite guest bedrooms. Two are on the ground floor, and one has a glorious four-poster bed. Most visitors plump for the dinner, bed and breakfast option, so that they can take advantage not just of the hearty and delicious breakfasts but

also the superb freshly-made dishes served at the evening meal. Non-residents can also dine here, but booking is essential at this superb and distinguished place.

202 WALTON HIGH RIGG FARM

Walton, Brampton, Cumbria CA8 2AZ
☎ 01697 72117 Fax: 01697 741697
e-mail: mounsey_highrigg@hotmail.com
🌐 www.waltonhighrigg.co.uk

Accommodation in spacious 18th-century
listed farmhouse with
large mature garden,
acres of farmland and
golf, fishing, sailing and
riding locally. Farmhouse
cooking.

203 SAMSON INN

Gilsland, Brampton, Carlisle,
Cumbria CA8 7DR
☎ 01697 747220

Beautiful early 18th-
century Free House open
all day, every day for ales,
great food (noon-9 p.m.)
and comfortable
accommodation. Booking
required at weekends.

Explore Britain and Ireland with
Hidden Places guides - a fascinating
series of national and local travel
guides.

www.travelpublishing.co.uk

0118-981-7777

info@travelpublishing.co.uk

204 HOLMHEAD GUESTHOUSE

Thirlwall Castle Farm, Hadrian's Wall,
Greenhead-in-Northumberland, Brampton,
Carlisle, Cumbria CA8 7HY
☎ 016977 47402 Fax: 016977 47402
🌐 www.holmhead.com

Built of stones from
Hadrian's Wall, within a
300-acre farm, quality
dinner and B&B or self-
catering accommodation.

VISIT THE TRAVEL PUBLISHING WEBSITE

Looking for:

- *Places to Visit?*
- *Places to Stay?*
- *Places to Eat & Drink?*
- *Places to Shop?*

*Then why not visit the Travel
Publishing website...*

- Informative pages on places to visit,
stay, eat, drink and shop throughout
the British Isles.

- Detailed information on Travel
Publishing's wide range of national
and regional travel guides.

www.travelpublishing.co.uk

Places of Interest in Cumbria

The selection of places of interest featured in this section includes museums, galleries, castles, historic houses, gardens, churches, cathedrals, gardens, country parks and many other places worth visiting in Cumbria. Each place of interest has an entry number which is used to identify its location on the map below and its name and short address in the list below the map. The entry number can also be used to find more information and contact details for the places of interest in the ensuing pages. In addition full details of places of interest in this section may be found on the Travel Publishing website – www.travelpublishing.co.uk This website has a large database of places of interest covering the whole of Britain and Ireland.

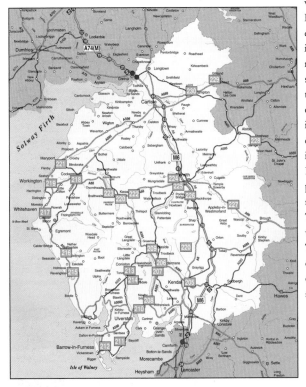

🏛 PLACES OF INTEREST

205	Abbot Hall Art Gallery & Museum, Kendal
206	Windermere Steamboats & Museum, Windermere
207	Blackwell, Bowness-on-Windermere
208	Aquarium of the Lakes, Lakeside
209	The Armitt Museum, Ambleside
210	The Lakeside and Haverthwaite Railway, Haverthwiate Station
211	Gleaston Watermill, Gleaston
212	The Dock Museum, Barrow-in-Furness
213	Ruskin Museum, Coniston
214	Brantwood, Coniston
215	Muncaster Castle, Ravenglass
216	Gosforth Pottery, Gosforth
217	The Beacon, Whitehaven

218	The Cumberland Toy & Model Museum, Cockermouth
219	Helena Thompson Museum, Workington
220	Cars of the Stars Museum, Keswick
221	Maryport Maritime Museum, Maryport
222	Threlkeld Mining Museum, Threlkeld
223	Whinlatter Forest Park, Braithwaite
224	Rheged Discovery Centre, Stainton
225	Dalemain Historic House & Gardens, Penrith
226	Lakeland Bird of Prey Centre, Lowther
227	The Bay Tree, Appleby-in-Westmorland
228	North Pennines Heritage Trust, Nenthead
229	Birdoswald Roman Fort, Gilsland
230	Border Heritage Trail, Brampton

205 ABBOT HALL ART GALLERY AND MUSEUM

Kendal, Cumbria LA9 5AL
☎ 01539 722464 Fax: 01539 722494

Abbot Hall Art Gallery forms part of a complex within Abbot Hall park and includes work by John Ruskin and the celebrated portrait painter, George Romney, who was born nearby at Dalton-in-Furness in 1734. The permanent collection also includes a wide range of 18th, 19th and 20th century British paintings and watercolours, and the Gallery hosts regular touring exhibitions.

A short walk from the Brewery Arts Centre is the **Museum of Lakeland Life and Industry** which is themed around traditional rural trades of the region, such as blacksmithing, wheelwrighting, agricultural activities, weaving, and printing. Here, too, are re-created cottage interiors, elegantly furnished period rooms and a

reconstruction of the study in which the celebrated author, Arthur Ransome, wrote the children's classic *Swallows and Amazons*.

At the other end of the town, near the railway station, is the **Museum of Natural History and Archaeology,** founded in 1796 and one of the oldest museums in the country.

Based on the collection first exhibited by William Todhunter in the late 18th century, the Museum takes visitors on a journey from prehistoric times, a trip which includes an interactive exhibit which tells the story of Kendal Castle.

The famous fellwalker and writer, Alfred Wainwright, whose handwritten guides to the Lakeland hills will be found in the backpack of any serious walker, was honorary clerk here between 1945 and 1974. Many of his original drawings are on display.

206 WINDERMERE STEAMBOATS & MUSEUM

Rayrigg Road, Windermere,
Cumbria LA23 1BN
☎ 01539 445565
🌐 www.steamboat.co.uk

The **Windermere Steamboat Museum** is a unique collection of Victorian and Edwardian steam launches which includes the *SL Dolly*, the oldest mechanically powered boat in the world. *Dolly* celebrated her 150th birthday in 2000 and still has her original engine in working order despite its having lain on the bed of Ullswater for more than 60 years before being recovered.

Some of the launches are still in working order and occasional cruises are possible. Private charters of an Edwardian steam launch can also be arranged. Facilities include a model boat pond, shop, tea room and picnic are.

207 BLACKWELL

Bowness-on-Windermere,
Cumbria LA23 3JR
☎ 015394 46139
e-mail: info@blackwell.org.uk
🌐 www.blackwell.org.uk

Occupying a superb position overlooking Lake Windermere, **Blackwell** is a treasure trove of the Arts and Crafts movement. Completed in 1900, the house was the work of the architect M.H. Baillie Scott who designed every last detail of this outstanding house, creating a symphony of art nouveau stained glass, oak panelling, intricate plasterwork and fanciful metalwork. As well as being a perfect work of art in itself, Blackwell provides the perfect setting for changing exhibitions of the highest quality

applied arts and crafts. Also here is a licensed restaurant with an outdoor terrace and a gift shop.

208 THE AQUARIUM OF THE LAKES

Lakeside, Newby Bridge,
Cumbria LA12 8AS
☎ 01539 530153
🌐 www..aquariumofthelakes.co.uk

The **Aquarium of the Lakes** boasts the largest collection of freshwater fish in the UK. Over 30 displays allow you to discover the world of both the fish and the wildlife which dwell in and alongside the water. A walk-through tunnel along a re-created lake bed provides great views of char, perch and diving ducks, whilst in the Morecambe Bay displays, visitors come face to face with sharks

and rays from around the local coast. A dramatic waterfall leads down to a moorland stream with salmon.

The mischievous otters on the riverbank are a special favourite with children and for the more earnest visitor there are educational displays on anything from leeches to lobsters. "The Quay" shop stocks a good range of quality gifts and souvenirs, and the "Café at the Quay" offers light refreshments and a good view of the lake.

209 THE ARMITT MUSEUM

Rydal Road, Ambleside, Cumbria LA22 9PL
☎ 01539 431212
e-mail: info@armitt.com
🌐 www.armitt.com

A short walk from the mill brings you to **The Armitt**, an attractive building which contains a gallery, museum and library dedicated to the area's history since Roman times and to its most famous literary luminaries, John Ruskin and Beatrix Potter. Visitors can "talk" to John Ruskin, watch a 19th century lantern slide show, and marvel at Beatrix Potter's pre-Mrs Tiggywinkle watercolours - exquisite scientific studies of fungi and mosses.

Other exhibits include a lock of Ruskin's hair, a life mask of Harriet Martineau, the political writer and author of an early *Guide to the Lakes*, and a fascinating collection of photographs by Herbert Bell (1856-1946), an Ambleside chemist who became an accomplished photographer, concentrating on lakeland scenes. The Armitt hosts regular exhibitions, lectures and concerts, and also has its own shop selling items produced exclusively for sale only at the museum.

210 THE LAKESIDE & HAVERTHWAITE RAILWAY

Haverthwaite Station, nr Ulverston, Cumbria LA12 8AL
☎ 015395 31594
🌐 www.lakesiderailway.co.uk

Beautifully restored steam locomotives of the **Lakeside & Haverthwaite Railway** haul comfortable coaches through the Leven Valley. With connections at Lakeside by way of Windermere Lake Cruises, the train offers a unique perspective from which to enjoy the ever-changing lake and river scenery of this picturesque part of the Lake District. This former Furness Railway branch line runs for 3.5 miles, with a journey time of around 20 minutes. The licensed Station Restaurant is an ideal way to start or end the journey with its superb home baking.

211 GLEASTON WATER MILL

Gleaston, Ulverston, Cumbria LA12 0QH
☎ 01229 869244   Fax: 01229 869764
🌐 www.watermill.co.uk

Where is **Gleaston Water Mill**? Take up the challenge and follow the signs from the A5087, down the country lanes of rural Cumbria and past the ruins of Gleaston Castle, to find it - it will be worth your efforts. The historic water driven corn mill is in

working order and abounds with atmosphere, artefacts, archaeologists and an apiary. Guided talks, walks and tours can be arranged. The Dusty Miller's café is fully licensed. Pig's Whisper is a rare treat for pig lovers of all ages. This gallery offers gift items from the sublime to the pigiculous.

212 THE DOCK MUSEUM 🏛

North Road, Barrow-in-Furness,
Cumbria LA14 2PW
☎ 01229 894444
e-mail: dockmuseum@barrowbc.gov.uk
🌐 www.dockmuseum.org.uk

The Dock Museum is a spectacular modern museum built over an orginal Victorian dock. Its displays trace the fascinating history of Barrow showing how it grew from a tiny nineteenth century hamlet to the biggest iron and steel centre in the world and a major shipbuilding force in just 40 years.

One permanent exhibition entitled

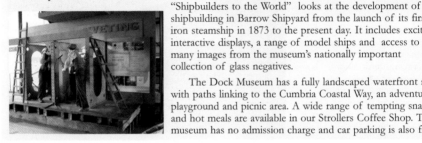

"Shipbuilders to the World" looks at the development of shipbuilding in Barrow Shipyard from the launch of its first iron steamship in 1873 to the present day. It includes exciting interactive displays, a range of model ships and access to many images from the museum's nationally important collection of glass negatives.

The Dock Museum has a fully landscaped waterfront site, with paths linking to the Cumbria Coastal Way, an adventure playground and picnic area. A wide range of tempting snacks and hot meals are available in our Strollers Coffee Shop. The museum has no admission charge and car parking is also free.

213 RUSKIN MUSEUM 🏛

Coniston, Cumbria LA21 8DU
☎ 015394 41164 Fax: 015394 41132
🌐 www.ruskinmuseum.com

The Ruskin Museum tells the Story of Coniston. From the dynamic geological history to 300 years of colourful but raw excavation in the old Coppermines. Guided walks are available on preset dates.
From the inspirational art work (including originals plus sketches on computer) and heart warming philosophies of John Ruskin, to the dramatic, suspense-filled saga of Donald Campbell's record breaking attempts on Coniston Water (poignant Powerpoint display of photos, including K7s recovery in 2001, plus video of the fatal crash and memorabilia)
the heritage of this unique area offers something for everyone.

214 BRANTWOOD 🏛

Coniston, Cumbria LA21 8AD
☎ 015394 41396 Fax: 015394 41263
🌐 www.brantwood.org.uk

Brantwood is the most beautifully situated house in the Lake District and enjoys the finest lake and mountain views in England. The home of John Ruskin from 1872 until his death in 1900, Brantwood became one of the greatest literary and artistic centres in Europe.
Tolstoy, Mahatma Gandhi, Marcel Proust and Frank Lloyd Wright can all be

numbered amongst Ruskin's disciples. The house is filled with Ruskin's drawings and watercolours, together with much of his original furniture, books and personal items. There is also an extensive programme of events at Brantwood, including concerts and exhibitions.

215 MUNCASTER CASTLE 🏛

Ravenglass, Cumbria CA18 1RQ
☎ 01229 717614 Fax: 01229 717010
e-mail: info@muncaster.co.uk
🌐 www.muncaster.co.uk

Muncaster Castle
is an impressive
castellated mansion
which has been
owned by the
Pennington family
since 1208. Back

in 1464 the Penningtons gave shelter to King
Henry VI after his defeat at the Battle of
Hexham. On his departure Henry presented
them with his enamelled glass drinking bowl
saying that as long as it remained unbroken
the Penningtons would live and thrive at
Muncaster. It remains intact and the
Penningtons are indeed still here.

Muncaster is also famous for its gardens
and, in particular, the rhododendrons, azaleas,
and camellias which are best viewed between
March and June. The woodland gardens
themselves cover some 77 acres.

216 GOSFORTH POTTERY 🏛

Gosforth, Cumbria CA20 1AH
☎ 01946 725296
e-mail: gospot@potterycourses.co.uk
🌐 www.potterycourses.co.uk

Found just 200 yards from the A595 at the
northern end of Gosforth, **Gosforth Pottery**
is a great place to find that unique and
beautiful piece of
tableware, vase, plant
pot, bowl, candlestick
or other housewares
made with skill and
craftsmanship.
Stocking the work of
over 20 potters, the
variety of designs and
techniques on display
is truly impressive.
The Pottery also hosts
a regular schedule of
lessons, short courses,

open days and 'pots and pizza' evenings.
Open May-Sept: Mon-Sat 10-5.30; Sun 12-
5.30. Oct-April: hours vary, please ring for
details.

217 THE BEACON 🏛

West Strand, Whitehaven,
Cumbria, CA28 7LY
☎ 01946 592302
e-mail: thebeacon@copelandbc.gov.uk
🌐 www.copelandbc.gov.uk

Situated on Whitehaven's attractive
harbourside, **The Beacon** is home to the
town's museum collection. It traces the social,
industrial and maritime heritage of the area,
using local characters, audio-visual displays
and fascinating museum pieces. The Met
Office Weather Gallery, where you can
monitor, forecast
and broadcast the
weather, offers
panoramic views
of the town and
coast. The
Harbour Gallery
offers free entry to
the changing
exhibitions and
there is a gift shop
and café. Guided
heritage walks
available.

218 THE CUMBERLAND TOY & MODEL MUSEUM 🏛

Banks Court, Market Place, Cockermouth,
Cumbria CA13 9NG
☎ 01900 827606
e-mail: Rod@toymuseum.co.uk
🌐 www.toymuseum.co.uk

This award winning museum exhibits a wide
selection of mainly British toys from c1900
to the present. There are many visitor
operated displays and buttons to press
including trains, Scalextric cars, Meccano,
Lego models and even a helicopter to fly.
Among the displays are prams, dolls' houses
and railways, and there
are worksheets linked
to National Curriculum
topics. Small children
can ride the rocking
horse or play with the
wooden bricks. The
museum entrance is
arranged as the inside
of an old toy shop and
there are always new
things to see.

219 HELENA THOMPSON MUSEUM

Park End Road, Workington,
Cumbria CA14 4DE
☎ 01900 326255 Fax: 01900 326256
e-mail: helena.thompson@allerdale.gov.uk

Visit the **Helena Thompson Museum** and discover Workington's fascinating social and industrial heritage. The Museum is housed in a fine, listed mid-Georgian building, bequeathed in 1940 by local philanthropist Miss Helena Thompson. Displays in the museum include pottery, silver, glass and furniture, dating from Georgian, Regency and Victorian times; women's and childrens dresses from the 18th to the early 20th century, together with accessories and jewellery; the social and industrial history of Workington, the coal mining, ship building, iron and steel industry for which Workington became world renowned. Admission is free.

220 CARS OF THE STARS MUSEUM

Standish Street, Keswick,
Cumbria CA12 5LS
☎ 017687 73757
e-mail: cotsmm@aol.com
🌐 www.carsofthestars.com

Located in the town centre, the **Cars of the Stars Museum** is definitely not to be missed. This fascinating collection, from film and television, includes such gems as Laurel and Hardy's Model T Ford, James Bond's Aston Martin, Batman's Batmobile and Mr Bean's Mini. Even Del Boy's shabby 3-wheeler Reliant van from Only Fools and Horses is here as is Chitty Chitty Bang Bang. Each car is displayed in its own film set, together with atmospheric lighting and sounds. Open from 10am to 5pm, daily between Easter and the New Year, weekends in December, and during the February half term.

221 MARYPORT MARITIME MUSEUM

1 Senhouse Street, Maryport,
Cumbria CA13 6AB
☎ 01900 813738 Fax: 01900 819496
e-mail: maryport.museum@allerdale.gov.uk

Did you know that Maryport has connections with the ill fated 'Titanic', or Fletcher Christian, of Mutiny on the Bounty fame? Visit **Maryport Maritime Museum** and discover the fascinating and proud maritime heritage of this delightful town. The building, formerly the Queens Head Public House, is built on one of the earliest plots of land developed by Humphrey Senhouse 11 when the town was built.

The Museum houses a wealth of objects, pictures, models and paintings that illustrate Maryport's proud maritime tradition; from a whale's tooth to a blunderbuss; from sailmakers' tools to telescopes; from a mutineer, Fletcher Christian, to a great shipowner, Thomas Henry Ismay of the great White Star Line, owners of the ill fated Titanic.

224

222 THRELKELD MINING MUSEUM

Threlkeld Quarry, Keswick,
Cumbria CA12 4TT
☎ 017687 79747

Entranced by the spectacular scenery of the Lake District, visitors are often unaware that in the past this was also a significant mining area. This industrial heritage is brought vividly to life at the **Threlkeld Quarry & Mining Museum** where visitors can browse through the collection of mining artefacts, wander through the locomotive shed and machine shop, or join the 40-minute tour through a recreated mine. At Threlkeld Quarry, men were employed from the 1870s until 1982 quarrying granite for railway ballast and road making, as well as producing granite setts and masonry stone. Several of the original buildings remain, including the locomotive shed which now houses various industrial diesel locomotives.

On display in the Museum is a fine collection of small mining and quarrying artefacts and more are now held at the new

Mining Museum in Keswick. There's also an excellent mineral collection and in the Geology Room a fascinating table top relief map of the Lake District, enhanced by rock specimens. The Museum Shop stocks the largest selection of mining, geology and mineralogy books in the north of England, (including a second-hand section), beautiful minerals from around the world, along with gemstone jewellery and a complete range of mine exploration and caving gear.

223 WHINLATTER FOREST PARK

Braithwaite, Keswick, Cumbria CA12 5TW
☎ 017687 78469 Fax: 017687 78049

The only Mountain Forest in England, **Whinlatter Forest Park** is also one of the Forestry Commission's oldest woodlands, providing a whole range of outdoor activities. The best place to start is at the Visitor Centre which has a wealth of information about the work of the Lakes Forest District and staff who will be happy to help you plan your day in the forest. Visitors can also book a forest classroom or a forest discovery walk with the Rangers. There's a shop and tea room here, with a terrace overlooking the woodlands and valley, an adventure playground close by and the Centre is also the starting point for several trails suitable for the whole family. The trails are clearly waymarked to provide easily followed routes taking in some spectacular views across the fells and forests of North Lakeland. Cyclists will find many miles of forest roads with some routes offering off-road and technical sections for the enthusiastic mountain biker. And if you have never tried orienteering, Whinlatter's permanent orienteering course is the perfect place to start. For children, there are Rabbit Run and Fox Trot orienteering trails, both starting from the Visitor Centre, while for those who prefer easier terrain or are less mobile, Europe's first permanent trail orienteering course combines the navigational skills of traditional orienteering with an easy-going route along forest roads and paths.

224 RHEGED DISCOVERY CENTRE

Redhills, Stainton, Penrith,
Cumbria CA11 0DX
☎ 01539 441164

Penrith's latest and most spectacular visitor attraction, **Rheged Discovery Centre,** opened in Easter 2000 and dedicates itself to "a celebration of 2000 years of Cumbria's history, mystery and magic - as never seen before". Open all year round, the Centre is housed in the largest earth-covered building in Britain, and is carefully designed to blend harmoniously with the surrounding fells.

Although it is built on 7 levels, from the outside Rheged looks like just another Lakeland hill. Inside, babbling brooks and massive

limestone crags replicate the Cumbrian landscape but the centrepiece is a 6-storey high, giant cinema screen, 60ft wide and 48ft high, on which is shown a specially commissioned film, *The Lost Kingdom,* which relates the story of the ancient Kingdom of Cumbria which once extended from Strathclyde in Scotland to Cheshire. Only a couple of minutes drive from Exit 40 of the M6, Rheged also offers visitors a retail shopping street, a useful information centre, special exhibitions, and restaurants and coffee shops which specialise in local delicacies and also provide panoramic mountain views.

225 DALEMAIN HISTORIC HOUSE & GARDENS

Penrith, Cumbria CA11 0HB
☎ 017684 86450 Fax: 017684 86223
e-mail: admin@dalemain.com
🌐 www.dalemain.com

Dalemain has been a much loved family home since 1679 and is set against the grandeur and picturesque splendour of the Lakeland Fells and Parkland.

Behind the impressive façade you will discover the surprise of Dalemain- its sheer variety. In the Georgian part of the house, the grand public rooms include the breathtaking Chinese Room with its original 18th century Chinese hand-painted wallpaper. Much of the house dates from Tudor times and here you will find a glorious confusion of winding passages, quaint stairways and unexpected rooms including the Fretwork Room with its magnificent 16th century plaster ceilings and oak panelling. The interior is full of fine furniture, family portraits, ceramics, dolls' houses and old toys, as well as housing the Westmorland and Cumberland Yeomanry Museum.

The gardens at Dalemain are a pure delight with a series of differing themes including a rose garden, a Tudor knot garden and a wild garden. A glorious woodland walk takes you high above Dacre Beck while other footpaths lead you by the walls of 14th century Dacre Castle or to Pooley Bridge. Besides the house and gardens, you can pause for refreshments in the Mediaeval Hall, with its range of home-made lunches and afternoon teas. A gift shop offers a selection of souvenirs and the Plant Centre sells a choice of English plants including old fashioned roses. The Agricultural and Countryside Collections can be found in the 16th century Great Barn. Open Sunday to Thursday March to October 10.30-5pm, (House and Gardens open 11am-4pm).

226 LAKELAND BIRD OF PREY CENTRE

Lowther, Nr Penrith, Cumbria CA10 2HH
☎ 01931 712746

The centre is a sanctuary for birds of prey,
set in the walled garden and parkland of
Lowther Castle. Visitors can see over 100
eagles, hawks, falcons and owls from around
the world. The aim of the centre is to
conserve birds of prey through education,
breeding and caring for injured and orphaned
birds before releasing them back to the wild.
There is also a tearoom as well as regular
courses and lectures.

227 THE BAY TREE

1 Bridge Street, Appleby-in-Westmorland,
Cumbria CA16 6QH
☎ 01768 353700 Fax: 01768 353700
e-mail: info@theybaytree.biz
🌐 www.thebaytree.biz

Ground-floor showroom with
crafts and gifts; upstairs there's
an excellent coffee shop
overlooking the river. Open
Fri-Sat and Mon-Weds 10-
4.30; Thurs 10-2.

Explore Britain and Ireland with
Hidden Places guides - a fascinating
series of national and local travel
guides.

www.travelpublishing.co.uk

0118-981-7777

info@travelpublishing.co.uk

228 NORTH PENNINES HERITAGE TRUST

Nenthead House, Nenthead, Alston,
Cumbria CA9 3PD
☎ 01434 382037
e-mail: info@ npht.com

Welcome to **Nent Valley**. Visit the 200-acre
centre at Nenthead, in the North Pennines, an Area
of Outstanding Natural Beauty. It offers a unique
insight into the lives of the miners who
transformed these fells. Visitors have the chance to
experience the underground world through guided trips in Carr's Mine, last commercially worked
for lead in 1920. There is the huge "Power of Water" interactive area, where visitors can open
sluice gates to operate water wheels and drive machinery. **Brewery Shaft** is an impressive 328 feet
deep, with a viewing platform for visitors to gaze down into the depths and be amazed at the
courage of anyone daring to descend.

Around the centre are various
restored buildings, which contain
exhibitions and interactive displays
about the geology of the area, the local
wildlife and social history of the area.
The 200 acre site includes woodland
walks, mountain streams and a
waterfall, whilst the surrounding area is
ideal for walkers of all ages and gives
access to the spectacular scenery of
the North Pennines. There is a café
where you can rest your legs and take
refreshments, and a well-stocked shop
to purchase postcards, books and gifts.

227

229 BIRDOSWALD ROMAN FORT 🏛

Gilsland, Carlisle, Cumbria CA8 7DD
☎ 016977 47602 Fax: 016877 47605
e-mail: birdoswald.romanfort@english-heritage.co.uk
🌐 www.birdoswaldromanfort.org

Located in a picturesque setting on Hadrian's Wall and overlooking the River Irthing, **Birdoswald Roman Fort** is one of the best preserved milecastles along the Wall and unique in that all the components of the Roman frontier system can be found here. This English Heritage Site is set high on a plateau with magnificent views over the surrounding countryside. The early turf wall, built in AD122, can be seen along with the fort, and a superb stretch of the Wall stretches from the fort

for a third of a mile. Originally, this fort would have covered five acres and it may have been the base for up to 1000 soldiers. During its 300-year occupation, the fort underwent substantial alterations and the turf wall, the stone wall, Harrow's Scar Milecastle, and the fort itself are all visible reminders of the occupation.

Between May and October, history comes to life at Birdoswald with a wide variety of events - battle re-enactments, music and drama, and the site also has an interactive Visitor Centre, a gift and tea shop, and a picnic area. A residential study centre with a range of excellent study facilities as well as accommodation is included in the site's amenities.

230 BORDER HERITAGE TRAIL 🏛

Contact: Tourist Information Centres at -
The Moot Hall, Brampton CA8 1RA
Tel: 016977 3433
Old Town Hall, Carlisle CA3 8JH
Tel: 01228 625600
3 High Street, Longtown CA6 5UA
☎ 01228 792835

The vast rural landscape around Carlisle, combines rich pasture land, gentle meadows and natural woodland with meandering rivers,

dramatic moorland and wild fells. From Hadrian's Wall to the Scottish Border, here is a captivating area containing numerous small villages and hamlets connected by a network of quiet roads lined with old hedgerows and wild flowers. The region offers a variety of outdoor activities including fishing, sailing, golf, horse riding, nature walks and cycle routes to suit all tastes. The Border Heritage Trail gives you the opportunity to access all of these.

As well as the scenery, the route will take you past an assortment of historical buildings and sites, including castles, churches, bridges, Roman forts and, of course, Hadrian's Wall.

The trail can be accessed at many points and walks can be made as long or as short as you want. Cycle routes and farm trails are also available. Contact the Tourist Information Centre for more information.

Tourist Information Centres

ALSTON MOOR

Town Hall
Front Street
Alston
Cumbria CA9 3RF
Tel: 01434 382244
Fax: 01434 382255
e-mail: alston.tic@eden.gov.uk
website: www.visiteden.co.uk

AMBLESIDE

Central Buildings
Market Cross
Ambleside
Cumbria LA22 9BS
Tel: 015394 32582
Fax: 015394 34901
e-mail: amblesidetic@southlakeland.gov.uk
website: www.amblesideonline.co.uk

APPLEBY-IN-WESTMORLAND

Moot Hall
Boroughgate
Appleby-in-Westmorland
Cumbria CA16 6XE
Tel: 017683 51177
Fax: 017683 51090
e-mail: tic@applebytowncouncil.fsnet.co.uk

BARROW-IN-FURNESS

28 Duke Street
Barrow-in-Furness
Cumbria LA14 1HU
Tel: 01229 894784
Fax: 01229 894703
e-mail: touristinfo@barrowbc.gov.uk
website: www.barrowtourism.co.uk

BOWNESS

Glebe Road
Bowness-on-Windermere
Cumbria LA23 3HJ
Tel: 015394 42895
Fax: 015394 88005
e-mail: bownesstic@lakedistrict.gov.uk
website: www.lakedistrict.gov.uk
Seasonal Opening

BRAMPTON

Moot Hall
Market Place
Brampton
Cumbria CA8 1RW
Tel: 016977 3433
Fax: 016977 3433
e-mail: ElisabethB@CarlisleCity.gov.uk
Seasonal Opening

BROUGHTON-IN-FURNESS

The Old Town Hall
The Square
Broughton-in-Furness
Cumbria LA20 6JF
Tel: 01229 716115
Fax: 01229 716115
e-mail: email@broughton-tic.fsnet.co.uk

CARLISLE

Old Town Hall
Green Market
Carlisle
Cumbria CA3 8JH
Tel: 01228 625600
Fax: 01228 625604
e-mail: tourism@carlisle-city.gov.uk

COCKERMOUTH

Town Hall
Market Street
Cockermouth
Cumbria CA13 9NP
Tel: 01900 822634
Fax: 01900 822603
e-mail: email@cockermouth-tic.fsnet.co.uk
website: www.gocumbria.co.uk

CONISTON

Ruskin Avenue
Coniston
Cumbria LA21 8EH
Tel: 01539 441533
Fax: 01539 441802
e-mail: conistonic@lakedistrict.gov.uk
website: www.lakedistrict.gov.uk

EGREMONT

12 Main Street
Egremont
Cumbria CA22 2DW
Tel: 01946 820693
e-mail: email@egremont-tic.fsnet.co.uk
Seasonal opening

GRANGE-OVER-SANDS

Victoria Hall
Main Street
Grange-over-Sands
Cumbria LA11 6DP
Tel: 015395 34026
Fax: 015395 34331
e-mail: grangetic@southlakeland.gov.uk
website: www.grange-over-sands.com

GRASMERE

Redbank Road
Grasmere
Cumbria LA22 9SW
Tel: 01539 435245
Fax: 01539 435057
e-mail: Grasmeretic@lake-district.gov.uk
Seasonal opening

HAWKSHEAD

Main Car Park
Hawkshead
Cumbria LA22 0NT
Tel: 01539 436525
Fax: 01539 436349
e-mail: hawksheadtic@lake-district.gov.uk
Seasonal opening

KENDAL

Town Hall
Highgate
Kendal
Cumbria LA9 4DL
Tel: 01539 725758
Fax: 01539 734457
e-mail: kendaltic@southlakeland.gov.uk
website: www.southlakeland.co.uk

KESWICK

Moot Hall
Market Square
Keswick
Cumbria CA12 5JR
Tel: 01768 772645
Fax: 01768 775043
e-mail: keswicktic@lake-district.gov.uk
website: www.keswick.org

KILLINGTON LAKE

Killington Lake Services
M6 South
Nr Kendal
Cumbria LA8 0NW
Tel: 01539 620138
Fax: 01539 621071
e-mail: killingtonlaketic@hotmail.com
Seasonal opening

KIRBY LONSDALE

24 Main Street
Kirby Lonsdale
Cumbria LA6 2AE
Tel: 01524 271437
e-mail: kitic@southlakeland.gov.uk
website: www.kirkbylonsdale.co.uk

KIRKBY STEPHEN

Market Street
Kirkby Stephen
Cumbria CA17 4QN
Tel: 01768 371199
Fax: 01768 372728
e-mail: ks.tic@eden.gov.uk
Seasonal opening

LONGTOWN

3 High Street
Longtown
Carlisle
Cumbria CA6 5PU
Tel: 01228 792835
Fax: 01228 792835
e-mail: ElisabethB@Carlisle-City.gov.uk

MARYPORT

1 Senhouse Street
Maryport
Cumbria CA15 6AB
Tel: 01900 812101
Fax: 01900 819496
e-mail: maryporttic@allerdale.gov.uk

PENRITH

Robinsons School
Middlegate
Penrith
Cumbria CA11 7PT
Tel: 01768 867466
Fax: 01768 891754
e-mail: pen_tic@eden.gov.uk
website: www.visiteden.co.uk

POOLEY BRIDGE

Finkle Street
Pooley Bridge
Cumbria CA10 2NW
Tel: 01768 486530
Fax: 01768 486530
Seasonal opening

RHEGED

Redhills
Penrith
Cumbria Ca11 0DQ
Tel: 01768 860034
Fax: 01768 868002
e-mail: tic@rheged.com

SEATOLLER

Seatoller Barn
Borrowdale
Keswick
Cumbria CA12 5XN
Tel: 01768 777294
Fax: 01768 777294
e-mail: Seatollertic@lake-district.gov.uk
website: www.lake-district.gov.uk

SEDBERGH

72 Main Street
Sedbergh
Cumbria LA10 5AD
Tel: 01539 620125
Fax: 01539 621732
e-mail: sedbergh@yorkshiredales.org.uk
website: www.yorkshiredales.org.uk

SELLAFIELD

Sellafield Visitors Centre
Seascale
Cumbria CA20 1PG
Tel: 01946 776510
Fax: 01946 727021
e-mail: julia.s.watson@bnfl.com

SILLOTH

Liddel Street
Silloth-on-Solway
Cumbria CA7 4DD
Tel: 01697 331944
Fax: 01697 331944
e-mail: sillothtic@allerdale.gov.uk

SOUTHWAITE

M6 Service Area
"Southwaite, Carlisle"
Cumbria CA4 ONS
Tel: 01697 473445
Fax: 01697 473445
e-mail: southwaite@scot-borders.co.uk

ULLSWATER

Main Car Park
Glenridding
Penrith
Cumbria CA11 0PA
Tel: 01768 482414
Fax: 01768 482414

ULVERSTON

Coronation Hall
County Square
Ulverston
Cumbria LA12 7LZ
Tel: 01229 587120
Fax: 01229 582626
e-mail: ulverstontic@southlakeland.gov.uk

WHITEHAVEN

Market Hall
Market Place
Whitehaven
Cumbria CA28 7JG
Tel: 01946 852939
e-mail: tic@copelandbc.gov.uk

WINDERMERE

Victoria Street
Windermere
Cumbria LA23 1AD
Tel: 01539 446499
Fax: 01539 447439
e-mail: windermeretic@southlakeland.gov.uk

WORKINGTON

21 Finkle Street
Workington
Cumbria CA14 3BE
Tel: 01900 606699
Fax: 01900 606699
e-mail: workingtontic@allerdale.gov.uk

Towns, Villages and Places of Interest

TRAVEL PUBLISHING ORDER FORM

To order any of our publications just fill in the payment details below and complete the order form.
For orders of less than 4 copies please add £1 per book for postage and packing.
Orders over 4 copies are P & P free.

Please Complete Either:

I enclose a cheque for £ [   ] made payable to *Travel Publishing Ltd*

Or:

Card No: [   ]   Expiry Date: [   ]

Signature: [   ]

Name: [   ]

Address: [   ]

Tel no: [   ]

Please either send, telephone, fax or e-mail your order to:
Travel Publishing Ltd, 7a Apollo House, Calleva Park, Aldermaston, Berkshire RG7 8TN
Tel: 0118 981 7777   Fax: 0118 982 0077   e-mail: info@travelpublishing.co.uk

	Price	Quantity		Price	Quantity
HIDDEN PLACES REGIONAL TITLES			**COUNTRY PUBS AND INNS**		
Cornwall	£8.99	....	Cornwall	£8.99	....
Devon	£8.99	....	Devon	£8.99	....
Dorset, Hants & Isle of Wight	£8.99	....	Sussex	£8.99	....
East Anglia	£8.99	....	Wales	£8.99	....
Lake District & Cumbria	£8.99	....	**COUNTRY LIVING RURAL GUIDES**		
Northumberland & Durham	£8.99	....	East Anglia	£10.99	....
Peak District	£8.99	....	Heart of England	£10.99	....
Sussex	£8.99	....	Ireland	£11.99	....
Yorkshire	£8.99	....	North East	£10.99	....
HIDDEN PLACES NATIONAL TITLES			North West	£10.99	....
England	£11.99	....	Scotland	£11.99	....
Ireland	£11.99	....	South of England	£10.99	....
Scotland	£11.99	....	South East of England	£10.99	....
Wales	£11.99	....	Wales	£11.99	....
HIDDEN INNS TITLES			West Country	£10.99	....
East Anglia	£7.99	....	**OTHER TITLES**		
Heart of England	£7.99	....	Off the Motorway	£11.99	....
North of England	£7.99	....			
South	£7.99	....			
South East	£7.99	....	**Total Quantity:**	[ ]	
Wales	£7.99	....			
West Country	£7.99	....	**Post & Packing:**	[ ]	
Yorkshire	£7.99	....			
			Total Value:	[ ]	

READER REACTION FORM

The *Travel Publishing* research team would like to receive reader's comments on any visitor attractions or places reviewed in the book and also recommendations for suitable entries to be included in the next edition. This will help ensure that the *Hidden Places series of Guides* continues to provide its readers with useful information on the more interesting, unusual or unique features of each attraction or place ensuring that their visit to the local area is an enjoyable and stimulating experience. To provide your comments or recommendations would you please complete the forms below and overleaf as indicated and send to:

**The Research Department, Travel Publishing Ltd,
7a Apollo House, Calleva Park, Aldermaston, Reading, RG7 8TN.**

Your Name:

Your Address:

Your Telephone Number:

Please tick as appropriate:

Comments ☐   Recommendation ☐

Name of Establishment:

Address:

Telephone Number:

Name of Contact:

READER REACTION FORM

COMMENT OR REASON FOR RECOMMENDATION:

....
....
....
....
....
....
....
....
....
....
....
....
....
....
....
....
....
....
....

READER REACTION FORM

The *Travel Publishing* research team would like to receive reader's comments on any visitor attractions or places reviewed in the book and also recommendations for suitable entries to be included in the next edition. This will help ensure that the *Hidden Places series of Guides* continues to provide its readers with useful information on the more interesting, unusual or unique features of each attraction or place ensuring that their visit to the local area is an enjoyable and stimulating experience. To provide your comments or recommendations would you please complete the forms below and overleaf as indicated and send to:

**The Research Department, Travel Publishing Ltd,
7a Apollo House, Calleva Park, Aldermaston, Reading, RG7 8TN.**

Your Name:

Your Address:

Your Telephone Number:

Please tick as appropriate:

        Comments ☐   Recommendation ☐

Name of Establishment:

Address:

Telephone Number:

Name of Contact:

READER REACTION FORM

COMMENT OR REASON FOR RECOMMENDATION:

....

....

....

....

....

....

....

....

....

....

....

....

....

....

....

....

....

....

....

READER REACTION FORM

The *Travel Publishing* research team would like to receive reader's comments on any visitor attractions or places reviewed in the book and also recommendations for suitable entries to be included in the next edition. This will help ensure that the *Hidden Places series of Guides* continues to provide its readers with useful information on the more interesting, unusual or unique features of each attraction or place ensuring that their visit to the local area is an enjoyable and stimulating experience. To provide your comments or recommendations would you please complete the forms below and overleaf as indicated and send to:

The Research Department, Travel Publishing Ltd,
7a Apollo House, Calleva Park, Aldermaston, Reading, RG7 8TN.

Your Name:

Your Address:

Your Telephone Number:

Please tick as appropriate:

Comments ☐   Recommendation ☐

Name of Establishment:

Address:

Telephone Number:

Name of Contact:

READER REACTION FORM

COMMENT OR REASON FOR RECOMMENDATION:

....

....

....

....

....

....

....

....

....

....

....

....

....

....

....

....

....

....

....

....

READER REACTION FORM

The *Travel Publishing* research team would like to receive reader's comments on any visitor attractions or places reviewed in the book and also recommendations for suitable entries to be included in the next edition. This will help ensure that the *Hidden Places series of Guides* continues to provide its readers with useful information on the more interesting, unusual or unique features of each attraction or place ensuring that their visit to the local area is an enjoyable and stimulating experience. To provide your comments or recommendations would you please complete the forms below and overleaf as indicated and send to:

**The Research Department, Travel Publishing Ltd,
7a Apollo House, Calleva Park, Aldermaston, Reading, RG7 8TN.**

Your Name:

Your Address:

Your Telephone Number:

Please tick as appropriate:

Comments ☐   Recommendation ☐

Name of Establishment:

Address:

Telephone Number:

Name of Contact:

READER REACTION FORM

COMMENT OR REASON FOR RECOMMENDATION:

Index of Advertisers

PLACES OF INTEREST

HIDDEN PLACES GUIDES

Explore Britain and Ireland with *Hidden Places* guides - a fascinating series of national and local travel guides.

Packed with easy to read information on hundreds of places of interest as well as places to stay, eat and drink.

Available from both high street and internet booksellers

For more information on the full range of *Hidden Places* guides and other titles published by Travel Publishing visit our website on

www.travelpublishing.co.uk
or ask for our leaflet by phoning **0118-981-7777** or emailing **info@travelpublishing.co.uk**

THE HIDDEN PLACES OF
DORSET, HAMPSHIRE AND ISLE OF WIGHT

THE HIDDEN PLACES OF
THE LAKE DISTRICT AND CUMBRIA

THE HIDDEN PLACES OF
NORTHUMBERLAND AND DURHAM

VISIT THE TRAVEL PUBLISHING WEBSITE

Looking for:

- *Places to Visit?*
- *Places to Stay?*
- *Places to Eat & Drink?*
- *Places to Shop?*

Then why not visit the Travel Publishing website...

- Informative pages on places to visit, stay, eat, drink and shop throughout the British Isles.

- Detailed information on Travel Publishing's wide range of national and regional travel guides.

www.travelpublishing.co.uk